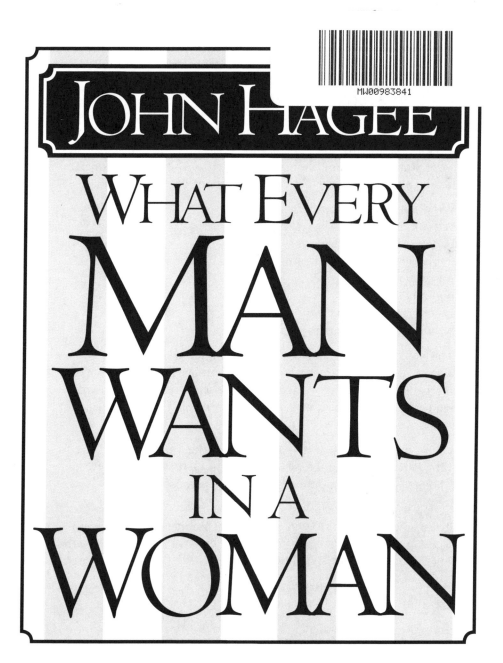

JOHN HAGEE

WHAT EVERY MAN WANTS IN A WOMAN

Charisma
HOUSE
A STRANG COMPANY

WHAT EVERY MAN WANTS IN A WOMAN;
WHAT EVERY WOMAN WANTS IN A MAN
by John and Diana Hagee
Published by Charisma House
A Strang Company
600 Rinehart Road
Lake Mary, Florida 32746
www.charismahouse.com

Scripture quotations marked PHILLIPS are from *The New Testament* in Modern English, revised edition. Copyright © 1958, 1960, 1972 by J. B. Phillips. Macmillan Publishing Co. Used by permission.

Scripture quotations marked THE MESSAGE are from *The Message: The Bible in Contemporary English*, copyright © 1993, 1994, 1995, 1996, 2000, 2001, 2002. Used by permission of NavPress Publishing Group.

Cover design by Rachel Campbell

International Standard Book Number 1-59185-723-6

People and incidents in this book are composites created by the author from his experiences in counseling. Names and details of the stories have been changed, and any similarity between the names and stories of individuals described in this book to individuals known to readers is purely coincidental.

05 06 07 08 09 — 10 9 8 7 6 5
Printed in the United States of America

*This volume is lovingly dedicated to my wife,
Diana Castro Hagee, who is the living portrait
of the Proverbs 31 woman of God!*

Acknowledgments

I would like to acknowledge my mother, Vada Swick Hagee, whose life of absolute devotion to Jesus Christ was the guiding light of my life. God placed in her hands the chisel that shaped every aspect of my life. I have become what my mother taught me to be!

I would also like to acknowledge the members of Cornerstone Church, whose love and prayers have sustained me through four decades of ministry. May the blessings of the Lord rest upon each of you and those you love!

"*Remember this: your marriage can be a better marriage, or it can be a bitter marriage. The choice is entirely up to you. Do not allow your past to control your future. You will never conquer, or change, what you refuse to confront.*"

JOHN HAGEE

John Hagee is the senior pastor of Cornerstone Church, a place of worship and teaching he founded in San Antonio, Texas. The nondenominational evangelical church now has more than 18,000 active members. Known best nationally for his End-Time writings, he has authored several fiction and nonfiction bestsellers, including *The Seven Secrets*.

CONTENTS

INTRODUCTION

WELCOME TO THE most exciting book on the mystery of marriage you will ever read—*What Every Man Wants in a Woman; What Every Woman Wants in a Man*.

Why is this book on marriage different from the other books you've read? Most books are written from the author's point of view. They are written from his experiences, his beliefs, and the unlimited research he has done on a particular topic.

This book is not written from my point of view, but from yours! I have surveyed thousands of men and women and asked them to write down the top ten things they want in a marriage partner. I am writing this book from the man's point of view as represented by those surveys. Diana will be writing to women from the woman's point of view.

TEN THINGS MEN WANT IN A WOMAN

The following ten statements reflect the results from the thousands of men surveyed. Here is what a man wants in a woman.

1. He wants sexual fulfillment.
2. He wants a recreational playmate.

3. He wants a beautiful wife.
4. He wants a committed homemaker.
5. He wants admiration.
6. He wants a woman of moral virtue.
7. He wants someone with a sense of humor.
8. He wants intelligence.
9. He wants someone he can totally trust.
10. He wants someone who is absolutely honest.

The story is told of a chemistry professor who was a world-class scholar in his field. His academic awards adorned the walls of his university office as evidence of his tremendous academic accomplishments.

The chemistry professor decided to write a book about love and marriage. After toiling over the manuscript for months, he proudly laid the finished product on his publisher's desk, beaming with pride in his new accomplishment.

The publisher read the manuscript, and to the horror of the professor, announced that he would not publish it. When the professor was informed of this decision, he pounded his fists furiously on his publisher's oak desk, shouting until his face turned crimson: "I want to know why you've rejected my manuscript on the principles of marriage."

The publisher responded firmly but kindly, "Professor, you are a world-class chemist whose life has been in the chemistry lab. You have never been married. You know nothing about love and romance. You have never had a serious date. You know nothing about sexual relationships or raising children. Write about something you know."

I am the pastor of eighteen thousand people and have been in the ministry for forty-six years. Much of this book will be gleanings from the pain, agony, and success of hundreds of these precious people whom I have known over the decades. They are people just like you, and they have battled through the same crises you are now facing. I have created composite stories that will illustrate the marriage issues I have discovered from my years of counseling. The names and details of the stories are not real, but the issues in marriage these stories illustrate are very real and may give you hope for being able to resolve the negative issues you are facing in your own marriage relationship.

I do this to show you what's possible. If you are willing for your marriage to be a better marriage, fasten your seatbelt and hang on as you read this book. This is going to be fast-paced and extremely funny, but it will be as hard hitting as the kick of a Missouri mule in the solar plexus.

In addition to the information I will share in this section for men, each chapter will contain a special section for women titled, "Hints for Her." These hints will aid a woman in giving a man what he needs.

Scattered throughout each chapter will be a parallel thought from my wife's section of this book, titled, *What Every Woman Wants in a Man*. You will find similar comments from me scattered through the pages of her section of the book. As you read these parallel ideas, you will recognize clearly the differences in the way a man thinks from the way a woman thinks. These comments will be titled, "He Says..." and "She Says..." They demonstrate the essence of this book—and these clearly recognizable differences are the reason why we thought it was important to write the book together.

At the end of each chapter you will have an opportunity to ask God to help you make the changes necessary to become the husband He wants you to be. Use the prayers I have included, and then continue praying your own prayer, committing to Him to do the work necessary to give your wife the husband she wants.

Welcome to *What Every Man Wants in a Woman*. After you read this portion of the book written by me from my male point of view, be sure you flip over to my wife's portion, *What Every Woman Wants in a Man*. By learning the principles Diana and I will share with you in this book, you can build your marriage to be an affair-proof marriage that will sizzle with joy and excitement every day of your married life. Remember this: your marriage can be a *better marriage*, or it can be a *bitter marriage*. The choice is entirely up to you. Do not allow your past to control your future. You will never conquer, or change, what you refuse to confront.

one

Has Your Marriage
LOST ITS SIZZLE?

THERE ARE THREE stages of marriage: lust, rust, and dust! Right now you know into which category your marriage falls.

In forty-six years of pastoral ministry, I've married hundreds of couples in every conceivable format. I've married them in churches, in magnificent cathedrals, under oak trees on a family farm, in public parks on a beautiful spring day, and on ships at sea with hundreds of our television Salt Covenant partners looking on during the John Hagee Ministry's annual cruise.

I have never been to a wedding where the room was not charged with joy, hope, and a sense of absolute delight for the future. The scene is always similar regardless of the setting.

The bride is glowing like an angel. Her face is radiant with joyous storybook expectations of the marriage she is about to speak into covenant. This is the pinnacle of her dreams. She holds the hand of the man she has chosen to be her partner for life and makes her covenant before God, saying, "I do."

Six months later, all hell breaks loose. She's in my office with tears dripping off her cheeks, gasping with convulsive sobs, saying, "What did I ever see in him?"

The groom stands in front of me holding her hand tenderly, pledging before God and man that he will "love, honor, protect, and provide" for his radiant bride. She is to be the queen of his life. She is the one whom God has sent into his life as the Proverbs 31 woman whose "price is far above rubies." She's priceless! You don't need to be Sigmund Freud to know that he has the urge to merge. A hormone hurricane is rapidly approaching category five just as he says, "I do."

Six months later, he's weeping in my office, head held in his trembling hands, sobbing like a child who has been slapped by a schoolyard bully, blubbering, "How did this ever happen to me? I thought I knew her. Who is this person I've married?"

I want to prevent this from being you! So, let's examine some of the basic reasons this scenario happens to good people just like you.

ENTERING INTO MARRIAGE WITH HIGH EXPECTATIONS AND LOW PREPARATION

It's absolutely amazing to me . . . no, actually it's unbelievable, that the courthouse will give any human being with brains enough to find the front door a license to get married. My father, who pastored for fifty-three years, often said, "If you have half a mind to get married, do it; that's all it takes."

Think about it! You must take a four-month driver's education course, learning how to put the key in the ignition, step on the gas to go forward, step on the brake to stop, work the windshield wipers when it rains, and turn the signal light right and left for the appropriate turn before you can climb behind the wheel of an automobile alone. This is not brain surgery. After four months, you get your license, and then you learn the really dangerous things like talking on the cell phone or putting on your makeup and lipstick while driving to work in rush-hour traffic. The state turns you loose on a freeway as financial fodder for every radar gun in your state.

A highway patrolman pulled a young executive over. The patrolman walked to the window of the Mercedes 500SCL and said, "Sir, your taillight is out."

The young executive leaped out of his car, ran to the back, and stared into space, screaming, "Oh, my God! Oh, my God! How could this ever have happened?"

The highway patrolman said, "Sir, don't become so emotional. It was just your taillight." The young executive responded, "Taillight?

I don't care about my taillight. Whatever happened to the fifty-thousand-dollar boat I was pulling?"

The point is this: You are supposed to know something about cars before you drive one. And you're supposed to know something about pulling trailers and boats before you do it.

Consider the science of cutting someone's hair. You can't cut someone's hair or trim their toenails without a license. You can't fish in a lake, a stream, or the ocean without a license. You can't go squirrel hunting or deer hunting without a license. If you're under fifteen years of age, you now have to take a gun safety course that costs fifty dollars to hunt something that can't shoot back.

But to get a license to get married, a license that empowers you to create new life, destroy your life, or crush the dreams and hopes of your spouse and family, all you have to do is have twenty-five dollars, and you are an instant player.

One man said, "Marriage is like fishing; you buy a license and take your chances." Marriage is made in heaven, but so are thunder and lightning.

One old maid said this concerning marriage: "What do I need with a man? I have a stove that smokes, a parrot that curses, and a cat that stays out all night." At least her expectations were realistic!

I asked a beautiful young lady just out of college, who sat in my office gushing about the "perfect marriage" she was going to have, "What kind of man would you like to marry?"

She joyously responded, "I want a husband who can dance, looks good, and likes what I feed him."

"That's great." I responded. "You've just described Trigger." (For those of you who have just recovered from your last case of acne, Trigger was Roy Rogers' show horse. Trigger could dance, he looked great, and he certainly enjoyed everything he was fed.)

Conflicting expectations are the source of most unhappiness in marriage. Which of the following expectations do you have that cause conflict with your spouse? Which of the following statements do you say?

- "You must like my friends and want to socialize with them."
- "Be sure you make our family priorities more important than your work."

- "You have to include me in all your activities."
- "Never do anything that upsets me."
- "Lose weight and stay in shape."
- "Make me happy—or else, because: 'If Mama ain't happy, ain't nobody happy.'"
- "You have to agree with me."
- "I wish you'd start making more money."
- "You need to be more affectionate and attentive."
- "You better never be attracted to anyone else."
- "You have to be the first to make up when we argue."

If you have these expectations, you are going to be extremely disappointed. There's more to marital readiness than a blood test. How sad that we spend so many years training for a career and so little time preparing for marriage.

A hasty courtship can often lead to a marriage relationship that is a disaster. Delaying your marriage by choice or because of financial or educational circumstances is usually beneficial. The passage of time allows all infatuation to die, while it tempers and develops true love and spiritual attraction.

Trying to escape from an unhappy home via marriage is like jumping from the frying pan into the fire. Over 60 percent of teenage marriages end in divorce. The more mature you are at the time of your marriage, the greater the probability of your success in marriage.

Marriage is more than a honeymoon; it's a lifetime contract. Through sickness and health, for richer and for poorer, marriage requires devotion and a mature ability to commit when it's the last thing you want to do. Marriage is the act of two incompatible people learning to become compatible via compassionate compromise.

MEN AND WOMEN FAIL TO RECOGNIZE THE DIFFERENCES BETWEEN THE SEXES

A man was walking along a California beach and stumbled across an old lantern. He picked it up, rubbed it, and out popped a genie. The beautiful genie said, "Thank you for releasing me from the lantern, kind sir. Ask me any wish you can imagine, and I will grant you your wish."

The man thought for a while and finally said, "I've always wanted to go to Hawaii, but I'm afraid to fly, and I get very seasick on a ship. Could you build me a highway from my beachfront home in California to Hawaii?"

The genie laughed, "That's impossible! Think of the logistics. How would the support beams ever reach the bottom of the Pacific Ocean? Think how much concrete and steel would be required, and imagine the engineering impossibilities of such a feat. Make another wish."

The man thought and finally responded, "My wife thinks I'm insensitive. Help me to fully understand women. Why do they cry when they are happy? Why do they cry when they are mad? Why do their moods change instantly and for no reason? Help me to fully understand women."

The genie looked at the man and said, "Do you want that highway to Hawaii to have two lanes or four?"

First Peter 3:7 gives the following command for all men: "Husbands, likewise, dwell with [your wives] with understanding...that your prayers may not be hindered." The fact is that before marriage, opposites attract; after marriage, opposites irritate.

Someone has said, "Women's faults are many. Men have only two: everything they say, and everything they do."

One of the major sources of friction in marriage is the inability or refusal of men to "dwell with [your partner] with understanding" (1 Pet. 3:7). The differences between the sexes remain when differences are misunderstood or unappreciated.

On one occasion, scientists gathered to determine if a computer should be called she or he. They divided into two groups, men and women, to discuss the differences in men and women.

The women scientists said that a computer should be addressed in the masculine gender. They gave these three reasons:

1. In order to get their attention, you have to turn them on.

2. They are supposed to solve problems, but half the time they are the problem.

3. As soon as you commit to one, you realize that had you waited a little longer, you could have gotten a better model.

The men scientists concluded that computers should be addressed in the feminine gender, and they gave these three reasons:

1. No one but the creator understands their internal logic.

2. Even your smallest mistakes are stored in long-term memory.

3. As soon as you commit to one, you find yourself spending half your paycheck on accessories for it.

Both men and women must accept this fact: men and women are different, and those differences will never change. You must understand those differences and dwell together according to knowledge.

Here are four differences every married man and woman must learn to accept.

1. The woman's right-brain caring vs. the man's left-brain logic

In 1981, Dr. Roger Sperry won the Nobel Prize in medicine and physiology for his breakthrough study on how the brain functions in male and female babies.[1] Dr. Sperry discovered that between the sixteenth and twenty-sixth week of gestation, boy babies have a chemical reaction in their brains that girl babies do not have.[2]

Two chemicals are released that slow down the development of the right side of the brain, which is the caring side. Dr. Sperry found out what all women already know—that all men are born brain damaged.

This right-brain and left-brain feature affects every phase of your married life. Mister, you may truthfully tell your wife that you are not rejecting her and are not being insensitive—that's how your brain works.

This right-brain/left-brain feature affects the memory of men and women.

For instance, my wife, Diana, can talk on the phone with her sister for thirty minutes, and when she gets off the phone, she wants to give me a word-by-word replay of the complete conversation. I do not care. I do not want to hear the conversation. Does that stop Diana from telling me every blessed word of that conversation? No.

When I talk to my mother for about twenty minutes, Diana will ask me, "What did your mother say?"

My response is, "Mother is fine!"

Diana probes, "What else?" Diana wants a word-per-word translation of what my mother has said over the past twenty minutes. It's just not going to happen.

This right-brain/left-brain feature is manifested immediately when a man and woman get married. Ask a man about his honeymoon, and he'll be able to remember he took one. Ask his wife, and she remembers what she was wearing on her wedding day, what she and her new husband wore every day of the honeymoon, the name of every restaurant they ate in during the honeymoon, how much they tipped the doorman when they left—and every other detail of the entire time! Why? Because a woman's memory is far more detailed in the right-brain caring area.

All husbands know that sinking feeling that comes when your wife asks you, "Do you remember when . . . ?" Then she describes the event in vivid detail—and you can't remember it ever happened. Why? Because the caring side of her brain is far more advanced than that of a man.

Ladies need to realize that there is a physical reason why men cannot remember. It isn't just that your husband doesn't care—his brain works differently than yours does. This is a scientific fact.

The right-brain/left-brain feature affects the way we respond to crisis. For example, where were you when John Fitzgerald Kennedy was shot?

I remember exactly where I was and what I was doing. I was a senior at Trinity University, waiting in the men's dorm for football practice to begin. When Walter Cronkite came on CBS saying that the president of the United States had been shot in Dallas, the world stopped.

I left the men's dormitory and ran down to the athletic center, where everyone was gathered around the television to witness that the impossible had just become reality. The Prince of Camelot was dead. The final football game of my senior year was canceled. It was a time of grief for our nation such as we had never known in our lifetimes. The American people dearly loved John and Jackie Kennedy.

How did men react to the crisis? We were asking each other, "Who's in charge of the country right now?" "What if Russia attacks right now?" "How many missiles do we have to respond to a crisis?" "How many soldiers do we have under arms?" This is left-brain logic.

What were the women saying across the campus? "Poor Jackie!" "Poor Caroline!" "Poor John John!" It was an entirely different way of seeing the same crisis. But it is a perfect illustration of right-brain caring vs. left-brain logic. There were two completely different reactions, neither wrong, but each dramatically different from the other. You must adjust to that reality, or your marriage will never have harmony.

If you apply this right-brain/left-brain feature to your marriage problem and try to solve marriage problems through pure logic—the man's forte—or pure emotion—the woman's disposition—you will experience perpetual disaster. Neither logic from the man nor emotion from the woman is the basis for settling marriage disputes. The only basis for settling any marriage dispute is the greatest marriage counseling text on Planet Earth, the Word of God.

Men aren't right!

Ladies aren't right!

But God's Word is always right. It says, "Dwell with them according to knowledge" (1 Pet. 3:7, KJV). Now, keep reading carefully. The statement used by wives that hurts their marriages more than any other is this: "When he changes to be like I want him to be, our marriage will be great!"

> **SHE SAYS...**
>
> **I try to relay to him the day's events as we lay in bed at night. I find this ritual to be the best sleep aid he has, for long before my diatribe is over, I hear the sounds of sleep coming from his side of the bed.**

Read my lips... *No, it won't!* Why? Because you will make the man into a right-brained creature, which by any other definition is a woman. What woman wants another woman just like her around the house? God made the man different for a reason. There is a dramatic and permanent difference between a man and a woman, and *vive la différence.*

If some women were married to Jesus, they would try to change Him. Here's biblical proof! Following His resurrection, Jesus fixed fried fish for breakfast for His disciples on the Sea of Galilee. (See John 21.) Husbands, what would your wife say if you asked for fried fish tomorrow morning for breakfast? Her response would probably be, "This is not Long John Silver's or Red Lobster. Here are pancakes. Enjoy."

2. Enjoying the process vs. accepting the goal

Women enjoy the process of reaching a goal. Men want to get to the goal as soon as possible—forget the process. Women will follow a twisting sidewalk to get to the front door of any office building. When a man gets out of his car, he will go through the hedges and through the rose garden straight to the door, because his objective is to reach the goal quickly.

My wife, Diana, loves to shop. She loves the process of looking. When she goes shopping, she will take a dress off the rack and say, "Look at this." She will take it to the mirror and look at it in the mirror, then bring it back and drape it over the rack. Then she starts the process all over. In thirty minutes she has half a dozen dresses draped over the rack, and she is still looking at all of them in total rapture. Like all women, she shops as though she is on a mission from God. How does anyone who works in a woman's clothing store keep from going insane?

And me? When I get ready to buy a suit, I call the store ahead of time and tell them what color of suit I'm looking for. "Please pull two or three out, and I will look at them as soon as I come in," I tell the clerk. I know what I want, and I want it quickly. Within fifteen minutes after walking in the door, I'm walking out of the door with my new suit. The shopping experience is over. The goal has been reached—upward and onward to the next adventure.

When we are driving on our vacations, Diana romantically gazes for minutes at something as monolithic as a sand dune. "Isn't that beautiful," she'll softly say.

My response is: "Watch out for radar, Diana. I'm trying to get there by five o'clock." Women love to smell the roses. Men will step on the roses if it will save them three steps. This is a difference that must be accepted. It will not change, not ever.

3. Spiritual authority vs. feminine manipulation

Ephesians 5:23 states, "For the husband is head of the wife, as also Christ is head of the church." Husband, it is your God-given assignment to be the prophet, priest, protector, provider, and promise keeper for your home. I'll say more about this later in the book.

Only a Spirit-filled woman can submit to her husband's lead. It is the natural desire of a woman to lead through feminine manipulation of the man. The battle of the sexes began in Genesis 3:16, when God said to the woman, "Your craving shall be for your husband and he shall rule over you."[3] In The Art Scroll Tanach Series, author Meir Zolotowitz stated, "Woman's punishment is measure for measure. She influenced her husband and he ate at her command. Her punishment was that she would now become subservient to him."[4]

Why did Saint Paul say, "I do not permit a woman to . . . have authority over a man" (1 Tim. 2:12)? It was because it is the natural thing for a woman to try to do. She is, by instinct, a manipulator of the situation. Fallen women will try to dominate the marriage. The man has the God-given role to be the loving leader of the home.

The Bible says, "For the husband is head of the wife" (Eph. 5:23). If you accept that difference, whether you are a husband or a wife, your marriage will be as the days of heaven on earth. If you resent and resist that difference, your marriage is going to be miserable from day one. That's God's plan, and it will endure. God is not in heaven saying, "Let's make a deal!" He's in heaven saying, "This is the deal!"

4. The Days of Wine and Roses vs. the Days of Thunder and Lightning

Within the body of every healthy woman who hasn't reached meno-pause or had a hysterectomy is a cycle known as *ovulation*. That means fourteen days of chemical balance, what I call the "Days of Wine and Roses," and fourteen days of chemical imbalance, or the "Days of Thunder and Lightning."

During the Days of Thunder and Lightning, moods change dramatically, inexplicably, and instantaneously. On one day a man comes home, and his wife is waiting at the door dressed in a negligee with a rose in her teeth. He scoops her up in his arms, provided she doesn't weigh three hundred pounds, and carries her off to the bedroom. He bangs on his chest and yells like Tarzan, "It must be the cologne I'm wearing!"

The next day, with his left-brain logic in high gear, he gets off work early. He races through the traffic and hurries home for a repeat performance from his wife. Except she is not at the door when he arrives. He searches through the house. She's not in the kitchen. She's not in the living room. She's not in the bedroom.

> *She Says* . . .
>
> **We do not become a slave to our partner when we surrender to him, and we do not give away our individualism, uniqueness, or dignity. Surrender within marriage simply means voluntarily yielding ourselves to one another in love.**

Finally he spots her huddled in a chair in the den crying her eyes out. He walks over and reaches out to comfort her, and she snarls like a half-starved junkyard dog, "Don't touch me, you big ape. All you ever want is my body. Sex, sex, sex, that's all you ever think about."

What happened? The Days of Thunder and Lightning have begun. Don't touch her, Bubba. If you do, you'll get hurt. If she has PMS . . . you'll get killed.

Do you know the difference between a woman with PMS and a snarling Doberman pinscher? The answer is *lipstick*. Do you know the difference between a terrorist and a woman with PMS? You can negotiate with a terrorist.

SEX IS GOD'S IDEA

The Bible is very specific about what God expects for men to be to a woman. First, consider Saint Paul's command to men: "Let each man have his own wife" (1 Cor. 7:2). The point is very clear. Sex outside of marriage is absolutely forbidden. There are no excuses. God has zero tolerance for sex outside of marriage. Safe sex is sex with a marriage license.

I have heard men in counseling sessions say, "But my wife is frigid."

My response is, "Find a way to light her fire, Bubba, but stay at home."

Some men say, "But my wife and I have an understanding."

I don't care what you and your wife have agreed upon. Let me give you God's understanding: "Do not be deceived. Neither fornicators, nor idolaters, nor adulterers, nor homosexuals, nor sodomites . . . will inherit the kingdom of God" (1 Cor. 6:9–10). God demands loyalty in the marriage covenant.

In 1 Corinthians 7:3, Paul gives a command to men: "Let the husband render to his wife the affection due her." In the King James version, it reads: ". . . render unto the wife due benevolence," which refers to sex, "conjugal duty." God not only expects the man to be loyal, but He also expects him to be a lover.

Sex is not just for procreation; sex is the symphony of the soul for married couples. Sex is joyous. It's a time of giving and sharing. It is tender and holy and should be as natural as drinking a glass of water. The Bible, written under the hand of the Holy Spirit, says, "Marriage is honorable among all, and the bed undefiled" (Heb. 13:4).

The phrase Paul uses in the King James Version, "due benevolence," means the payment of what is due. When you rent a house, the rent is the payment of what is due. When you buy a car, the car payment is the amount due. When you get married, sex is the payment of what is due.

What's the difference between your honeymoon and your fiftieth wedding anniversary? The answer is that on your honeymoon, it was *Niagara*; on your fiftieth anniversary, it's *Viagra*.

A wife took her husband to the psychologist and said, "My husband has no life, no fire, no passion. I need your help to sustain this marriage."

The psychologist walked around the desk, kissed her on the lips passionately, and, looking fiercely at the milquetoast husband, said, "That's what your wife needs."

The milquetoast husband looked at the psychologist and said, "OK. I'll bring her in every Tuesday and Thursday at ten o'clock."

> *S*HE *S*AYS . . .
>
> **What are my husband's needs? What does the Word of God say about our sexual relationships? How can I change and be a better spouse?**

I repeat: the Bible is a book for lovers. In Genesis 2:18, God said, "It is not good that man should be alone." God created Eve and brought her on His arm down the grassy slopes of the Garden of Eden. She was a perfect ten. She was absolutely naked and totally stunning. Adam started singing the well-known song, "I Just Feel Like Something Good Is About to Happen."

Jesus said, "The two shall become one flesh" (Matt. 19:5). "One flesh" means sexual union. Proverbs 18:22 says, "He who finds a wife finds a good thing." And in the life of a man, his wife is the best thing that ever happened to him.

In the book for lovers, Solomon fell in love with a peasant Shulamite girl. In chapter 1 of the Song of Solomon, he sees the Shulamite girl for the first time. He describes her from the chin up, because that's all he could see. He could see her eyes, and he could see her nose, and he described it as sensually as possible.

As time passes, women seem to wear less and less. A hundred years ago, it took a cotton gin all day to produce enough cotton to make a woman's dress. But today, a silk worm can do it on his lunch break.

In chapters 4 and 5 of the Song of Solomon, Solomon and the girl get married, and he describes her even more passionately. If you don't believe the Bible is a book for lovers, listen to this:

Behold, you are fair, my love!
Behold, you are fair!
You have dove's eyes behind your veil.
Your hair is like a flock of goats,
Going down from Mount Gilead.
Your teeth are like a flock of shorn sheep
Which have come up from the washing....
Your lips are like a strand of scarlet,
And your mouth is lovely.
Your temples behind your veil
Are like a piece of pomegranate.
Your neck is like the tower of David,
Built for an armory,
On which hang a thousand bucklers,
All shields of mighty men.
Your two breasts are like two fawns,
Twins of a gazelle,
Which feed among the lilies....
You are all fair, my love,
And there is no spot in you.

—SONG OF SOLOMON 4:1–5, 7

The message? "You're perfect and absolutely beautiful." Husband, have you told your wife that lately?

Then the Shulamite girl describes Solomon, saying:

His head is like the finest gold;
His locks are wavy,
And black as a raven.
His eyes are like doves
By the rivers of waters,
Washed with milk,
And fitly set.
His cheeks are like a bed of spices,
Banks of scented herbs.
His lips are lilies,
Dripping liquid myrrh.

His hands are rods of gold
Set with beryl.
His body is carved ivory
Inlaid with sapphires.
His legs are pillars of marble
Set on bases of fine gold.
His countenance is like Lebanon,
Excellent as the cedars.
His mouth is most sweet,
Yes, he is altogether lovely.
This is my beloved,
And this is my friend,
O daughters of Jerusalem!

—SONG OF SOLOMON 5:11–16

It's touch and tell. Don't tell me the Bible is not a romantic book. Sex is a divine symphony between two lovers, and God is leading the orchestra.

Hints for Her

These hints will aid a woman to give a man what he needs. Try them—they work!

Don't forget that it is God's Word that is always right—not woman's . . . and not man's! Instead of constantly trying to change your husband, celebrate your differences and use them to bring excitement and diversity into your marriage.

Remember that your husband has a God-given role as leader of your home. Allow the Holy Spirit to help you willingly submit to his loving, godly leadership. Avoid the natural desire to manipulate his leadership and dominate in situations that arise in your family's life.

CONCLUSION

I began this chapter by identifying three stages of marriage: lust, rust, and dust! By beginning to incorporate the principles in this book for men and women by my wife, Diana, and myself, you will soon realize that these are not the only three stages of marriage. There is that joyful, fulfilling, covenantal "oneness" that truly *sizzles*! Determine now that you will allow God to direct your marriage toward a symphony of godly love and satisfaction.

ASKING GOD'S HELP

Father, I don't have any trouble recognizing the differences in the way my wife and I think. So many times I just can't understand why she is acting the way she is or saying the things she says. But I have a lot of trouble figuring out how You want me to respond to her and learning how to say the things to her that You want me to say. Help me, Father! Teach me to listen for Your direction before I open my mouth. Make me sensitive to her needs and wants, and willing to figure out—with Your help—what will please her and bring fulfillment to her instead of just trying to do what I want. I really love her, Lord. Help me to do a better job of showing her my love every day. Amen.

O N ONE OCCASION a woman gave me a book titled, *What Men Know About Women*. I opened it, and every page was totally blank.

Here are seven things God says women want from men:

1. Women want a man to love them completely, passionately, and romantically.

The Bible commands every husband, "Husbands, love your wives, just as Christ also loved the church and gave Himself for her" (Eph. 5:25). In short, be a passionate and devoted lover.

Women are sick and tired of domestic Hitlers who try to dominate them for their own purposes. They are tired of macho men who rule with an iron fist and have to be right all the time. They are weary with men who show little affection until they want sex.

Women are tired of men who offer little compassion or communication and act like a warden and treat everyone in the house like prisoners. No one can live with that macho monster.

What do women want? Women are tired of spiritually weak, milquetoast husbands who refuse to lead the family spiritually. They want a husband who will provide for the family financially, one who protects them emotionally, and one who leads them spiritually. They are tired of powder-puff husbands who demonstrate all the robust leadership of a parked car.

What do women want? Women do not want a playboy husband. Playboy husbands will get AIDS sooner or later. Some men say, "I practice safe sex. I use a condom." What a joke! Dr. Teresa Crenshaw, a member of the U.S. Presidential AIDS Commission, has this warning: "Saying that the use of condoms is 'safe sex' is in fact playing Russian roulette. A lot of people will die in this dangerous game."[1] You will bring death and disease to your wife with your mate-to-mate, bed-hopping lifestyle. Stop it!

My advice for women married to playboy husbands is this: if your husband has refused to change his adulterous ways, for your safety and the safety of your children, terminate that marriage.

2. Women want nonsexual affection.

When a wife says "Come and hold me" to her husband, he rubs his hands together as his testosterone meter explodes and responds, "All right..." He is ready for raw sex. She simply wants affection.

In counseling sessions, I have asked men and women this question: "How would you feel if you knew you would never have sex again with your mate?"

> SHE SAYS...
>
> **It is very important to show affection to your husband every opportunity you get. Take his hand when you are walking together, or pat his shoulder as you pass by him. Kiss him often.**

Almost all women respond, "It's really no big deal if I never have sex again with my husband, but it would be a big deal if we never touched or kissed or romanced again." That's nonsexual affection.

When I ask men the same question, "What if you could never have sex with your wife again?", their eyes bulge, their nostrils flare, and sweat begins to drop off their forehead.

They shout in terrified response, "Give up sex? Not in my lifetime!" To ask a man to give up sex is like asking him to give up eating and breathing.

Why is there this huge difference between men and women? This is a very sensitive issue, so hang on. God placed in a man's body an atomic bomb called *testosterone*. It fires him up sexually, and it doesn't take much to set him ablaze. It takes very, very little, as a matter of fact.

To give wives better perspective on this issue, imagine this: You have just been informed by mail that you've won the grand prize in a national contest. You and your husband will be taken to a tropical island for ten days of first-class service at a five-star hotel.

You'll be given twenty-five thousand dollars for spending money! You'll be furnished unlimited usage of a luxury limousine. You will be taken by private jet to and from the resort. You will have maids, chefs, and butlers. This will be the most thrilling ten days your mind can imagine.

As a wife, you can't wait for your husband to walk through the door so you can tell him the good news. Now imagine that when he comes through the door, you greet him by saying, "I have wonderful news! We have just won a grand prize!"

He responds, "Not now, dear. I'm tired, and I have a headache—we'll talk about it later."

Here is the point: A man's testosterone level makes him feel like he has won the grand prize almost every day. He can't wait to tell you about it. When you show disinterest, his frustration factor runs off the page. You drift off to a dreamy sleep on your side of the bed while he's chewing the corner of the pillowcase and clawing the paint off the wall.

3. Women want a man who can truly understand that women are divinely different—and that they aren't going to change.

In the movie *My Fair Lady*, Professor Henry Higgins took on the unenviable task of trying to transform Eliza Doolittle, a commoner, into a sophisticated socialite in London. After weeks of extreme effort to correct her diction and the manner in which she walked and greeted people, he yelled in exasperation, "Why can't a woman be more like a man?"

A woman cannot be like a man, and a man cannot be like a woman, because each is divinely different from the other—and that fact will never change. God created man and woman that way, and the sooner you adjust to and accept it, the happier you will be.

4. Women want open communication.

If you don't know how to listen, you don't know how to communicate.

> **SHE SAYS...**
>
> **We have no business changing that which God has ordained. But we must learn to adapt to these differences.**

If you always have to give your opinion, you don't know how to communicate.

SHE SAYS...

Reveal to your husband as much information about yourself as you know: your thoughts, feelings, habits, likes, dislikes, personal history, daily activities, and plans for the future.

If you always raise your voice to make your point, you don't know how to communicate.

If you don't let the other person speak, you don't know how to communicate.

If you must always have the last word, you are a dictionary, not a communicator.

If you speak to another adult in the same way you speak to a small child, you don't know how to communicate.

Has your wife ever misunderstood you? Have you ever told your wife something as clearly as you can speak, and she got it wrong...all wrong? We have developed technology that permits men on earth to talk to people on the moon, yet husbands often can't talk openly with their wives across the breakfast table. Why?

What is communication? Communication is an exchange of feelings or information. Communication is giving your wife the freedom to disagree with you completely without you flying into a rage or pouting or sulking for a week.

Communication happens when you, as husband and wife, can honestly tell each other who you are, what you think, how you feel, what you love, what you honor, what you esteem, what you hate, and what you fear, desire, hope for, believe in, and are committed to without fear of a prolonged argument.

Are you ready to improve on your own communication techniques with your wife? Here are seven ways to find time to talk to your wife in meaningful communication:

- Set aside a fifteen-minute period when you both get home from work at the end of the day just to talk. Turn off the television, throw the cat out the back door, put the newspaper down, and talk to each other about everything significant that happened in your lives that day. You will discover that those fifteen-minute periods become thirty minutes—and longer.

- Make a rule that the TV is off during dinner. For that hour, do not answer the phone. Let the answering machine take all phone calls.

- Write a monthly date night into your schedule that cannot be broken.

- Get together for lunch once a week, even if you just brown bag it in a public park.

- Attend one of your children's sports games or other performances as a couple. You will be amazed how much talking can take place during nine innings of a slow baseball game! As a matter of fact, I never missed a single baseball, basketball, or football game that any of my children ever played in.

- Take a walk together after dinner. It's a good time to talk, and, besides, it's physically good for you.

- Plan a weekend getaway once each year just for the two of you. Take the Song of Solomon with you—and read it together.

5. Women want emotional intimacy.

Emotional intimacy includes touching, caressing, hugging, kissing, and romancing. There are approximately five million touch receptors in the human body. More than two million receptors are in the hands alone.

The right hand of touch releases a pleasing and healing flow of chemicals in the bodies of both the *toucher* and the *touched*. Studies have shown that even the tender touch of a pet dog or cat can cause people to get healthier. Everyone wins when we touch each other in the proper way. To paraphrase Southwestern Bell telephone company, "Reach out, and touch someone."

My mother was a person who could hug you and make the world go away. She was a master of touch. From my earliest childhood, I watched her reach out and hug all the people she loved, and many others, too. I adopted that practice as a teenager, and I practice it until this day. I believe it's beneficial for every person to receive affection from another person through touch.

Listen to me! Without the emotional intimacy of touch, and warm personal communication, sex with your wife is little more than domestic rape.

6. Women want spiritual intimacy.

As husband and wife, pray together, and for each other, every day. The Bible says, "A threefold cord is not quickly broken" (Eccles. 4:12). A man and a woman talking to God, bound together in prayer, is an unbreakable union. Do you know how hard it is to pray for someone when you are mad at that person? It's impossible. Do you know how I know that? Try it; you'll like it.

7. Women want mutual submission.

In Ephesians 5:21, Paul says this: "...submitting to one another in the fear of God."

Here are some ways to improve sexual intimacy.

Be romantic! I know a man who didn't kiss his wife for ten years, and then shot somebody who did. Men, you know what your wife likes—do it! That's what the Bible means when it says, "Dwell with [your wife] with understanding" (1 Pet. 3:7).

For some women, being romantic means buying her flowers. For others, it means sending carefully chosen greeting cards. For others, it means scheduling regular date nights. For others, romance is as simple as sharing the work around the house. But whatever spells *romance* for your wife, all women respond to romance and want more of it.

Make yourself physically attractive. In one counseling session, a man expressed irritation because of his wife's cool responses to his invitations for physical affection. When I quizzed his wife, it turned out that "John Wayne" was coming into the house sweaty, dirty, smelly, and unkempt, looking for instant romance. That was not going to happen.

There is sexual intimacy when there is reverence for each other. Paul wrote: "Nevertheless let each one of you in particular so love his own wife as himself, and let the wife see that she respects her husband" (Eph. 5:33).

> ### SHE SAYS...
> **When my husband leaves our home, I pray a prayer of blessing over him. He not only needs the prayer, but he also needs the encouragement that comes as the person he loves and partners with is putting a cover of blessing over his life.**

Reverence means to "stand in awe." Men, would you like for your wife to follow you around the house saying, "Awe...awe...awe"? Then love her as Christ loved the church. Give her nonsexual affection. Understand her differences without trying to change her. Give her open communication. Give her emotional and spiritual intimacy. Reverence her, honor her, and provide for her. Love her as your own flesh. You *are* one flesh, and God sees both of you or neither of you. This is the mystery of marriage.

MARRIAGE CHECKLIST

1. Do you find a way to make your wife feel good about herself once each day? Diana and I have something between us we call *O.W.E.* It's an acronym for One Way Every day. One way, every day, I seek to find a way to make Diana feel good about herself or to help her accomplish a task that is becoming overwhelming. Last night we washed dishes together. Some days, it's a rose from the rose garden. Other days, it's a card. Other times, there is a date night. But one way every day there has to be the transmission of my effort to make that day a better day.

2. Can you express your wants, beliefs, hopes, goals, and plans to your wife without World War III breaking out in your home?

3. Can your wife tell you how she honestly feels about the negative things you do and the negative things you say to her without you responding by pouting for a week...a day...or even for a mere hour?

4. When your wife wants to talk (and without fail it will be in the fourth quarter of the Super Bowl, with the score tied, and your team getting ready to kick the winning field goal), do you scream, "Not now!"? Or do you regularly respond by saying calmly, "Give me about ten minutes, and then we'll talk"? Remember, if Mama ain't happy, ain't nobody happy.

    When the television is on and Diana wants to talk, she has this irritating habit of walking in front of the television, spreading her arms out like a flying eagle, and saying, "Let's talk." There's no chance even to see the television screen. There's no need to reach for the remote! Would your wife say you are a good listener, or would she say that you are forced to listen because she stands in front of the television?

5. If you've been married for two years or more, answer this question: If you met your wife today, knowing what you know about her, would you marry her again?

6. Do you know your wife's emotional needs, and do you look for ways to meet those needs?

7. When your actions offend your wife, do you have the courage to go to her and say, "I'm sorry"?

8. Would your wife say you are her protector and her provider? Would your wife say that you are loyal and that you are her lover?

9. Are you the priest and prophet of your home?

10. Do you have emotional problems (anger, resentment, rejection, insecurity) that produce a lack of confidence? Does jealousy cause constant turmoil and torment in your marriage?

Considering these questions will help you to make your marriage affair proof.

Hints for Her

Review the *ifs* for open communication earlier in this chapter, and ask yourself these important questions:

- Do I *listen* carefully to my husband, or do I do all the talking?

- Can I hear what my husband is saying without needing to express my opinion?

- Do I speak louder when I'm trying to make a point?

- Do I keep my husband from talking by talking so much myself?

- Do I always have to have *the last word?*

- Do I speak to my husband in the same tone of voice I use to address my preschooler?

Commit to improving your own communication techniques with your husband. He will be trying to do the same thing after he finishes reading this chapter.

CONCLUSION

This chapter included many things that you can do to understand your wife better and to work at building an even better marriage relationship. Discuss the marriage checklist with your wife, and determine together to take those ten steps to a more fulfilling marriage relationship.

ASKING GOD'S HELP

Father, I want to be the man, in every way, that my wife wants. Teach me to love her completely, passionately, and romantically. Help me to recognize that sometimes all she wants is my affection. Help us both to celebrate our differences and to communicate openly about them every day. Father, forgive me for the times when I have been unwilling to pray with my wife. Help me to refuse to let anything interfere with our prayer times together. Teach me the joys of mutual submission. Show me ways to reverence and respect her. And, Lord, give me Your creative help for keeping the romance in our relationship. Amen.

three

Love Secrets Every
MAN MUST KNOW

A LASTING AND JOYOUS marriage relationship doesn't just happen; you create and sustain it with continuous effort. Love, like a tree, grows stronger when it is planted in good soil, nurtured with clean water, fertilized often, and pruned. Many times a new tree must have support stakes to keep it from being destroyed by fierce winds and adverse weather while it comes to maturity.

Love fades in the environment of neglect, hostility, and resentment. Love secrets will empower you to create a great relationship. You must become a lover, a skilled communicator in the language of the heart. Most married couples spend less than thirty minutes each week sharing their most intimate feelings. Love is not enough. It must be cultivated, or it will die.

LOVE SECRET NUMBER ONE:
WHAT YOU ARE WILLING TO WALK AWAY FROM
WILL DETERMINE WHAT GOD CAN BRING YOU TO.

Let me give you three illustrations that will emphasize this point.

Samson was a handsome and athletic young man in ancient Israel. He was not attracted to any woman of his faith. In spite of his parents' warning, he chose to give his heart to Delilah, an unbeliever.

Samson should have walked away instantly from Delilah, because the Bible says, "Do not be unequally yoked together with unbelievers" (2 Cor. 6:14). Samson's bitter reward for not walking away was a cheap haircut that cost him his power with God. The anointing left him, and he didn't know it. When the Philistines came to capture him, Samson said, "I will go out as before, at other times, and shake myself free" (Judg. 16:20). He engaged the Philistines in combat and was quickly conquered. They burned out his eyes with a hot poker and forced him to grind corn like an ox all the days of his adult life, all the while mocking him in their capital city.

All he had to do to have a successful and happy life was to walk away from Delilah. He could not, and it totally destroyed his life.

David should have walked away from Bathsheba. He did not, and committed adultery with her. David entered into a conspiracy to murder the husband of Bathsheba, Uriah, to hide Bathsheba's pregnancy before the eyes of Israel. Their lust produced a child, who died shortly after birth.

The prophet Nathan walked into the palatial chambers of King David, pointed his bony finger in the ashen-white face of the sovereign, and said, "You are the man!" (2 Sam. 12:7).

Because David did not walk away from Bathsheba, God promised that the sword would never depart from his house (2 Sam. 12:10). Their first-born child died at birth. Absalom became a rebel who wanted to murder his father and take his kingdom from him. David's daughter Tamar was raped by David's son Amnon. David's wives were used sexually by Absalom in the sight of all Israel. David lived in shame and public ridicule until the day he died because of his illicit relationship with Bathsheba.

Is there someone in your life from whom you need to walk away? Remember that good is the enemy of better, and better is the enemy of best. Before God can give you something that is better, He has to take that which is good away from you. And before He can give you what is the best, He must take what is better away. If you do not trust God to bring you to your divine destiny and absolutely believe that your best interest is His top concern, you will live in torment, worrying over your relationships.

Let me tell you about Barbara and Bill. Barbara was a college graduate who had a bright future in the field of hotel management. She was dating a young man who was trying to stretch four years of college into eight. His only two skills were that he played basketball with a local city league team, and he enjoyed line dancing. Barbara was raised in the home of devout parents and in the environment of faith. Bill was raised as an American pagan.

The relationship between Barbara and Bill grew and blossomed into engagement. A moral crisis came into the life of this engaged couple, and Barbara broke the engagement. She decided to walk away from Bill. It turned out to be the best decision she ever made in her life. However, at the moment, with her face covered in tears, she felt as though her true love was walking out the door.

Six months after she ended the engagement, Barbara met a brilliant young man who became an outstanding financial institution executive. They married, and, decades later, they have one of the most beautiful marriages that I've ever known. The point is very clear. Because Barbara was willing to walk away from a relationship that compromised her moral convictions, God rewarded her with a husband who was literally Prince Charming, and remains so to this day.

Don't be afraid to walk away from a relationship in your life if that person does not meet your spiritual requirements for a lifetime partner.

LOVE SECRET NUMBER TWO:
LOVE IS NOT A LICENSE TO CHANGE
OR TO CONTROL YOUR PARTNER.

Let me tell you the story of Mary and Harry. Mary and Harry attended the same church, where they met and, sometime later, married.

On a counseling sheet during their premarital counseling, all of the requirements for an exciting marriage and a prosperous future were evident. However, shortly after they were married, storm clouds formed on the horizon. Mary was a control freak. She tried to put an iron yoke around the neck of Harry and make him accountable for every minute of his day. She gave him a cell phone and demanded that he stay in touch with her every instant. If he left work to go to the bank, get his haircut, or shop for a new suit, she wanted to know about it before it happened.

Mary also became extremely jealous. She checked the phone bill of his cell phone to see whom he called and how long they talked, and she interrogated him about the calls. Her father had been a blue-ribbon whoremonger, and she believed it was the universal curse of all men.

Mary controlled the checkbook, and any questions about how the funds were spent led to World War III with Harry. Harry was gregarious, yet Mary wanted him to stay at home. Mary was given the choice of loosening up or of losing her marriage. In her case, she lost her marriage. It was more important to her to have control of her husband than it was to hang on to the marriage relationship.

It has been said, "If you love something, set it free. If it is truly yours, it will return. If it doesn't return, it was never yours."

A struggle for control between two people is often a struggle to the death. As one struggles to

> SHE SAYS . . .
>
> **We must let go of trying to be in total control of every situation and let God have His sovereign way in our lives and in our marriages.**

get free, the other struggles more intensely to control that person. The only possible solution is for the one trying to do the controlling to set that person free, or else the relationship will be totally destroyed.

How controlling are you in your relationships?

LOVE SECRET NUMBER THREE:
THE FOLLY OF BELIEVING, "I UNDERSTAND HER."

"I understand her" has to be one of the most stupid remarks I hear young men make about their future wives.

No, you don't. She doesn't understand herself. She cries when she's happy, or for no reason whatsoever. At times she doesn't even know why she cries. If you ask her why she's crying, she will tell you, "I don't know."

Stop believing that you understand her. Try to make every day an adventure of good will, rather than trying to be a young Sigmund Freud who is psychoanalyzing your partner and structuring a relationship that will not survive the storms of life.

LOVE SECRET NUMBER FOUR:
STOP PLAYING THE BLAME GAME.

The "me" generation in America has been taught not to accept responsibility for their actions. Sir Winston Churchill said, "Responsibility is the key to greatness."

Why do you do what you do? The answer is very simple. You do what you do because you are who you are. If you cannot accept responsibility for who you have become and for the things you do, no marriage counselor on earth could keep your marriage together.

Blaming your partner and complaining about what she does doesn't work. Most of us try to blame others for the emotional agony we experience. We say things like: "Stop making me feel guilty." "After all I've done for you, this is the thanks I get." "It's your fault. Don't come crying to me because of your choices."

How often have you told your wife to make a decision for both of you, and then complained about the outcome? You tell her to pick a place to eat supper, yet when she does, it's the wrong place. You tell her to choose the movie to go see, and when she picks the movie, it's the wrong movie.

Don't become like the man who complained about everything his wife did. On one particular morning, he told her, "I want you to fry one egg and boil the other." Graciously, she did so. When she brought both eggs on a plate to the table and set it before him, he looked at his wife and snarled, saying, "You boiled the wrong egg."

Tragically, I know husbands who criticize everything their wives do. Stop it! You are systematically destroying her self-esteem and every feeling of self-worth she has. You are blaming her for your faults, your failures, and your emotional insecurities.

You can break the blaming habit by praising your wife sincerely and publicly when she does something good. Shift your attention from nagging about everything she does that does not satisfy you to blessing her for those things she does that make your life as sweet as the days of heaven on earth.

LOVE SECRET NUMBER FIVE:
WHEN YOU MAKE A MISTAKE,
ACKNOWLEDGE IT AND APOLOGIZE.

Every person in every married relationship makes major mistakes despite the best intentions and all the wisdom in the world. Minor shortcomings add humor to affection. Perfection is not necessary. Love allows room for disagreements, mistakes, and sadness. However, love *does* mean that you have to learn to say, "I'm sorry."

On one occasion I came home late one Saturday afternoon from the ranch. I was tired and wanted to take a shower and get ready for the Sunday services the next day.

When I got out of my Chevy truck, Diana told me we had a massive leak in the plumbing that was in the wall of the garage. That was the last thing I wanted to hear. When I looked in the garage, I saw the water seeping from the lower wall onto the floor. I grabbed my electric ripsaw and cut a four-foot piece of paneling out of the wall, ripping it loose to examine the faulty plumbing.

All the while I was working, Diana was telling me, "I think there has to be an easier way to solve this problem."

I just looked at her like she had lost her mind and continued the surgical sawing. When I pulled the four-foot-square piece of plywood off the wall, I looked through into the wall. From my vantage point in the garage, suddenly I could see that in the wall was a dripping hot water faucet—and that the wall on the other side had a door that had been put there for easy access to the plumbing! All I had to do to solve the problem was turn the corner, open the door, turn off the faucet, and it was done.

Did I have egg on my face? At least a plate full. Did I have to look at Diana and say, "I'm sorry"? Absolutely.

That night for supper, I ate a large plate of crow. You must learn to apologize when you make a mistake. It is a love secret you may not enjoy, but you must do it to maintain honesty and integrity in the relationship.

LOVE SECRET NUMBER SIX:
LEARN TO LAUGH.

My mother has the spirit of joy. She loves laughter. I believe that people who learn to laugh live long and joyous lives. Mother is ninety-one years of age at this writing, in great health, and living her life joyously.

I know many people who, when they think of love, usually think of passion and romance rather than the joy of laughter. Yet a shared joke, a knowing wink, and a sense of joyous living can make your life delightful.

It's important to learn to laugh together, not *at* each other, but *with* each other. This kind of laughter does not signal mocking or contempt, but it expresses understanding and love.

Laughter is not only a great connector; it's also a great healer. Sophisticated studies are being made in medical science to verify that when you laugh, the brain releases powerful endorphins that heal sickness. The Bible says it this way, "The joy of the LORD is your strength" (Neh. 8:10). The Bible also says, "A merry heart does good, like medicine" (Prov. 17:22).

How much laughter is there in your relationship? When you see your wife and loved ones at the end of your day, do you find ways to share joy and laughter? Or have you become so obsessed with work and toil that you have forgotten to develop the sound of laughter in your home? Do it! The rewards are better than streams in the desert.

LOVE SECRET NUMBER SEVEN:
A MARRIAGE BUILT UPON SEXUAL EXCITEMENT ALONE IS DOOMED TO FAILURE.

I have been the pastor of thousands of people for nearly forty-six years. I have never seen a marriage built on sexual excitement that was successful. At the beginning of this book, I stated that there are three phases of marriage: "lust, rust, and dust." If you are building a dating relationship on sexual excitement, you are violating the laws of God as a fornicator, and your relationship in the future is doomed without total repentance and reformation.

When you become romantically involved, you experience an intense adrenaline and endorphin high. Romantic love can be very exciting. Sex ups the ante even more. However, the body can keep the flow of adrenaline and endorphins going for just so long.

Soon you become exhausted, depressed, and bored. The relationship is dumped, and you go on to someone else who will give you that same excitement. But soon that new relationship dies also because it has a faulty foundation.

Almost everyone has experienced the physical sensations of romance—the pounding of the heart, butterflies in the stomach, goose bumps, chills, tingling, trembling, and sexual excitement.

That is not *love*; it is *romance*. Many people become addicted to romance. As a result of such an addiction, there are many disappointments in love, and many marriages fail. Relationships built on the excitement of sex alone are doomed to failure.

Are you addicted to the excitement and rush of romance? The consequences will be a perpetual merry-go-round of relationships that never develop into marriage because of the faulty foundations upon which you build.

LOVE SECRET NUMBER EIGHT:
JEALOUSY IS THE WAY TO DRIVE YOUR WIFE OFF WITHOUT TRYING.

As I look back over forty-six years of ministry, I see a graveyard filled with marriages that were murdered by jealousy. Jealousy destroys the very love it seeks to develop. Jealousy turns conversations into inquisitions: "Where were you?" "What did he look like?" "How do I know you're not lying?"

It is ironic that the more possessive you become, and the more love you demand, the less love you will receive. But the more freedom you give, and the less love you demand, the more love you will receive.

The Bible says, "Jealousy [is] as cruel as the grave" (Song of Sol. 8:6). Let me share with you the story of a man who discovered love letters in his wife's dresser drawer. This particular man was a man driven compulsively by the spirit of jealousy. Everything his wife did created intense suspicion in his mind. Telephone conversations that lasted more than just a few moments became the basis for interrogation. When his wife went somewhere without him, upon her return he drilled her with: "Where were you? Whom did you see? What did they say?" And so on.

When he found the letters in the drawer, he went into a rage, knowing *for certain* that his wife was having an affair with another man. He was sure that he had lost her. Enraged, he beat her brutally with his fists. When he was put in jail and the lawyers started going through the letters, they made a shocking discovery. They were letters he had written her in his youth that she had saved for thirty years to remember a love that had been lost, a marriage that was killed by jealousy.

LOVE SECRET NUMBER NINE:
LEARN TO FORGIVE YOURSELF FOR NOT BEING PERFECT.

There is no perfect man!

There is no perfect woman!

Stop looking for her. She doesn't exist. At the present time I know several young men in my church who are looking for a woman who is the combination of Catherine Zeta-Jones, Betty Crocker, and Mother Teresa. That woman does not exist on the face of the earth.

They read Proverbs 31 and brazenly declare, "That's the kind of woman I'm looking for." Let me assure you that Proverbs 31 does not speak of one particular woman. It is God's composite of the characteristics of good women. No one woman possesses all those characteristics. Proverbs 31 is a *goal*; it's not a *god*.

Many people feel they are not "made of the right stuff" because they were rejected by their parents or peers, or because they failed at their first marriages or had a series of business failures. As a result, they feel they are fatally flawed.

Unnecessary guilt may be the result of having been told inappropriately that you are flawed. As a result of internalizing a harsh criticism, people wind up treating themselves worse than their parents ever did.

Many years ago when I was a young man in evangelism, traveling the nation and speaking from church to church, at one church I observed a young man sitting on the back pew. His hair was white as snow. Although his face was young, his eyes and expressions were haggard and old.

On that particular night, I chose the theme of "The Peace of God That Surpasses Understanding!" As I presented the message, I saw tears flowing down his face. After the service, he came forward for prayer, and I spoke with him at length. Here is his story.

> ## SHE SAYS...
>
> **Only the Master Potter can mold each of us into the design He wants and make every lid fit perfectly with every pot. To have a "perfect fit" we must let Him work His plan.**

He was a soldier serving our country in the Korean War. He was a demolition expert whose responsibility it was to go into a given area, search for any buried bombs or demolition devices, and then pronounce the area to be clear. One day he and his team went into a particular area, performed their search, and then announced to their comrades, "This area is clean of land mines and explosives."

Within minutes, his dearest friend stepped on a land mine and was killed. It was a moment in time that changed his life, and his black, wavy hair became white as snow in a matter of weeks. Emotionally, he was a living dead man. He blamed himself for the death of his friend to the point that he preferred death to the life he lived.

I met with that young man for more than one hour following the service and encouraged him that God had forgiven him, and he should forgive himself. There are many people who have a dark page in their lives. Perhaps you are reading this book right now, and you have an area in your life that requires you to accept the forgiveness God has already given. None of us are perfect. "For all have sinned and fall short of the glory of God" (Rom. 3:23). The sooner you recognize your imperfection and the fact that you are, on your best day, a fatally flawed mortal, living day to day by the grace of God, the sooner you will be happy.

Hints for Her

In this chapter and the next, your husband is learning eighteen important love secrets that will help him to cultivate your marriage relationship for fresh, new growth. The real-life stories that demonstrate the importance of each of these love secrets enabled many couples to have fresh, vibrant relationships with their mates. In a marriage, there are two people who must grow. Think about these love secrets, and see if God is asking for some *cultivation* on your part for a new harvest of love for your husband. Ask yourself these questions:

- Are there relationships in your life that should be less important so your marriage relationship can be more important?

- Are there areas where you should stop trying to control your husband?

- Are you trying to help your husband understand you better?

- Are there things you should stop nagging your husband about?

- Are you willing to admit your mistakes and apologize quickly?

- Do you laugh *with* your husband—or *at* him?

- Have you realized that it takes more than *romance* to build a marriage?

- Do you continually avoid all thoughts of jealousy that surface?

- Do you admit your own imperfections—and *forgive, forgive,* and *forgive* your husband for his?

CONCLUSION

We will take a look at some more love secrets in the next chapter. But the greatest truth about love is no secret at all—it's a demonstration of love from Jesus Christ Himself: "By this we know love, because He laid down His life for us. And we also ought to lay down our lives for the brethren [or your wife . . . or your husband . . .]" (1 John 3:16).

ASKING GOD'S HELP

Father, I'm just an ordinary man who needs to learn—and to prac-tice—the love secrets You are showing me in this book. I trust You, Lord, to lead me away from anything that could interfere in my relationship to You or to my wife. May I never forget that it is not my place to try to control my wife or to blame her for the things that might not be working in our marriage. Forgive me for not taking the time to try to understand her better. Thank You, Father, for giving her to me. Forgive me for my stubborn unwillingness to admit my mistakes and apologize quickly. Help us to laugh about our imperfections as we commit our lives to becoming the husband and wife You want us to be. Amen.

I N THE LAST chapter we learned about nine important love secrets every man should know. With nine secrets, you should be well on your way to becoming the husband your wife has always dreamed of having. But you're not finished yet. I want to tell you about nine more love secrets that will increase your ability to be the godly husband you were meant to be.

LOVE SECRET NUMBER TEN: NO PAIN, NO GAIN.

You may have heard this: "If it has to be, it's up to me." You may have heard your athletic coach tell you, while running wind sprints on a football field or dashing up and down the basketball court, "If it doesn't hurt you, it's not doing you any good."

In the development of a marital relationship, whenever you take a new step and venture into the unknown emotionally, you're bound to experience some anxiety. Some fear is natural when you commit to a new relationship or confront a problem in your marriage.

By remaining stuck, you can try avoiding reality. By refusing to work out the difficulty in your relationship, you can convince yourself that the relationship is basically sound and will last. Sooner or later, this bubble of self-delusion will burst.

Stop thinking of yourself as fragile. You won't realize how strong you are until you stop putting up with problems in your love relationship and take steps toward change. Change is painful. But if there is no pain, there is no gain.

Ask yourself, "What are the most painful events in my life?" What did you learn from those difficult times that caused you to be the person that you are today? Or have you put your head in the sand to avoid reality, refusing to face the problems you need to face to become the person God wants you to be?

LOVE SECRET NUMBER ELEVEN:
DON'T LET YOUR PARENTS' MARRIAGE CONTROL YOURS.

The Bible says, "For this cause shall a man leave father and mother, and shall cleave to his wife: and they twain shall be one flesh" (Matt. 19:5, KJV). Notice the words *leave* and *cleave*.

SHE SAYS . . .

If you have an argument with your husband, don't share that argument with your parents. It could take much longer than you desire for your husband to regain respect in the eyes of your parents.

When you get married, you leave the authority your parents have to control your life. You do not have to call home to see where you will have Thanksgiving or Christmas dinner. You do not have to call your mother or father to get their approval for anything you are doing. You are a new family unit with the sovereign blessing of Almighty God to do and to become what your divine destiny dictates. When your parents invade your space with their opinions, you may listen politely and totally ignore everything they say.

You may be blessed with parents who are wise and whose counsel you seek out. This is an entirely different manner than allowing your parents' marriage to control your marriage. Was your parents' marriage an ideal marriage, or was it a perpetual war zone?

Do you explode in anger over small matters and later regret what you said because of the conduct of your father? Do you have an alcohol, drug, or food addiction that destroys the relationship with your wife or fiancée because you are allowing your parents' marriage to control you? Do you suffer from fears of rejection, disapproval, or abandonment because your parents' relationship is still affecting you?

Ask yourself this question: "Do I want a marriage just like that of my parents?" The vast majority of times, the answer will be a resounding *no*. Then, with the guidance of God, take your spouse by the hand and determine that you will leave your parents and cleave to your wife to produce heaven on earth in your home.

LOVE SECRET NUMBER TWELVE:
HOW TO PUT LOVE FIRST TO MAKE LOVE LAST.

The Bible describes the complexity and majesty of God with these three words "God is love" (1 John 4:16). When Jesus completed His ministry on this earth, He gave His disciples a command, known as the eleventh commandment, which was, "Love one another as I have loved you" (John 15:12). Christ gave His love when it was not deserved to people who did not deserve it. That's a principle you're going to have to practice in your marriage if it's to be an exciting and enduring marriage.

There will come a time when you will need to give love to your spouse, love that is not deserved, and give it joyfully. We are all angels with one wing, and we need each other to fly. Marriage is God's idea, and it is the microcosm of heaven on earth. But the glue that holds it together is the unconditional love of God one for the other. Love is the one ingredient of which our world never tires and of which there is never an overabundance. The world will never outgrow its need for love. God created us in His own image, which means we were created to function on the fuel of love. The apostle Paul said, "Our love for God and for our neighbor is the fulfillment of all the Law of God." (See Romans 13:8.)

The world cries out for genuine love, love that heals, love that unites, love that forgives, love that encourages. Dr. Karl Menninger, famed American psychiatrist, found that people who are able to give and receive love recover more quickly from their illness. He stated, "Love

> *S*HE *S*AYS . . .
>
> **You and your husband have to partner together in order to make a good family. One of the areas needing your partnership efforts is in the area of family relationships.**

cures people—both the ones who give it and the ones who receive it."[1] In contrast, individuals who lack love often develop personality scars and often die. Love is essential to our emotional, physical, mental, and social well-being. Our lives are shaped by those who love us and by those who refuse to love us.

My cousin, who is an accomplished surgeon, told me the story of a twelve-year-old boy for whom he performed a surgery that was considered routine. The boy was healthy, and there was no physical reason why he should not have recovered from this surgery. However, my cousin observed that no one came to see the boy after he was admitted. There was no one there when he went into surgery. When he returned to his room after surgery, no one from his family was there. When my cousin asked him about his family, it became obvious that no one truly loved this boy.

That night, a twelve-year-old boy—who was healthy and had every medical reason to live—died. With tears in his eyes, my cousin said, "He died from the lack of love. Love would have kept him alive."

For sure, love will keep your marriage and the children that come from that marriage alive. If you give love away, it will be renewed each day and become stronger and purer. There is a poem that I have learned over the years, which says:

> A bell is not a bell until you ring it.
> A song is not a song until you sing it.
> Love in your heart is not put there to stay,
> Love is not love until you give it away.[2]

Whom do you love? Have you told them *today* how much you love them? Do it!

LOVE SECRET NUMBER THIRTEEN:
WHAT YOU BELIEVE TO BE SO BECOMES SO.

The Bible says, "For as he thinks in his heart, so is he" (Prov. 23:7). If you believe your marriage to be beyond the point of redemption, no one can save it. Now that our church has eighteen thousand members, I no longer do marriage counseling. We have hired a very outstanding professional staff to handle the perpetual avalanche of marriage counselees.

But for twenty years, every Thursday, which I called "Tylenol Thursday," I listened to the marital sicknesses of my congregants. I asked each man and woman who walked through my doors to answer this question as soon as they were seated: "Do you want this marriage to survive?"

I would accept no answer other than *yes* or *no*. Answers like "I'm not sure" or "Well, that depends on what he (or she) does" would cause me to shut down the counseling session. In the final analysis, if you don't want your marriage to work, even God Himself can't help you. God has given you the power of choice. As powerful as God is, He cannot answer prayer until it's prayed. You must choose to pray. As powerful as God is, He can't force you to love Him. You must choose to love Him. As powerful as God is, He cannot force you to love your wife. You must choose to love her. Many times that has to be an act of your will…not emotion.

LOVE SECRET NUMBER FOURTEEN:
YOUR ATTITUDE IS CONTAGIOUS.

How you respond to other people will dictate how they respond to you. One wife said to her husband, "I'm not a grouch; I've just been in a bad mood for forty years."

I get an attitude going to the airport. On one occasion I checked my luggage in at the Washington DC airport and saw mistletoe tied over the luggage rack. I asked the attendant behind the desk, "Why is that mistletoe tied to that luggage rack?"

He looked at me with a smirk on his face and said, "That's so you can kiss your luggage good-bye." That's an attitude.

What is an attitude? Your attitude is the advance man of your true self. Its roots are hidden, but its fruit is always visible. Your attitude is your best friend or your worst enemy. It draws people to you or repels people from you.

Your attitude is never content until it's expressed. It determines your success or your failure. It does not depend on the circumstances of your life.

Your speech is a reflection of your attitude. Stop saying, "I can't," and start saying, "I can do all things through Christ." Stop saying, "If…," and start saying, "I will by God's grace." Stop saying, "It's impossible for my marriage to improve," and start saying, "If you have faith…nothing will be impossible for you" (Matt. 17:20).

Stop saying, "I don't know the right people." If you know God the Father, God the Son, and God the Holy Spirit, you know the right people.

Stop saying, "I'm too old." Moses was eighty years old when God called him to set Israel free from Egyptian bondage. He died at one hundred twenty years of age and walked to his own funeral.

Old is when your friends compliment you on your new alligator shoes, and you are barefooted. Your attitude will determine the quality of your marriage. Have you been hurt? Get over it. Have you been unjustly criticized? Get over it. Have you been rejected? Get over it.

One of my favorite quotations of all times is one by President Calvin Coolidge, who said, "Press on. Nothing in the world can take the place of persistence. Talent will not; nothing is more common than unsuccessful men with talent. Genius will not; unrewarded genius is almost a proverb. Education will not; the world is the full of educated derelicts. Persistence and determination alone are omnipotent."[3]

Life can be a grindstone. Whether it grinds you down or polishes you depends on what you are made of. Are you made of the right stuff? Grinding makes a diamond shine with brilliant radiance. Grinding reduces dirt to dust. Are you diamond or dust?

Adversity is the opportunity for your marriage to improve. Your attitude toward adversity will determine whether you make progress or self-destruct.

A rubber band is effective only when it's stretched. A turtle gets nowhere until it sticks its neck out. Kites rise against the wind, not with it. A tiny seed has to struggle and push its way up through the rock and hard soil. It fights its way up to the sunshine, only to wrestle with storms, then snow, and then frost before it becomes a mighty oak.

Your marriage must learn to endure adversity to reach achievement. Your attitude toward adversity will determine your accomplishments.

LOVE SECRET NUMBER FIFTEEN:
NO ONE CAN MAKE YOU FEEL INFERIOR WITHOUT YOUR CONSENT.

Eleanor Roosevelt made the above statement as she championed the civil rights of black Americans to be treated fairly and equally in America.[4]

When the Founding Fathers penned the words "We the people," they did not mean black people. The Supreme Court ruled in the Dred Scott

Decision of 1857 that black people were the same as cattle.[5] They were possessions; not people. One of the great stories of conquering the feeling of being inferior to become the person God designed you to be is the story of Rosa Parks. Rosa Parks was born Rosa Louise McCauley. She was born ninety years ago in rural Alabama. This woman, who had no more than a high school education, would go on to become an American icon of unwavering resistance to oppression.

Many of Rosa Park's early memories were laced with trepidation—listening to nearby lynchings by the Ku Klux Klan, fearing that her house, too, might be ravished and burned to the ground. At the time, her birthplace, Tuskegee, was enjoyed as an illustrious place in African American history, the home of Booker T. Washington.

This graceful, soft-spoken graduate of slaves grew up to commit an act of defiance of such magnitude that the law and America were changed forever. On one particular day, Rosa Parks "sat down" for justice and equality.

When Rosa was just two, and her brother, Sylvester, was an infant, their father, James, headed north and was rarely heard from thereafter. With their mother, a teacher, they moved to tiny Pine Level, Alabama, to live on their grandparent's farm. Surrounded by her extended family, Parks matured with a profound sense of fairness and dignity. Deeply engrained in her were the lessons of her mother, Leona. Rosa Parks recalled, "My mother taught me self-respect. There's no law that says people have to suffer."

Learning to love to read at an early age, Parks attended a black-only, one-room schoolhouse for the five months a year it was open. The Parks family moved to Montgomery when she was eleven. Her education was put on hold five years later so that she could take care of her dying grandmother, and then later, her mother.

At nineteen, Rosa McCauley met and soon married a skilled and handsome barber, Raymond Parks. He was ten years her senior and a passionate civil rights activist. In her first autobiography, ***Rosa Parks: My Story***, she recalled what had impressed her most. "He didn't seem to have that meek attitude, what we call an 'Uncle Tom' attitude."

The couple's lives were constrained daily by laws that enforced segregated elevators, segregated buses, segregated water fountains and restaurants and houses—all made legal by a set of Supreme Court decisions in the late 1800s that remained valid for over seventy years.

On December 1, 1955, when forty-two-year-old Rosa Parks refused to give up her seat to a white man on a Cleveland Avenue bus after a long day's work as a seamstress, she was painfully reminded of an experience with the same driver twelve years earlier. That event had ended with her humiliated eviction from the bus. This time, she recalled, "God sat with me as I remained calm and determined not to be treated with less dignity than any other citizen of Montgomery."

She was summarily arrested and then released on bail. As the news spread throughout the African American community, a movement to boycott the municipal bus system quickly began. Dr. Martin Luther King Jr., a twenty-six-year-old unknown, added his voice to the bus boycott already being organized for December 5, Park's day in court.

As expected, she was convicted for her act of rebelliousness. Her fine was $14. The black community joined, and untold thousands of African Americans walked, carpooled, took taxis, road mules, and even missed work and school, leaving the city buses to run nearly empty.

Both Park's faith and the boycott endured for 381 days. In late 1956, the Supreme Court ruled that Montgomery's segregation laws were unconstitutional. Rosa Parks refused to hand her dignity on a silver platter to anyone. Her single act of refusing to be humiliated changed America forever.[6]

Take charge of your life, or someone else will.

LOVE SECRET NUMBER SIXTEEN: HAPPINESS IS A CHOICE.

> **SHE SAYS . . .**
>
> **Life is more than wants. Don't make the mistake of always making your wants your goals. Satisfaction will still be nowhere to be found.**

Abraham Lincoln said, "People are just about as happy as they make up their minds to be."[7]

When Jesus Christ of Nazareth preached His first sermon, the Sermon on the Mount, it contained the nine principles of happiness. He said, "Blessed are the pure in heart...Blessed are the meek...Blessed...Blessed...Blessed...Blessed." (See Matthew 5.)

The word *blessed* translates "happy." No amount of striving is going to produce happiness. No amount of manipulation, control, or berating is going to lead to fulfillment. The less able you are to experience inner peace, the more you will require material symbols like a bigger house, faster car, bigger boat, or larger salary to satisfy your thirst for happiness.

Let your highest principles guide your life, and you will find happiness on the way. Orienting your life to creative expression, the well-being of others, or the improvement of mankind will give you pleasure and happiness.

Giving yourself to another person in their hour of need creates happiness. The Bible says, "It is more blessed to give than to receive" (Acts 20:35).

You become a lover of life not by just taking a philosophical stance, but through a passionate commitment to integrate your personal growth with what you give away. It has often been said that we make a life by what we earn, but we enrich the world by what we give. You have the gift of happiness to give away every day.

Ask yourself this question: "Am I truly happy?" If not, why not? The answer lies within you.

LOVE SECRET NUMBER SEVENTEEN:
FEEL GREAT ABOUT YOURSELF.

The Bible says, "Love your neighbor as yourself" (Lev. 19:18, NIV). It is certain that if you do not like yourself, you will not like your neighbor. There is a difference between being selfish and having self-interest. To be selfish is cyanide of the soul. To be interested in your self is intelligent behavior. It is in your self-interest to go to heaven, because the alternative is to be lost forever. That's self-interest. It is in your self-interest to prosper, which is achieved in the kingdom of God by giving.

How do you feel about yourself?

When you look in the mirror, what do you see? Do you see ugliness? Do you see beauty? Do you like what you see? Do you want to change what you see? Do you like to think about your future? Who are you?

Every person on the earth is a unique creation of the hand of God. When you were born, the genius of heaven exploded. There is not another person on the planet quite like you. You have a destiny that no other person can fulfill. God has placed you on this earth for a purpose that no one but you can achieve. You need to feel good about yourself.

Let me share this personal story with you. When my father pastored in Houston, Texas, I worked at Weingarten Supermarket #16, located at Washington Avenue and Shepherd Drive. I was thirteen years of age, and my mother got me the job even though I was under age because, in her mind, if a child was not going to church or school, that child should be working. The idea of a child sitting around and watching television was absolute insanity in my mother's mind.

There was a woman who was a checker at the supermarket who was absolutely delightful. I'll call her *Nancy*. Nancy was 6'2" and weighed every ounce of 200 pounds. When you are thirteen and only 5'0" tall and weigh only 125 pounds, someone as tall as Nancy looked very large! The truth is, Nancy *was* pretty. She was happy, and she was constantly smiling. People waited in her line to be checked out because she imparted to them a sense of well-being. Nancy had more dates than ten women, and she married a husband who was very successful. Why? It was because she felt good about herself.

Over the years I have seen individuals, particularly women, who are extremely critical about their physical appearance. They are so unhappy about themselves that their misery translates into their relationships. That misery is transferred by osmosis into the life of every person with whom those individuals come into contact. Their romantic lives become merry-go-rounds of endless relationships, which never mature because the individuals do not feel good about themselves and cannot make other people comfortable with who they are.

Ask yourself these questions: "Do I really like me? What are the changes I need to make to become acceptable to me?" If you see things you can improve upon, and you refuse to do so, you are only compounding your misery. Take action!

LOVE SECRET NUMBER EIGHTEEN:
THE LOVE YOU REFUSE TO GIVE YOU LOSE.

As of this writing, I have been to Israel twenty times. Every time I go, I enjoy it beyond description. It is the land of the Lord, and it is the vortex of the world tomorrow. Every significant thing that will happen from this moment until Christ returns to earth the second time is tied to the state of Israel and to the city of Jerusalem.

One of the perpetual spiritual lessons in Israel is that of the Dead Sea and the Sea of Galilee. The Sea of Galilee flows into the Dead Sea. It continuously brings living water to a dead sea, one that is full of salt. I have swum in the Dead Sea, and its salt concentration is so intense you can literally sit in the water and read a newspaper, just like sitting on a couch. But the phenomenal thing about the Dead Sea is that in spite of all the fresh water it receives on a daily basis from the Sea of Galilee, nothing lives in it. It's absolutely dead.

Why? Because the Dead Sea only receives; it never gives. There is no place around the perimeter of the Dead Sea where it sends water to some other destination. For centuries it has been receiving the living water of the Sea of Galilee. Yet it is just as sterile today as it was in the days when Jesus Christ lived and died in the city of Jerusalem.

The love you refuse to give away will be lost to you. As your love develops, your appreciation of your own dependence upon other human beings will grow as well. The more love you feel, the more love you want to share. Personal growth and social contribution become woven into one relationship. Today there is a rising spirituality, some-times imperceptible, but becoming increasingly more evident, a respect for the sacredness of every person, occurring because of the spirit of love at work through people. You will overcome old, negative habits and experience more love and pleasure when you learn to break through old barriers and push past resistances to new levels of spiritual strength and honest communication.

Hints for Her

Think about the additional love secrets in this chapter. How can you use these concepts to cultivate a new harvest of love for your husband? Ask yourself these questions:

- Are you willing to reveal the painful areas of your marriage that need to be changed, and to work with your husband to grow beyond them?

- Does your husband know that you put your love for him ahead of everything else but God?

- Have you chosen to love your husband—every moment of every day?

- What is your attitude toward adversity?

- Are you working constantly to develop a better self-image?

- Are you a lover of life? Do you give away happiness daily?

- Do you really like yourself? If not, why not?

- Have you discovered that the more love you give away, the more you have?

CONCLUSION

Ask yourself this question: "To whom am I giving my love each day?" If you are not giving it away, you have become like the Dead Sea. Soon your life will be stagnant and sterile. Today, look for someone who needs to feel the love of God, and then give that person the love God has given to you. For all of us, our lives are shaped by the people who love us—and by the people who refuse to love us.

Choose to be a man of God who gives away love daily. Give it to God, to your wife, to your family, and to each person you meet each day. Remember this: "We love ... because He first loved us" (1 John 4:19).

ASKING GOD'S HELP

Father, I still have more to learn about the secrets of a happy marriage. Thank You for revealing some of these to me in this book. Thank You for the painful reminders that You are trying to change me into the man You want me to be. Teach me genuine love ... Your love! Help me to be giving and loving and hopeful and faithful in everything I do for my wife. I choose to be happy, Father, and to make her happy. I'll do everything I can to help her feel great about herself—and about me! Show me how to give her my love in everything I do, in everything I say, and even in the times when no words are necessary to express to her how much I love her. Amen.

E VERY MARRIAGE COUNSELEE who walks through the door of my office believes his or her marriage is the absolute worst marriage on Planet Earth. They multiply their problems on a calculator and count their blessings on their fingers. Marriage used to be a contract. Now many regard it as a ninety-day option.

One man said, "I've been unlucky in both my marriages. My first wife left me, and my second wife won't." Marriage is the art of two incompatible people learning to live compatibly.

I heard an illustration depicting the degeneration of the romance factor in marriage by showing one husband's reactions to his wife's illness with the common cold during seven years of their marriage. He responded as follows:

The first year the husband says, "Sugar Dumpling, I'm really worried about my baby girl. You have a bad sniffle, and there's no telling about these things with all the strep going around. I'm putting you in the hospital this afternoon for a general checkup and a good rest. I know the food is lousy, but I'll be bringing your meals from Zios. I already have it all arranged with the floor superintendent."

The second year of the married cold, the husband says, "Listen, darling, I don't like the sound of that cough, and I just called Dr. Miller to rush over here. Now you go to bed like a good girl, just for me."

The third year of the married cold, the husband says this: "Maybe you better lie down, honey. Nothing like a little rest when you feel lousy. I'll bring you something. Do we have any canned soup?" Notice the degeneration?

The fourth year of the married cold, the husband says to his wife, "Now look, dear, be sensible. After you have fed the kids, done the dishes, and mopped the floors, you'd better lie down."

The fifth year of the married cold, the husband says, "Why don't you take a couple of aspirin?"

The sixth year of the married cold, the husband says to the wife, "I wish you would just gargle or something instead of sitting around barking like a seal all day."

The husband says on the seventh year of the married cold, "For Pete's sake, stop sneezing! Are you trying to give me pneumonia?" The romance factor is g-o-n-e! Now, it's a matter of survival, and this is not a reality TV show. It's life!

Marriage is like a computer. You get out of it what you put into it. Trash in; trash out. If there is no investment of yourself, of your emotions, of your heart, you will receive nothing in return.

When I was eight and earning my money by picking cotton on the farm of a man who attended my father's church, that family of seven and all the hired hands got their drinking water out of a well that functioned with a manual pump. Before you could get water out of the well, you had to pour water down the shaft to wet the leather that created the suction sufficient to bring fresh cool water to the top. If you put no water down the well, you could pump the handle until you had blisters, and there would be no water. No water in; no water out.

> **SHE SAYS...**
>
> **Thank the Lord every day for your husband, and call out in him the traits that God wants in him to be the man He has destined him to be.**

Marriage is the same. No love in; no love out. No tender communication in; no tender communication out. If you nurture your marriage, it will be your oasis. If you neglect it, it will become your Sahara Desert.

In this chapter, I will share some composites from true-life stories of people who have walked into my office over the years with marital problems that were colossal in nature. I share these living testimonies of unspeakable suffering with you to show you that you can recover if you're willing to save your marriage. The names have been changed, but the facts are absolutely true. You will see yourself in some of these relationships.

CAN THIS MARRIAGE BE SAVED FROM ADULTERY?

Let me tell you the story of Bob and Betty. Bob was a dentist with an outstanding practice in the northeast section of the United States. He was handsome and had an outgoing personality. He was, in fact, tall, athletic, and a high-energy, type-A go-getter.

In addition to his accomplishments as an outstanding dentist, he was a loving father and fantastic husband. He was every woman's dream for a husband. He had been a faithful, loyal, loving husband for nearly twenty years without fail. He provided handsomely for his wife and children, and he believed his marriage was bulletproof. He was wrong.

His wife, Betty, was an intelligent, modestly attractive woman, but not nearly as attractive as Bob. People wondered how in heaven's name she ever attracted Bob.

Betty was short and stocky, and she wore thick glasses that distorted the shape of her blue eyes. She had straight, reddish-brown hair that she wore pulled back in a ponytail. She was not outgoing and did not seem to make friends easily. Bob and Betty were polar opposites in many ways. Remember, opposites attract before marriage and irritate after marriage.

The day came when Bob walked into my office, his face ashen white. He sat down looking like a mule had kicked him in the stomach, and without my saying a word, he blurted out, "Betty is having an affair with the contractor who has been building our house."

I was stunned. Both of us sat in total silence for a prolonged period of time. Tears began flowing down Bob's face.

"When did it begin?" I asked him.

He responded stoically, "Over a year ago when we began planning to build."

"How did you find out?"

"She told me this morning at breakfast that her relationship with him had developed to the stage that she could no longer hide her deep feelings for him. She wants a divorce and plans to marry him and move to another state with our children."

I asked bluntly, "Are you telling me that you had no clue before today that your relationship with Betty was drifting? How can a woman have sex with one man during the day, then come home and get in bed with her husband without the husband knowing something is wrong?"

Bob shrugged his shoulders, absolutely shell-shocked. "I absolutely had no clue. There have been no arguments. There have been no disagreements. I thought our marriage was a work of perfection until this afternoon."

There was a long pause, and then Bob asked, "What are my options as far as God and the Bible are concerned?" I waited for a long moment, looking at a man who had just been emotionally gutted. His world of absolute perfection was imploding. All he had worked for his adult life was burning to the ground.

I answered Bob by saying, "Biblically you have the right, according to Christ's teaching in Matthew 19:9, to divorce your wife. Jesus said, 'And I say to you, whoever divorces his wife, except for sexual immorality, and marries another, commits adultery.' Your wife has committed adultery. You are free to divorce and remarry if you choose to."

Then I continued by saying, "But you have another option also. You can forgive her—totally and completely forgive her. That's always an option in Christianity."

Bob looked at me with glazed eyes. He stared at me without speaking. I had no idea what he was thinking. Would he opt for divorce . . . or try to save the marriage?

I interrupted the silence saying, "Bob, that means if she is willing to confess her sin with a contrite spirit, asking for forgiveness, you have the option to say, 'Yes, I forgive you.' But if you say, 'All is forgiven and forgotten,' then she is totally and completely forgiven. You can't bring up her adultery six months from now when you are in a heated argument. Total forgiveness means you never speak of it again—not ever! I want you to look deep into your soul and ask yourself, 'Can I do that?'"

Bob looked at me with a fresh flood of tears dripping off his face. He gasped for breath beneath sobs and blurted out: "I have to forgive her. But the problem is greater than just adultery."

I almost levitated out of my chair. "What can possibly be greater than adultery?" I had to make a conscious effort to keep my voice under control.

"She just found out that she's pregnant with the contractor's baby."

Bob looked at me like a child looking at his father for my reaction.

My heart almost stopped! Here was sweet, quiet Betty teaching a children's Sunday school class on Sunday but living an adulterous lifestyle Monday through Saturday—and carrying another man's child. I wanted to scream. The spirit of slap came into both my hands.

"Bob, are you sure you even want to try to save this marriage?" I was almost yelling!

Without hesitation, and very firmly, he responded, "Absolutely."

I sat for an extended period of time in stone-cold silence. I thought to myself, *He's in shock. He doesn't know what he's saying. When he goes home and thinks this through, reality will set in, and he's going to explode in a demonstration of rage and violence. There's no way this marriage can survive adultery, which has led to pregnancy. It's time for reality therapy.*

"Bob," I roared more like a marine drill instructor than a marriage counselor, "are you telling me you are ready to forgive your wife totally without a trace of malice or lingering hostility, and to raise another man's child as your own?"

Bob looked at me through piercing brown eyes and fired back firmly: "Yes! That's exactly what I mean."

A complete book could be written as a classic study for absolute marital impossibilities based on this particular case. Can this marriage be saved? Not one man in ten thousand would even try to save this marriage. But I am here to bear witness that by God's sovereign grace, this marriage was miraculously saved and has survived for many years with genuine love and mutual affection one for the other.

> *S*HE *S*AYS...
>
> **There is a mercy bank in all of our lives. The more you deposit mercy into your bank, the more you will receive when you need it.**

Bob and Betty are happily living together as man and wife, and they have two grown children, one his adopted son from his wife's adulterous affair, and a couple of grandchildren, because "if you have faith—nothing will be impossible for you" (Matt. 17:20). Now what did you say is the problem in your marriage?

CAN THIS MARRIAGE BE SAVED FROM ABUSE?

Let me tell you the story of Ruth and Roy. Roy was the athletic supervisor for recreational sports through the public parks in his county. He was 6'4" and weighed about 250 pounds. He was a physical powerhouse. He was an avid collector of antique cars, and he spent enormous sums of money traveling to all parts of the world to buy them. He and Ruth had been married for about ten years when they walked through the door of my office for marriage counseling.

Ruth was an attractive woman. Moderately tall herself, she carried herself graciously, had a very outgoing personality, and was dearly loved by her children as a devout mother and loyal wife. Ruth was tender and loving…but push her too far, and you had a wildcat in high heels.

One night I received a phone call from Roy, who said he wanted to "drop by the office with his wife and discuss a marital problem." The church, at that time, was quite small, less than five hundred people, and my schedule in those days was flexible, so I agreed.

They walked into my office, introduced themselves, and sat down on the couch across the desk from me. Roy reached into his suit pocket and pulled out a letter from a physician authorizing Roy to have his wife admitted to a mental health facility without her approval. He handed me the document with an air of official condemnation, and I read through it. I laid it on my desk, knowing his mind was concrete—thoroughly mixed up and firmly set.

"Roy," I said to him, "you have come to my office to talk about saving your marriage. Why are you handing me a letter to have your wife committed to a mental hospital?"

Roy looked at me without blinking and said, "That's where she needs to be."

I asked him, "Why do you feel your wife needs to be admitted to the mental hospital?"

He responded, "Because she is thoroughly addicted to prescription drugs and high all the time. Therefore, most of the time she is sleeping. She does not keep the house clean, and when I come home, supper is not ready. When she is in one of her depressive episodes, she leaves our young children completely unsupervised."

I looked at Ruth, who was sizzling at the accusations being made toward her. I was about to see the wildcat turned loose.

"Ruth, do you take prescription drugs excessively?"

She responded, "I probably do, but I'm constantly fighting depression over Roy's multiple adulterous relationships." Roy's calm demeanor was instantly transformed. His face turned crimson red with rage.

Roy reached back his right hand to slap Ruth, but he was a half second too late. Ruth had cocked her right fist and landed a haymaker right on the side of Roy's jaw. I am here to tell you that there was a battle royal between husband and wife on that couch so violent it broke the legs off my couch. I sat right there and watched them go at it. I was not about to get in that fight. My mother didn't raise an idiot.

When they had literally beat the thunder out of each other, I asked them to please be seated so we could continue. It was so bizarre that it was all I could do not to laugh. They were sitting on a broken couch trying to heal a broken marriage after a fight ESPN would love to telecast. Could this marriage possibly be saved?

I hit Roy with my standard shot over the bar: "Do you want to get rid of your wife, or do you want to save this marriage?"

Roy looked at me like I had stabbed him with a sword. "I want to save our marriage, but it has too many problems."

I responded tartly, "And you are the source of the problem. You expect your wife to perform flawlessly in the midst of your perpetual adulterous relationships. Your demands in the marriage are unreasonable. Her response to your actions is predictable. Do you want this marriage to be saved?"

"Yes, I would like for the marriage to continue. We have two beautiful children, and they deserve a home without chaos."

I looked at Ruth and asked her, "Ruth, are you willing to forgive Roy for his adulterous relationships and work to save this marriage?"

"Absolutely. There's nothing on earth I will not do to save my marriage. I freely and gladly forgive him of everything that he has done in the past."

I picked up the phone and called the doctor who had signed the letter to commit her to the mental hospital. I told him that Roy had misled him about his wife's condition and that I was tearing up the document and throwing it in the garbage. He gave his consent. The "put the wife in the mental hospital approach" to the marital problem was over.

Roy and Ruth went through months of counseling. In their first session, I asked them to write everything they could think of in answer to these four questions:

1. What do you like about your marriage?
2. What do you dislike about your marriage?

3. What changes do you want your spouse to make?
4. What changes are you willing to make?

When they came back to my office the second week, they each came back with a stack of papers as thick as a telephone book. They had both written enough to put *Gone With the Wind* to shame. It was a beginning. I had a new couch, and both Roy and Ruth had a new attitude.

Several months of confession and repentance led to restoration with reconciliation. That marriage was gloriously and divinely saved. There is no adversity that cannot be overcome if two human beings are willing to totally forgive each other and not allow the past to control their future.

> **SHE SAYS . . .**
>
> **Remember that it isn't *honesty* that drives a wedge of distance into your marriage—it is *dishonesty*.**

CAN THIS MARRIAGE SURVIVE HARD TIME IN PRISON?

The following statement may shock you, but it's a statement of absolute truth. Some of the sweetest, most generous people I have ever met are people who have spent time in prison.

Never look at a person who has been to prison and write that person off as a second-class citizen. Some people in prison are there because they made a mistake they will regret for the rest of their lives. Others experience a real conversion experience in prison and come out different people. Some who are there are not even guilty of the crime that put them there. There are people who are sent to prison because they had an incompetent lawyer. In America, tragically, it is true that your defense is just about as good as your bank account. When your bank account is exhausted, so will your defense be exhausted.

When I was attending graduate school at North Texas University where I received my master's degree, I worked for a man who had spent eight years in the penitentiary. He had been reared in a church by a godly father, but he started running with the wrong crowd as a teenager. He was sent to prison with a sentence of sixty-six years for selling drugs.

While in prison, a Christian group held a chapel service, and a woman gave him a New Testament. To alleviate the boredom behind prison walls, he read the New Testament for the first time, searching for the Christ he had never found in a church. Behind prison walls, he was gloriously converted.

My friend became such a model prisoner that at the end of his eighth year, he was released from prison. He returned to his family in the Dallas area, where some close relatives were very successful commercial building contractors. They gave my friend a job pouring sidewalks. Gradually he progressed from pouring sidewalks to pouring foundations for homes and apartment complexes. Bit by bit, he learned to be a skilled contractor. Within a few years he was happily married, wealthy, and the father of two beautiful children.

When I was attending North Texas University, he gave me a job taking care of an apartment complex. My payment was a rent-free apartment at a point in my life when every dime had to count. No other person has been more gracious or generous to me than this man, who came from behind prison walls.

Sitting each Sunday in the pews in the sanctuary of my church are a number of people who have been to prison. Most of them received justice, but some were innocent. Believe me, we live in a world where innocent people do go to prison.

Here is a fact about prison that few people ever consider: when a man goes to prison, his wife and his children go with him. The breadwinner is gone. Economically, the family is devastated. Emotionally, the children are in instant disarray. The wife flounders while trying to recapture a life that has suddenly been scattered in this cataclysmic experience.

Every year at Cornerstone Church, we give away thousands of toys to children whose fathers are behind prison walls. Without those gifts, those children would have no Christmas. We tell those children the gifts came from their fathers, so that they have a love relationship sustained for someone who is not there.

Can marriage survive hard time in prison? Let me tell you the story of Jack and Jo-Ann. Jack was sent to prison, and, with all of my heart, I believe he was innocent. He received a four-year sentence for a nonviolent offense. Jack had lived every day of his adult life as a Bible-believing Christian.

The day federal marshals handcuffed him and led him out of the courtroom, he looked over his shoulder at his wife and children with tears running down his face. It was an absolute nightmare. It was unbelievable, but it was happening.

Jo-Ann went home, and life suddenly began to unravel. The bank foreclosed on their home. Every financial calamity you can imagine began to happen to her. Their lives were being scattered like straw in the grip of a vicious tornado.

Jo-Ann was like a bleeding victim in the ocean whose blood attracted sharks, and the feeding frenzy was on.

They lost their home and all their possessions. Jo-Ann moved into a trailer house owned by one of their grown children. She did not get bitter.

Her husband called her from the penitentiary and told her that he had found a way to make money by washing the clothes of some of the inmates. The penitentiary gave a limited amount of hand soap to every prisoner. It was insufficient to wash your clothes, so he was going to wash the other prisoner's clothes and charge them a small fee.

Jo-Ann went to the supermarket and bought large boxes of laundry soap. At night, she carried them to the field where her husband would be working each day and hid the soap for her husband to find the next day. He used the soap to generate enough income to have the seed money for a new start when he was released four years later.

Jack has been out of prison for ten years. His business is thriving again. He never misses a day in the house of the Lord. He did not become bitter for a situation that has no rational explanation. Only God in eternity will be able to explain why it happened and what the purpose was for that experience.

Because Jack and Jo-Ann had sustaining faith in Christ, they went through a prison experience that brought them closer to Christ and to each other. Although they lost all their material possessions, they discovered that life does not consist in the abundance of *things*. The greatest treasure in life is the love that a man and a woman have for each other.

Can a marriage endure a prison experience? Can it go through the fire of financial loss and survive? Can it survive public ridicule? Can it endure the self-righteous snobbery of fellow church members? The answer is absolutely *yes!*

If you have a loved one in prison, pray for that person, because life behind bars is life in a living hell. If you have a friend in prison, remember that his wife and children are struggling. Reach out to them, and help them. Remember Jesus Christ, who said, "I was...in prison and you did not visit Me" (Matt. 25:43).

Hints for Her

No woman would choose to marry a man who told her before they married that he would have an adulterous affair; abuse her physically, sexually, or emotionally; or commit a crime that would require him to be imprisoned. These may not be issues that have affected your marriage. But if they have, I pray that the real-life stories in this chapter have given you hope and courage to face your circumstances and ask God for wisdom to help you follow His will for you in your marriage.

If you have never been confronted with these problems in your own marriage, do more than merely thank God that He has protected you from adultery, abuse, and imprisonment. Ask Him what you can do to help someone else who is facing one of these situations. Then go on and ask Him what you can do to build a wall of protection that is even stronger around your own marriage relationship so that you need never face a devastating problem that could threaten your marriage.

CONCLUSION

Can God save a marriage threatened by an adulterous affair? Is there any hope for a marriage where physical, emotional, or sexual abuse has taken root? Will a marriage survive when one of the marriage partners is doing hard time in prison?

Bob and Betty, Ruth and Roy, and Jack and Jo-Ann discovered that God is greater than these devastating circumstances. When they were willing to turn to Him for wisdom and direction—and willing to work hard at what He told them to do—their marriages were not only saved, but also they were made many times better than anything they had previously experienced.

God is greater than anything you may face in your marriage. Remember this: "If you have faith...nothing will be impossible for you" (Matt. 17:20).

Asking God's Help

Father, may we never experience the pain of facing adultery, abuse, or imprisonment. Show me ever more clearly how to avoid the temptations—even in my thought life—that could lead to one of these problems. Help our marriage to be a beacon of light to other couples, a light that leads them to Your will and Your guidance and love. Help me never to forget the lesson in this chapter that says, "God is greater than anything you will ever face in your marriage." Hold me closely to You with the cords of love, and give me opportunities to walk in faith believing that "nothing will be impossible" for me with Your help. Amen.

ADDICTIONS, ALCOHOLISM, OR HOMOSEXUALITY?

six

AMERICA HAS BECOME the mecca of addiction. The cost and consequence of alcoholism and drug dependence place an enormous burden on America's society. Substance abuse is America's number one health problem. It strains the health care system and the economy, and it harms family life while threatening public safety. At the same time, America is facing the problem of addictive lifestyles. Homosexuality is on the increase, often causing devastation to families as its insidious tentacles reach into homes and marriages and rip them asunder. Is there hope for marriages suffering the agony of overwhelming addictions?

CAN THIS MARRIAGE BE SAVED FROM ADDICTIONS?

Substance abuse crosses all societal boundaries. The problem of addiction affects each gender, every ethnic group, and people in every tax bracket. America has become addicted to alcohol, drugs, pornography, and ideological concepts that have become a cancer on the soul of America.

The scope of the problem can be seen in the following facts.[1] There are more debts and disabilities each year in the United States from substance abuse than from any other cause. About eighteen million Americans have alcohol problems. About five to six million Americans have serious drug problems. More than half of all adults have a family history of alcoholism or problem drinking. More than nine million children live with a parent dependent on alcohol or illegal drugs.

The consequences of addiction are as follows: one-fourth of all emergency room admissions, one-third of all suicides, and more than half of all homicides and incidents of domestic violence are commonly related. Heavy drinking contributed to illness in each of the top three causes of death: heart disease, cancer, and stroke. Almost half of all traffic fatalities are alcohol related. Between 48 and 64 percent of people who die in fires have blood alcohol levels indicating intoxication. Fetal alcohol syndrome is the leading known cause of mental retardation.

The cost of addictions to America is staggering. Alcohol and drug abuse cost the American economy an estimated $276 billion per year in lost productivity, health-care expenditures, crime, motor vehicle crashes, and other conditions. Untreated addiction is more expensive than heart disease, diabetes, and cancer combined. Every American adult pays nearly one thousand dollars per year for the damages caused by the addictions of other Americans.

Anyone involved in family counseling is going to confront the addiction problem immediately. Yes, there are people attending your church, sitting on the pew in front of you and beside you, who have addictions that are destroying their lives. These people come to church, sing songs like "Victory in Jesus," and yet are living in a literal hell because of their bondages.

Let me tell you the story of Bill and Beverly. Bill was a very successful businessman in the health supplements industry. During World War II, as an Army medic, he developed a formula for a topical ointment that was unique and that promoted healing of surface wounds very quickly. When he was released from the Army, he began to promote this formula; he caught the attention of a major health products manufacturer and was instantly rewarded with wealth beyond his wildest imagination.

At the age of nearly forty, Bill met Beverly. She was fun loving and vivacious. Beverly and Bill

SHE SAYS . . .

She told me that . . . because of her repentant spirit before her husband, their relationship was better than it had ever been before. She had been freed from the accuser. The only way to stop paying his ransom is to expose him.

had many interests in common, and they were married within just a few months. Shortly thereafter, Bill discovered that Beverly was addicted to alcohol. She came from a drinking family, and she had continued the family tradition.

"I take her to a social event where no liquor is being served," Bill told me, "and she is sober as a judge when we arrive. But before the event is half over, she's drunk. How does that happen?"

I asked Beverly how she managed to do this, and she responded, "I shop for little bottles of liquor that I can tie to my petticoat when I go out in public. I have six to eight little bottles tied to my petticoats when we leave the house. I go into the lady's restroom, and I come out intoxicated. I simply cannot live without alcohol. I took a drink, and the drink took me. Some people can drink and stop. I am not one of those people. When I start drinking, I don't stop until I'm looking at the bottom of the bottle."

I won't tell you how much she drank or what she drank, but I don't know how she lived through those drinking binges. How her body avoided alcohol poisoning is beyond comprehension.

After weeks of counseling with Bill and Beverly, during which both of them had to make deep confessions of everything that had happened in their lives before they came together, and covenants of what they would do with their lives from that moment forward, Beverly was liberated from alcoholism. I am here to tell you she was set free from the absolute addiction to alcohol.

Bill and Beverly were in my church for twenty years before they passed into eternity. From the moment of her deliverance, Beverly lived every subsequent day of her life in sobriety. Every day was a day of conquest. However, she retained one evidence of her years of substance abuse. She had lived in a drunken stupor for so long that she had developed a slur when she talked. Until the last day of her life, she talked with the slurred speech of an inebriated person.

Can your marriage survive alcohol? If you are willing to confess everything in your life that resents and resists the perfect will of God, yes, you can. Otherwise, it's not possible in your own strength. The Bible

> **SHE SAYS...**
>
> **Righteousness is only attained through the blood of Jesus Christ. It's by His sacrifice that His white robe of purity is put over every sinner at the cross.**

says, "Therefore if the Son makes you free, you shall be free indeed" (John 8:36). "'Not by might nor by power, but by My Spirit,' says the LORD of hosts" (Zech. 4:6). You must have the help of God every day to be victorious over whatever addiction you may have.

CAN THIS MARRIAGE BE SAVED FROM ALCOHOLISM?

Quality research supports the fact that there is no alcoholic personality. Many people believe the alcoholic is more dependent, more anxious, more childish, more self-centered, and less self-controlled. Dr. George E. Vaillant of Harvard University confirms that whatever common personality traits exist among alcoholics, those traits develop *after* the addiction, not before.[2]

Psychological similarities are a consequence of addiction…not a cause.

Alcoholism has no known physical cause. Some scientific experiments have tried to prove that there are physical differences between alcoholics and nonalcoholics prior to addiction. To date, no one has succeeded. Research on brain neurochemistry to determine if this is a cause has occurred, but there is no proof.

An unhappy childhood is not a primary cause of alcoholic addiction. For every alcoholic who had an unhappy childhood, there is an alcoholic who had a happy childhood.

Alcohol abuse is involved in most murders, assaults, child abuse cases, traffic fatalities, drowning accidents, and fire accidents.

Alcoholism destroys a person's health, marriage, children, and productivity on the job, and it enslaves that person in a literal hell. First, the person takes a drink, and then the drink takes the person.

I have known alcoholics to vomit blood and shake like a leaf while saying, "I can quit anytime I want to," or "I don't drink as much as Harry." Most alcoholics don't stop drinking until the graveyard, but you can stop through Christ's help. Alcoholism, or drunkenness of any kind, is clearly forbidden in Galatians 5:19–21.

In Sweden, where adoption records are well kept, sons of alcoholic fathers placed at birth in nonalcoholic homes were found to have a nine-to-one chance of becoming alcoholics. Girls were found to have a three-to-one chance of becoming alcoholics. If you have a parent or a grandparent with a drinking problem, be careful…alcoholism can kill you and is trying to attack you.

There is a difference between an alcohol abuser and an alcohol addict. The *abuser* is a heavy drinker or someone who drinks regularly until he or she experiences a mood change. The *addict* is a person who cannot control how much he or she drinks. An alcoholic cannot stop drinking without someone else's help, even if the alcoholic loses a job, loses his or her family, and even loses his or her physical health. The addict drinks to stop the pain, not to feel good.

There are several stages of drinking. First, the person drinks to be social, and then he drinks to relax. Then he drinks to go to sleep. Finally, he drinks to forget, and, in the final stages, he drinks to stop the pain.

The physical signs of an alcoholic are obvious—the red face, the bulbous nose, sclerosis of the liver, morning nausea and vomiting, diarrhea, and hand tremors. An additional problem for men is impotence. As the addiction progresses, the face flushes and the nose becomes enlarged and inflamed. The palms of the hand may turn red and take on the appearance of what is commonly referred to as "liver palms."[3]

The late stages of addiction are withdrawals and severe headaches. Then come the shakes and DTs (delirium tremens). The alcoholic is tormented by his poisoned, malfunctioning brain and sees terrifying visions.

An emotional indication of alcohol addiction is rationalization. There's always a reason to drink. The alcoholic plans his or her day around drinking. There is the projection of self-hatred. A man will say, "My wife is a nag," when, in fact, she's an angel. He will continue the blame game saying things like: "My children are ungrateful." "My boss is a bum." "My preacher puts me down." The alcoholic goes into severe mood swings. An alcoholic can go from happy to angry in a moment's time. Alcoholics display the "Jekyll and Hyde" syndrome—there are two personalities in one body.

Another manifestation of alcohol addiction is mental blackouts. The person can physically function, but has no memory of where he was or what he did. In his book *I'll Quit Tomorrow*, Dr. Vernon Johnson tells of a real estate broker who said, "They tell me that last night I drove my car through three kids on bicycles and killed one. I just can't remember it."[4]

The way out of alcoholism is as follows:

1. Make an absolute confession that you are an alcoholic.

2. Acknowledge your dependence on Jesus Christ, and ask Him to set you free from alcoholism.

3. Find a support group. At Cornerstone Church, we have the SAVED Group (Substance Abusers Victoriously Experiencing Deliverance). Every person in the group has an addiction of some kind, and each person is accountable to each other for daily living the victorious life over that substance abuse.

4. Let the alcoholic experience the consequences of his addiction. Almost every alcoholic suffers from the delusion that he is in control of himself. Let the consequences of his drinks run over him. If he gets a fine, make him pay it. Let him clean up his own vomit. Let him explain to his boss why he's late or sick again. If he gets arrested, let him go to jail where the reality can set in that he's out of control. The point is, his or her illusion of self-control must be shattered.

   Also, don't agree with an alcoholic. The more silence you demonstrate, the more unnerved the alcoholic becomes. Don't be afraid to lose your alcoholic husband or wife. If he or she threatens to leave, do not try to make him stay. After a few days, he'll come home when he realizes that stunt didn't work.

5. Confront the problem! A well-planned confrontation with your husband and his boss, with a doctor or minister, is a valid way to bring reality to the alcoholic. You will not conquer what you will not confront. Do not allow your past to control your future.[5]

CAN THIS MARRIAGE SURVIVE HOMOSEXUALITY?

As I write this book, the issue of same-sex marriage rages on the front pages of America's newspapers and is seen on national telecasts each evening. Massachusetts has just agreed to recognize same-sex marriages. For a fact, Sodom and Gomorrah are being reborn in America.

The only hope morality has to survive in America is for a constitutional amendment to be passed stating that the only marriage recognized in America will be between a man and a woman of legal age.

I have carried seventy-five thousand petitions from our television partners to Washington DC and personally placed them in the hand of Senator John Cornyn of Texas. Senator Cornyn is the chairman of the subcommittee that will hear all evidence and expressions from the American people of their desire for a constitutional amendment.

I encourage every person who has biblical beliefs to contact their congressman and their senator on a regular basis and implore them

> **SHE SAYS...**
>
> **Embrace the freedom of truth. The Word of God tells us that the knowledge of the truth will set us free—free from the chains of the past, and free from the fear of tomorrow.**

to pass this constitutional amendment recognizing only the marriage between a man and a woman. If we fail to achieve this, the gates of hell will be opened. It will open the door to incest, to polygamy, and to every conceivable marriage arrangement demented minds can possibly conceive. If God does not then punish America, He will have to apologize to Sodom and Gomorrah.

What does the Bible call homosexuality? Let's look at Leviticus 18:22. It reads: "You shall not lie with a male as with a woman. It is an abomination."

Leviticus 20:13 states: "If a man lies with a male as he lies with a woman, both of them have committed an abomination. They shall surely be put to death. Their blood shall be upon them."

The word *abomination* in Hebrew means "something disgusting, and abhorrent," the strongest Bible word for the denunciation of sin. It is impossible to call yourself a *Christian* and defend homosexuality. There is no justification or acceptance of homosexuality. How many ways can you say "abomination" in Hebrew?

In Romans 1:18–32, Saint Paul certifies homosexuality as rebellion against the Law of God.

The Bible story of homosexuals demanding the guests of Lot for their sexual pleasure in Genesis 19:1–5 is the portrait of homosexuality out of the closet. In this story about the homosexuals who came to Lot's house to demand that he turn over to them his guests, the homosexuals came from every part of the city. They encircled the house. They were young and old, and they had no intention of leaving without Lot's guests. They were as aggressive as a pack of wolves.

They were even willing to break down the door (vv. 6–9). They were willing to disregard the rights of Lot's property, the rights of his home, because they wanted sex with his guests. Why did Lot offer his two unmarried daughters in verse 8 to these homosexuals? Because he knew their lust was for men…not women.

The homosexuals attacked Lot for standing in the way between them and the two angels. They were very aggressive. Even after the angels struck them blind, they did not scatter in the fear of God. They wearied themselves groping about in darkness trying to find the door of Lot's house.

What was the result? You can read it in Genesis 19:24. God executed an urban renewal program with fire and brimstone. God's opinion of homosexuality has not changed. Malachi 3:6 states: "For I am the LORD, I do not change." In the beginning, God created Adam and Eve, not Adam and Bruce. Homosexuality means the death of society because homosexuals can recruit, but they cannot reproduce.

Once homosexuality gets out of the closet, it becomes aggressive. We are receiving every signal that intelligent humanity can receive from the homosexual community. They do not want mere acceptance; they want to be in charge.

Can your marriage survive homosexuality?

Let me tell you the story of Robert and Rachel. Robert was a very successful stockbroker. He was extremely meticulous. He had feminine characteristics, and he was homosexual. He came to the church and confessed that he wanted to make a change in his conduct and become a Christian. He began to serve and serve well in a number of ways in our church.

He met Rachel, who was far more successful in her business than Robert. Rachel was extremely intelligent, a type-A, turbo-charged woman who lived in a man's world and was extremely successful. They met and were married within six months.

For the first year, life seemed to be a thing of beauty. And then the thing that I had feared from day one began to manifest itself. Robert told Rachel he was having an affair with another man.

Rachel came to my office shaken, but committed to solving the problem. She said, "If it were another woman, I know how to fight that fight. But how do you fight a relationship with another man?" I had no intelligent answer.

I asked Robert and Rachel to come to my office together, and I asked Robert the question I asked everyone in the first five minutes of the first counseling session: "Do you want to save your marriage?"

Robert said *yes,* and we began to work toward removing the roots in his past life that would bring him to reconciliation with God and Rachel. What we did and said and experienced is in and of itself worthy of a book, but the point of this story is to say that, years later, Robert and Rachel are living together in divine harmony with their children without another homosexual manifestation. Yes...your marriage can survive homosexuality.

Hints for Her

This chapter has dealt with some of the more difficult situations facing some marriages. Are you carefully avoiding any substances that could become addictive to you? Even that morning cup of coffee or those headache pills that help you get to sleep faster can become addictive. Decide to be the *family watchdog* to guard each family member from tumbling into an unplanned addiction. Offer your family wholesome, nutritious meals, and create a relaxed, stress-free family life. Teach your family to go to God with their problems—not to a bottle or some other addictive substance.

CONCLUSION

In this chapter we have seen evidence of God's supernatural grace and power transforming the lives of Bill and Beverly, out of the bondages of addiction, and Robert and Rachel, out of the bondages of homosexuality. There is nothing too hard for God: "I am the LORD, the God of all mankind. Is anything too hard for me?" (Jer. 32:27, NIV). Trust Him with your marriage, and He will make it a testimony of God's supernatural grace and power at work in your lives.

ASKING GOD'S HELP

Lord, Your supernatural grace and power can transform any life. Thank You for beginning the work of transformation in my life. Continue that work, O God, and free me from anything that could become more important to me than You. Protect my wife and my family from the threat of addictive substances or feelings or behaviors. Let our lives be testimonies of Your keeping power. Take from me anything that robs my life of Your presence. Forgive me for putting other things—work, TV, sports, fun, even sleep—above You or in place of the relationship You want me to have with my wife and family. Amen.

Can a Marriage Survive Poor Communication,
LACK OF PASSION, OR POOR MONEY MANAGEMENT?

seven

T HE PROBLEMS WE will take a look at in this chapter are problems that affect many, many marriages. There are times in every marriage when these three issues rise up and threaten the peace in that ·marriage relationship. The important thing to remember is that whether these are little annoyances that can quickly be resolved, or great big insurmountable problems that threaten your marriage, is largely up to you and your wife. You may be able to just not speak to each other one day because you are in the midst of an argument. But if you do that too many days in a row, you may actually build a wall of noncommunication that threatens the very life of your relationship. As you read this chapter, determine to guard against these "little foxes that spoil the vines" (Song of Sol. 2:15).

CAN THIS MARRIAGE BE SAVED
FROM POOR COMMUNICATION?

A couple was celebrating their fiftieth wedding anniversary. They cut the cake and celebrated with friends and family. After all of their guests had left the home, the wife said, "After all these years, I find you tried and true."

73

Her aged husband put his hand behind his ear and yelled, "What did you say?"

She said, "After all these years, I have found you tried and true."

Once again, he put his hand behind his ear and said, "I didn't quite hear you. Would you say that again?"

This time his wife of fifty years yelled at the top of her lungs, "After all these years, I found you tried and true."

Her husband responded, "Well, after all these years, I'm tired of you, too."

Poor communication is generally more than the result of poor hearing. We have developed communication systems that permit men on earth to talk to men walking on the moon, yet often husbands can't talk to their wives as they sit across from them at the breakfast table.

Problems and differences in marriage are not dangerous, but not being able to communicate with each other about those problems *is* very dangerous. Communication is to love what blood is to the body. When it stops flowing, your marriage dies. Communication is not outyelling your wife, and communication is not the art of winning an argument. You can win an argument and lose your marriage.

In the midst of a marital argument or disagreement on any matter, the question each person must ask himself or herself is this: "Do I want to be *reconciled* to my mate, or do I merely want to be *'right'*?" If you want to be reconciled . . . give your jaws a rest. Silence is golden.

Communication is not winning the argument. Arguing with your wife is as useless as trying to blow out a light bulb. Trying to intimidate your wife through anger is not communication.

A man and a wife were on vacation. She was the navigator with the map in her hands, and he was driving their new Mercedes across country. She decided to take a nap. After a while, she woke up, looked at the map, and shouted, "We're lost!" She looked at her husband and said, "You're going the wrong way."

He exploded in anger. After two hours of pouting, they passed a mule in the field. "Is that a relative of yours?" the husband asked his wife.

The wife responded, "Yes . . . by marriage!"

Communication is when your wife can tell you how she feels, what she thinks, and what she loves, honors, esteems, hates, fears, desires, hopes for, believes in, and is committed to without starting World War III.

Words are a transcript of the mind. Matthew 12:34 says, "Out of

the abundance of the heart the mouth speaks."
A few verses later, the Bible says, "For every idle
word men may speak, they will give account of
it in the day of judgment. For by your words you
will be justified, and by your words you will be
condemned" (vv. 36–37).

Be careful what you say to your wife or your
husband. Be careful what you say about your
wife or your husband. God is listening, and you
are going to answer to Him on Judgment Day for
every word that you have said about your spouse
that is less than kind.

If you really want better communication, don't
show up in combat gear.

> **SHE SAYS . . .**
>
> **Criticism causes men to become defensive, but admiration motivates and energizes them. A man expects and needs his wife to be his most enthusiastic fan.**

CAN THIS MARRIAGE BE SAVED FROM A LACK OF PASSION?

A wife took her husband to the doctor and told the doctor, "My husband has no passion. He has no fire. He has no desire to be around me. Give him a physical examination to see what problem he has."

The doctor examined the husband, and after a thorough examination, he excused the husband and invited the wife into his office to speak to her alone. The doctor said to the wife, "If you would cook three square meals every day for your husband and have a meaningful sex relationship with him, he would be OK."

On the way home, the husband asked his wife, "What did doctor say to you in his office?"

The wife responded, "The doctor said you are going to die."

Has your marriage lost its passion? Has it lost its fire and excitement? Is the sizzle gone? The first step toward making your marriage an affair-proof marriage is to determine that both of you want to improve your marriage. Every marriage can be a better marriage. Turn off the football game. Put down the newspaper, and plan a date night. Sit down and make a list of exciting things you would like to do together, and then do them. Insanity defined is "doing the same things the same way and expecting a different result." Your marriage can sizzle, but not without your planning to make it happen.

CAN THIS MARRIAGE SURVIVE POOR MONEY MANAGEMENT?

A rich wife yelled at her husband, "If it weren't for my money, that Rolex on your arm wouldn't be there. If it weren't for my money, that easy chair you're sitting in wouldn't be there. If it weren't for my money, that Mercedes you drive wouldn't be there."

The husband responded tartly, "If it weren't for your money, sweetheart, I wouldn't be here."

Many of America's marriages are destroyed by the lack of money management. Jesus gave us thirty-six parables in the New Testament. Thirty of them deal with how to manage material wealth. The Bible says in Proverbs 22:7, "The rich rules over the poor, and the borrower is servant to the lender." Many marriages are enslaved by American Express and MasterCard charge cards. The joy of the relationship has been destroyed because they are in debt beyond their capacity to pay back. If you can't control your spending any other way, do it with plastic surgery—cut up your credit cards and start living on a cash basis.

> ### SHE SAYS…
> **Remember this rule: You will seldom find something as much fun to own as it is to *look forward to owning*.**[1]

Money management is a lengthy and involved topic, but the road to getting your life on an even keel financially is to begin by admitting you spend too much. Both husband and wife need to sit down with a financial counselor and plan an airtight budget, and then stay with it.

Don't let your marriage be destroyed by your inability to control your financial spending.

SEVEN STEPS TO MARRIAGE SURVIVAL

1. Totally forgive and forget the past.

I have given you composite stories based on the lives of real people who battled to save their marriage against impossible odds. The foundation for every marriage reconstruction begins with absolute and total forgiveness. In the Lord's Prayer, Jesus taught us, "Forgive us…as we forgive…" (Matt. 6:12). Forgiveness is not optional. If you will not forgive other people, God cannot forgive you. Forgiveness is the key that unlocks the door of resentment and loosens the handcuffs of hatred.

Forgiveness is a full pardon. Forgiveness is a fresh start. Forgiveness is another chance and a new beginning. Sooner or later, you will fail, and you will need to be forgiven by someone. If you do not forgive others, God Himself will not forgive you.

2. The husband is the king, priest, and prophet of his family.

As king, he governs the family. As priest, he guides the family spiritually. As prophet, he guards his family and blesses his children.

> **SHE SAYS...**
>
> **Forgiveness is not a feeling we achieve but a choice we make. Granting forgiveness is not always easy. At times it is the hardest thing we will ever do.**

I encourage every father to put your hands on the head of your child every day and bless that child. It does not have to be a long, ceremoniously conducted prayer, but you should do it. I have a six-hour teaching series on "The Power of the Blessing," which instructs fathers, as the priests of their homes, to know how to release the supernatural abundance and blessing of God into the lives of their children by blessing them.

If you don't know how to speak the blessing over your children and your wife, get that teaching series and begin to bless your wife and children every day.

3. Realize that submission in the Bible means mutual submission.

When Paul writes of submission in Ephesians 5:21, he says, "...submitting to one another in the fear of God."

Husband, you don't submit to your wife's lead, but you must submit to her need. That means if she needs you to help her clean the kitchen, you do it. That means if she needs you to help her wash the dishes or to go shopping, you do it. That means if she needs you to go to the opera with her instead of to the country and western concert, you do it.

Submission does not make a man the "Hitler" of the house. Submission means that he does have leadership, but he is a loving, compassionate leader who loves his wife as Christ loved the church and is willing to die for her in an instant to redeem her.

4. Eliminate the absentee father.

Saint Paul writes in Ephesians 6:4: "You, fathers, do not provoke your children to wrath, but bring them up in the training and admonition of the Lord."

I am truly tired of hearing milquetoast fathers say, "I just can't train my son to do the right thing." Listen to me. I have been to Sea World, and if Sea World can train a porpoise to play basketball, you can train your child to carry out the trash and to obey you.

America's number one problem is the absentee father. Gangs run in the streets of America like packs of wild wolves, because sons are looking for leadership. They are looking for authority. They want someone to tell them what to do. They want a role model, and because they can't find it at home in the absentee father, they go to the streets to find it.

If you are an absentee father who has abandoned his children for a lover or a new wife, you are required by God in heaven to be a father to those children. You may have divorced your wife, but you never, ever divorce your children. Go home and rear those children in the fear and admonition of God, or face the wrath of God on Judgment Day for your negligence as a father.

5. Start communicating today.

Communicate openly and honestly.

I never cease to be amazed that a woman can walk into my office for a counseling session and reveal the most secret sexual frustration in her soul. But when I ask her if she's told her husband this, the instant answer is, "No, I could never tell him that."

If there is anything in your heart, soul, or mind that frustrates you in your marriage relationship toward your spouse, start talking about it today. To deny your emotional feelings is disaster delayed. Holding your emotions in check is something like holding a beach ball under water. You struggle to hold the ball beneath the water and fight furiously to keep it in check. But sooner or later, you will lose your grip, and the beach ball will explode up and will be gone.

Your emotions cannot be held in check year after year without exploding. Sooner or later you must have a genuinely cathartic conversation with your mate, during which you explain the deepest secrets of your soul to your spouse with no holds barred. Only then will you have a successful marriage. Until then, your marriage has no emotional foundation for intimate, meaningful communication.

6. Live in sexual freedom.

In 1 Corinthians 7:4, Paul states, "The wife does not have authority over her own body, but the husband does. And likewise the husband does not have authority over his own body, but the wife does." Manipulating your partner with sex is witchcraft! Witchcraft has these three manifestations: manipulation, domination, and ultimate control. Any married person who tries to manipulate his or her spouse through sex is committing sin in the counsel of heaven. If you're doing it, stop it.

7. Reverence for the marriage relationship.

The Bible says, "Husbands, love your wives, just as Christ also loved the church and gave Himself for her. . . . Nevertheless let each one of you in particular so love his own wife as himself, and let the wife see that she respects her husband" (Eph. 5:25, 33).

The word *reverence* means "to stand in awe." Husband, would you like for your wife to follow you around the house saying, "Awe...Awe... Awe"? If you will love her as Christ loved the church, that may happen in your marriage.

Can this marriage be saved? Only if you're willing to forgive completely and to begin anew. Any marriage can be saved if both partners are willing to practice total forgiveness.

> ### SHE SAYS...
> **Your husband has true value in the eyes of God, just as you do. It is unfair to treat him as anything but royalty.**

Hints for Her

By now you should be thoroughly convinced that whatever the problem, God is bigger! There is no problem in your marriage He cannot solve—*if you are committed to working at His direction.* Use the Seven Steps to Marriage Survival to help you make some necessary changes. Don't just assume that your husband has all the work to do. You can take these steps along with him.

1. Use the key of forgiveness to unlock the door of resentment.

2. Encourage your husband to fulfill his role as king, priest, and prophet of your family.

3. Practice mutual submission in your marriage relationship.

4. Make your home a place your husband *never* wants to leave—even for a moment.

5. Start communicating today—openly, honestly, and consistently.

6. Never attempt to manipulate your husband through sex.

7. Revere your husband.

CONCLUSION

If you truly have a revelation of the supernatural love, grace, and power of God to impact your marriage relationship, you will never need to ask the question, "Can my marriage be saved?" Without a doubt, God can transform the mediocre into the miraculous, the problematic into the problem free, and the dying into the living. A more important question for you to consider should be: "Am I willing to do whatever God directs me to do to make my marriage better?" If you will make that commitment—and never forget it, your marriage can be like heaven on earth.

ASKING GOD'S HELP

Father, sometimes I am such a failure at communicating positively with my wife. I have such a big mouth—and I use it sometimes when I should be listening to her—or to You—instead. I want our marriage to be full of fun, full of excitement, full of You, Lord. Teach me how to surprise her with little things that let her know how much I love her. Show me ways to make her heart beat faster when she thinks of me. And keep us from the mistakes of believing that we have to spend money we shouldn't spend to enjoy our time together. Lord, I remember when just catching a glimpse of her smile was enough for me—take us back to the simple joys of spending time together doing nothing but enjoying each other's presence. Amen.

PORTRAIT

F ROM THE BEGINNING of time, poets and prophets have put their pens to parchment trying to describe the power and passion of love. No one has ever equaled Saint Paul's description of love found in 1 Corinthians 13. Not Shakespeare, not Byron, not Shelley, not Keats, or even Browning with his magnificent "How do I love thee? Let me count the ways."

- What does love look like?
- What does love feel like?
- What does love sound like?
- Have we forgotten what genuine love truly is?

Our lives are shaped by people who love us and by those who refuse to love us. If a man says that marriage hasn't changed him, he's not out of the church yet.

Psychologists say that girls tend to marry men like their fathers. I believe that's why mothers cry at weddings. One of the greatest mysteries of love and marriage to me is this: how can that dumbbell who married your daughter last year become the father of the world's smartest grandchild this year?

The average woman would rather have beauty than brains. Why? Because the average man can see far better than he can think.

WHAT LOVE IS NOT!

Love is not emotion. A young man sat in my office describing his future bride and said, "When I get around her I can't breathe."

I responded, "It's asthma...it's not love. Either that, or you have a nineteen-inch neck and you're wearing a sixteen-inch shirt."

Jesus didn't say, "I was hungry, and you felt sorry for Me." Jesus didn't say, "I was naked, and you felt shame for Me." He didn't say, "I was in prison, and you were embarrassed for Me." He didn't say, "I was sick, and you were sympathetic with Me."

No! He said, "I was hungry and you gave Me no food; I was thirsty and you gave Me no drink; I was a stranger and you did not take Me in, naked and you did not clothe Me, sick and in prison and you did not visit Me" (Matt. 25:42–43).

Love is not what you feel. Love is what you do. **Works**...not words...are proof of your love.

Love is not sex!

Love is not the urge to merge.

Love is not a hormonal response to a plunging neckline or short skirt. As I said earlier, it used to take a cotton gin all day to make enough cotton to make a woman's dress. In the twenty-first century, a silk worm can do it on his lunch break.

There is "free love" and "covenant love." And you better know the difference. Free love takes, and covenant love gives. Free love will give you AIDS and a home in the lake of fire. Covenant love gives you a ring and makes your life as the days of heaven on earth. Your choices have consequences.

America's TV generation watches Britney Spears get married one day and divorced just forty-eight hours later. J.Lo married recently, and a week after the wedding, pundits were joyfully responding to the fact that she stayed married for seven whole days. With these examples from Hollywood's elite, it is no wonder the concept of covenant love seems strange to America's young generation.

LOVING LIKE CHRIST

Saint Paul dips his pen in ink and gives the world God's portrait of love. Paul said, "[If I] have not love, I am nothing" (1 Cor. 13:2).

Without love you are spiritually dead! The Bible says, "We know that we have passed from death to life, because we love the brethren" (1 John 3:14). Anyone who does not love remains in death.

If love is lacking, "we are dead." Unless we love, we are not the sons and daughters of God, no matter what church membership we claim or spiritual experience we profess. The Bible says, "He who does not love does not know God, for God is love" (1 John 4:8).

The three evidences of salvation in Scripture are these:

1. The confession of the Lord Jesus Christ: The Bible says, "If you confess with your mouth the Lord Jesus…you will be saved" (Rom. 10:9).

2. Water baptism: Water baptism is a public testimony that you have left your old life and are now walking in the newness of your faith in Christ. Your old life has been washed away, and you are standing absolutely clean before God. If you reject water baptism, you need to hear the verse that says, "Whoever denies Me before men, him I will also deny before My Father who is in heaven" (Matt. 10:33).

3. Love for the brethren: The acid test of conversion is "love for the brethren." Some confessions that are made with the mouth are less than truthful. There are water baptisms where the person has gone under the water but is not under the blood. But you cannot fake your love one for the other. Jesus said, "By this all will know that you are My disciples, if you have love for one another" (John 13:35).

The missing ingredient in the majority of churches in America is the basic love of Christ. Jesus commanded us to "love one another as I have loved you" (John 15:12). Christ loved us unconditionally. And He loved us when we did not deserve to be loved. The people who deserve love the least need it the most.

So often, these are the qualifiers of our love: We love others because they love us first. We love others because they come up to our expectations. Or we love others because they are made of the *right stuff*. We love others because they have money and affluence. We love others because they are physically attractive.

But Christ has no qualifiers on His love. Christ loved us "while we were still sinners" (Rom. 5:8). He loved us when we were covered with the stench of sin. He loved us unconditionally.

Christianity without love is just another cult. The world does not care what we know until they know that we care.

Without love, you have no value. Without love, you are less than junk. Junk is something that can no longer make a contribution to anything or anyone. Junk reminds me of the first car I bought when I was in the ninth grade. When I was twelve years old, my father told me that I could buy a car whenever I could pay cash for it and insure it for one year with cash. In 1954 I bought a four-door, straight-8 1948 Pontiac that was as long as the Queen Mary. If you looked close, you could see my head slightly above the window seal level.

I drove it through high school and drove it to Bible college. It had four "may-pop" tires, meaning they may pop at any time. It burned oil so badly it looked like a brush fire coming down the road with a bumper on both ends.

When I was in Bible school, I went to the junkyard to buy a used tire. I said to the owner of the junkyard, "You have a lot of junk here." I was looking at acres of car bodies, bumpers, tires, and hubcaps—every conceivable, mechanical, abandoned device your mind can imagine.

The owner of the junkyard looked at me and said, "Young man, this is not a junkyard. Junk has no value. You are here looking for a used tire because it has value. What you are looking at here," he said as he extended his hands over the acres of mechanical debris, "is unlimited possibilities." Potential is everywhere you look.

WITHOUT LOVE, YOU ARE NOTHING

Saint Paul writes, "Though I speak with the tongues of men and of angels..." (1 Cor. 13:1). I personally have studied Latin, Greek, Hebrew, Spanish, and English, and have mastered none of them. But what if I was eloquent in every language on the earth? What if I was eloquent in every dialect on the planet? It would be a human instinct to say, "I am something." But, through the pen of Paul, God says, "Without love, you are nothing."

Paul writes, "Though I have the gift of prophecy..." (v. 2).

What if I knew the future?

What if I could predict tomorrow with 100 percent accuracy?

What if I could tell the *Wall Street Journal* what the stock markets of the world were going to do tomorrow?

What if I had the ability to predict earthquakes and tornadoes?

What if I could tell the president what was going to happen in the Middle East tomorrow?

The president would be calling me every morning. Alan Greenspan would want to live next door. Night and day, financial advisors would besiege me from around the world. I would have the human tendency to say, "I am something because I know the future." But God says, "Without love, you are nothing."

Paul writes, "And [if I] understand all mysteries..." (v. 2).

I walk the corridors of hospitals every week. I see legions of people suffering from every conceivable disease known to man. The cure for cancer continues to be America's greatest medical mystery. I sit beside children diagnosed with cancer and pray this prayer: "O God, let us solve the mystery of cancer." Brilliant men and women are working day and night all over the earth trying to solve this single mystery. Billions of dollars are being spent to find the answer.

But what if I could call the American Cancer Society and say, "I, John Hagee, have solved the mystery to cancer." I would win the Pulitzer Prize. My picture would be on the cover of every magazine in the world. Every newspaper would come running to my office for an interview. Television reporters would be stacked in my front yard like cordwood. I would have the human instinct to say, "I am something because I have solved this great mystery."

But God says, "Without love, even if you have solved all the mysteries on Planet Earth, you are nothing."

Paul writes, "...and all knowledge..." (v. 2).

In every field of knowledge, there are men who study for a lifetime to master a portion of that field. It was my pleasure to sit in some of the great universities of America and listen to some of America's brightest minds. They had studied one subject their entire adult lives, and they shared the pearls of knowledge they had gleaned over decades of diligent scholarship. Each of those magnificent scholars would profess publicly that they did not know everything about their field of study, but they were striving daily to stay abreast of the infinite ocean of knowledge.

But what if I had all knowledge in every field of academia? What if I knew enough about chemistry to make Linus Pauling blush? What if I knew enough about mathematics to intimidate Albert Einstein? What if I knew enough about political science that Henry Kissinger would hide in the closet when I came into the room? There would be the natural human instinct to say, "John Hagee, you are really something."

But God says, "John Hagee, without love you are nothing."

Paul writes, "...and though I have all faith, so that I could remove mountains..." (v. 2).

Faith is a subject that has forever intrigued me. The Bible says, "This is the victory that has overcome the world—our faith" (1 John 5:4). Faith starts out before you know how it's going to turn out. Faith does not demand miracles, but faith creates the environment in which miracles happen. Nothing is impossible to those who believe. Everything heaven has to offer comes with the currency of faith. Without faith, it is impossible to please God.

In my sixty-four years of living, it has been my privilege to see great men of faith in colossal arenas praying for tens of thousands of people who had come from the four winds of Planet Earth to be healed. As a nine-year-old child in Houston, Texas, I heard, for the first time, an evangelist called Oral Roberts from Oklahoma who had a powerful healing ministry. My father's church filled the church bus every night of that healing campaign. We drove from our home in Channelview, Texas, to Houston, Texas, to hear this great man of God.

When we arrived, the tent that held five thousand people was full, and the crowds were gathering outside the tent to stand and catch a glimpse of God's power. For the better part of an hour, Oral Roberts preached a message about "The Fourth Man." Then the healing ministry began. He prayed for several hours for those who had come previously to be taught the principles of healing.

Electrifying, visible miracles happened in that service that convinced the greatest skeptic that the healing power of God was alive and well on Planet Earth.

Smith Wigglesworth was a mighty man of faith. On one occasion, God told him to get up and go across town to pray for a woman who was sick. He instantly obeyed, but when he arrived at the home of the sick woman, relatives informed him she had just died.

Smith Wigglesworth said, "God sent me here to pray for her. Whether she is dead or alive does not affect me."

He entered the house and was escorted to the room of the deceased. He picked her up out of the bed and leaned her against the wall and shouted, "Live, in Jesus' name!" Instantly the woman returned to life. I must confess I do not bat in that league.

But God says that if you have "all faith, so that [you] could remove mountains..." If you can raise people from the dead...if you have a miracle ministry that packs stadiums and auditoriums on every continent of Planet Earth...and have not love, you are nothing.

"And though I bestow all my goods to feed the poor..." (1 Cor. 13:3).

The Bible tells the story of the rich, young ruler who kept all of the commandments. He was an outstanding person, because the commandments are truly a supernatural document of spiritual excellence. When he met Jesus of Nazareth, Jesus told him, "Sell all that you have and distribute to the poor" (Luke 18:22). The Bible says this about that young man's response: "He became very sorrowful, for he was very rich" (v. 23). Why was he so sorrowful? Because he loved his possessions more than he loved Jesus Christ.

Most of us are willing to give *some* to God...but *all?* Seventy-five percent of America's church members will not tithe to their local church. The Bible says, "Though I bestow all my goods to feed the poor...but have not love, it profits me nothing" (1 Cor. 13:3).

SHE SAYS...

I minister to many wives who are tormented by the fact their husbands refuse to give back to the Lord one-tenth of what the Provider has allowed them to earn.

Love As Described by the Apostle Paul

Paul gives fourteen definitions in the portrait of love. The first seven deal with you, and the last seven deal with other people. We will look at several of these definitions in this section of the book.

1. Love is patient (v. 4, NIV).

Paul writes, "Love is patient."

Patient love endures. It never gets tired of waiting. Patient love never gives up! Patient love doesn't give up on your alcoholic wife, your drug-addicted son, your loveless marriage. Love locks its jaws and refuses to give up.

Are you impatient? Do you stand in front of the microwave screaming, "Hurry up!"? Do you grow impatient while brewing instant coffee? I'm not saying I prefer fast-food restaurants, but the other day I caught myself ordering into the mailbox and driving around the house.

The American attitude toward waiting is reflected by the sign, "Antiques Manufactured Here While You Wait."

We can't understand a God who is powerful and patient. When God does not do what we want, we get fidgety and fretful. We want what we want, and we want it when we want it, and if God doesn't give it to us, we scream, "You don't love me!" Listen to me! God's delays are not God's denials. Greatness is slow to anger, and part of the greatness of God is His eternal patience.

Look at God's patience in the plan of salvation. God sent Moses to Israel, and Moses was rejected. God sent prophets, and they were stoned. God sent kings, and they became corrupt. Saul went to the witch of Endor. David was seduced by Bathsheba. Solomon's wives led him into idolatry.

Finally, God sent His only begotten Son, not on a white horse, not pushing and shoving humanity like a supreme sultan, not strutting with a swagger stick like a supreme commander, but nestled in Bethlehem's manger as a tiny baby wrapped in swaddling clothes.

He didn't come to a throne in Caesar's palace. He came touching the untouchable lepers. He hugged and kissed the castoffs of society. In the final days of His life, He wrapped a towel around His waist and washed the dirty feet of His disciples in the upper room.

In the greatest demonstration of love, He allowed Herod's men of war to slap Him, spit on Him, mock Him, crown Him with a crown of thorns, and, finally, nail Him to a crude Roman cross outside the eastern walls of Jerusalem. Why? Because God's love is patient.

Through the pen of Saint Paul in 1 Corinthians 13, God is saying, "If you have My love, you will be patient with those you love. You will be patient with your wife, your husband, and your children. You will be patient with your boss at your place of employment. You will be patient with your pastor and other spiritual leaders."

2. Love is kind (v. 4, NIV).

Paul writes, "Love is kind." The Phillips' translation states, "It [love] looks for a way to be constructive." Kindness is love in action. Kindness is the ability to love people more than they deserve.

On one occasion, a woman who was in my office for marriage counseling said, "My husband doesn't deserve kindness."

I said to her, "Give it to him on credit; you do everything else on credit." She was not amused.

Do you want to do something great for God? Be kind to His children! Kindness is a language that the deaf can hear and the blind can see. People will overlook the faults of anyone who is truly kind.

Treat a dog with kindness. Pet him often and feed him well, and he'll never leave you. That same system generally works for husbands. Be as kind as you can be today; you may not be here tomorrow.

Years ago, a husband who attended my church left for work with his wife screaming at him over a silly matter that amounted to nothing. On the way to work that morning, he was killed in a car crash. She walked to his casket sobbing, "I'm so sorry." She lived the rest of her life with those silly, hateful words burning in her ears over a matter that amounted to absolutely nothing. Those words were the last thing she said to the man she said she loved.

> *S*HE *S*AYS . . .
>
> **I try to bless my husband every day before he leaves our home. There is a battlefield outside of the doors of our home, and he needs all the help he can get.**

3. Love does not envy (v. 4, NIV).

Do you think someone loves you? Go buy yourself a new Mercedes with steam-heated doorknobs, Posturepedic seats, and the luxury package of accessories, and drive up in front of that person's house. It takes little discernment to see the steam coming out of his ears. Nothing depreciates your car faster than having your neighbor buy a new one. Most of us would be better off if it weren't for the extravagance of our neighbors.

A person generally criticizes the individual whom he secretly envies. The man who belittles you is trying to cut you down to his size. When you feel yourself turning green with envy, you are ripe for trouble. Love envieth not. Love is not jealous. Love is not possessive.

One husband told me, "My wife isn't jealous of my secretary. She doesn't care how good looking my secretary is, just as long as he's efficient."

I have heard wives confess to me, "My husband is so jealous he gets mad every time anyone looks at me."

My advice is simply, "Don't get angry when someone admires your wife. They are complimenting you on your intelligent choice. If they put their hand on your wife, cut it off at the elbow and hand it back to them."

James Dobson said, "If you love something, set it free. If it comes back to you, it's yours. If it doesn't, it never was."

There's another version: "If you love something, set it free. If it doesn't come back to you, track it down and beat it to death."

Envy possesses, and love releases. When you possess someone, you smother that person. The more you smother and hover, the more that person fights to get free. The harder you try, the harder the struggle. It's a fight for emotional survival. Turn loose! Love your partner without envy! Love without jealousy. Set him free; if he is yours, he will not leave you. If she is not yours, there's nothing on earth you can do to keep her.

4. Love does not boast (v. 4, NIV).

Love does not boast about its existence. Love doesn't say, "I know you're fat, freckled-faced, have false teeth, wear a wig, and look like a mobile home in a skirt—but I love you."

Love does not put itself on display. Love makes no parade. Love has no pride. Love is needed most by those who deserve it least. To love the world is easy; it's that jerk next door that's the real problem.

A honeymoon is often defined as "that brief period of time between 'I do' and 'You'd better.'" Compare this to your attitude. Do you want a twenty-one-gun salute for bringing colored toothpicks to the church picnic? Is everything you do the act of a prima donna? Are you pretentious? Are you pompous? Do you strut like a peacock?

5. Love is not proud (v. 4, NIV).

Remember: God has no superstars! He only has servants. His servants are loving and humble. Servants are willing to be poured out in an endless stream of the love of God. Service is merely love in work clothes. When you get to heaven, you will be welcomed with these words: "Well done, thou good and faithful servant." Are you a servant? If not...why not?

6. Love is not rude (v. 5, NIV).

Paul writes that love is never rude. Love does not behave indecently. Love has good manners.

America's society revels in its crudeness. Recently the Federal Communications Commission (FCC) in America fined major media outlets for allowing absolute filth to be visually transmitted across the airwaves and spoken over radio stations. In America, the "gentleman" is being replaced by something that resembles an enraged orangutan. The "lady" has become a hip, vulgar, promiscuous, tattooed, loud-mouthed, hell-raising feminist.

What's wrong with being mannerly?

It's still all right to carry on a conversation without four-letter words. It's still in order to pull the chair out for the lady before she sits down—not as she sits down. It's still all right to open the car door for your wife, even if you've been married twenty-five years. It's still OK to send a "thank you" card to friends and family thanking them for their kindness.

7. Love is not self-seeking (v. 5, NIV).

Paul writes that love is not self-seeking. Love does not insist on its own way. Love does not pursue a selfish advantage.

During the Holocaust, a Catholic Jewish mother with three children dashed into the woods before the approaching Nazi army. For days they lived on roots and grass in the forest.

One morning, a farmer and his son discovered them. The farmer demanded they come out of the brush. He saw in an instant that they were starved, and he told his son to give the mother a loaf of bread. The mother took it eagerly. Like a famished animal, she broke it into three pieces and gave it to her children.

The farmer's son said, "She kept none for herself because she is not hungry."

The father quickly responded, "She kept none for herself because she is a mother."

Love does not seek its own. Love looks for a way to give! Money can build a house, but it takes love to make it a home.

8. Love is not easily angered (v. 5, NIV).

The Bible says, "Love is not easily angered." The word *easily* was added in the King James translation. It is not in the original Greek text. Love is not irritable. Love is not touchy or fretful. Love is not quick to take offense. Love does not walk around with a chip on its shoulder, looking for a reason to pout.

A mother said to her son, "Son, it's time to get dressed for church."

The son responded, "Mom, I don't want to go to church. I don't like those people down at that church, and they don't like me. Give me three reasons why I should go to church today."

The mother looked at her son and said, "It's Mother's Day, and I'm your mother, and I want you to go. Second, you are forty-five years of age and should go. Third, you are the pastor of the church."

LOVE IS LOYAL!

There is no greater portrait of loyalty than the statement Ruth made to Naomi as they were about to enter the nation of Israel. Ruth and Naomi stand at the border of a Jewish nation. Ruth is a Gentile, moving into a Jewish society without hope of marriage, without hope of ever being accepted, without hope of ever having children. For this Gentile woman in a Jewish society, her only future would be serving her mother-in-law. Now listen to her words:

> Entreat me not to leave you,
> Or to turn back from following after you;
> For wherever you go, I will go;
> And wherever you lodge, I will lodge;
> Your people shall be my people,
> And your God, my God.
> Where you die, I will die,
> And there will I be buried.
> The LORD do so to me, and more also,
> If anything but death parts you and me.
>
> —RUTH 1:16–17

What was the result of her loyalty? She met and married Boaz, a mighty man of wealth. Their first child was named Obed, and he became the great-great-grandfather of Solomon and an ancestor of Jesus Christ. Ruth was listed in the genealogy of Christ. Her loyalty brought her to a position of immortality.

May I ask you this question? Is your love loyal?

Hints for Her

Do you personify these characteristics of love? When your husband thinks about you, does he remember that you are patient, kind, humble, and gentle? If you will try to live your life in demonstration of these characteristics of love in 1 Corinthians 13, you will reap the blessings of Proverbs 31:28–29: "Her children respect and bless her; her husband joins in with words of praise: 'Many women have done wonderful things, *but you've outclassed them all!*'" (THE MESSAGE, emphasis added).

CONCLUSION

Earlier in this book I quoted a poem about love that I memorized years ago and have never forgotten. Read it again, and think about its message.

A bell is not a bell until you ring it.
A song is not a song until you sing it.
Love in your heart is not put there to stay.
Love is not love until you give it away.[1]

You have just seen God's portrait of love. Ask the Holy Spirit to show you the areas in your life where you fail to possess the love of Christ for other people as He loved you.

ASKING GOD'S HELP

Father, I know that without You, I am nothing. Your love is all that I need to be the man You created me to be. I want to exemplify Paul's portrait of love. Make me so much like You that my wife describes me as "patient, kind, humble, helpful, and sweet!" Lord, I want to be loyal in every way to my marriage commitment. I know that the words of Proverbs 31:28–29 are talking about a wife, Lord, but it would make me so happy to hear my wife tell me, "Honey, there are a lot of great guys out there, but you outclass them all!" Amen.

Notes

CHAPTER 1
HAS YOUR MARRIAGE LOST ITS SIZZLE?

1. Ray Mossholder, *Marriage Plus* (Lake Mary, FL: Charisma House, 1990).

2. Ibid.

3. Meir Zolotowitz, *The Art Scroll Tanach Series* (Brooklyn, NY: Mesorah Publications, 1977), 131.

4. Ibid.

CHAPTER 2
WHAT WOMEN WANT

1. "Condom Warnings—Beware! Doctors Speak Out About Condom Failures," Pro-Life America, www.prolife.com/condoms.html.

CHAPTER 4
MORE LOVE SECRETS EVERY MAN MUST KNOW

1. "Quote Me On It," http://www.quotemeonit.com/menninger.html.

2. This quote is attributed to Oscar Hammerstein II, who gave it as advice to Mary Martin.

3. "Quotes to Inspire You," http://www.cybernation.com/victory/quotations/authors/quotes_coolidge_calvin.html.

4. Ray Spangenberg and Diane Moser, *Eleanor Roosevelt: A Passion to Improve* (N.p.: Facts on File, 1997), 42.

5. "The Dred Scott Decision," Historical Documents and Speeches, http://www.historicaldocuments.com/DredScott.htm.

6. The information on Rosa Parks was adapted from Internet sources about her and the Civil Rights movement. The majority of the information came from the Academy of Achievement, the Hall of Public Service, the Profile, Biography, and an Interview with Rosa Parks. See http://www.achievement.org/autodoc/page/par0pro-1.

7. See ThinkExist Quotations, http://en.thinkexist.com.

Chapter 6
Can a Marriage Survive Addictions, Alcoholism, or Homosexuality?

1. Statistics quoted in the following three paragraphs were obtained from the National Institute on Chemical Dependency, found at http://www .ni-cor.com.

2. George E. Vaillant, *The Natural History of Alcoholism Revisited* (Cambridge, MA: Harvard University Press, 1995).

3. The information about alcohol addiction in the previous paragraphs are adapted from Vaillant, *The Natural History of Alcoholism Revisited*.

4. Vernon Johnson, *I'll Quit Tomorrow: A Practical Guide to Alcoholism Treatment* (San Francisco: HarperSanFrancisco, 1992).

5. Ibid.

Chapter 7
Can a Marriage Survive Poor Communication, Lack of Passion, or Poor Money Management?

1. James Hewett, *Illustrations Unlimited* (Chicago, IL: Tyndale House, 1988), 342.

Chapter 8
Love's Portrait

1. This quote is attributed to Oscar Hammerstein II, who gave it as advice to Mary Martin.

You have just finished *What Every Man Wants in a Woman* by Pastor John Hagee. The information you read about marriage was presented from a man's point of view. The principles the author shared will help you build a loving relationship with your mate.

Now you will want to flip this book over and read *What Every Woman Wants in a Man,* written from a woman's point of view by Diana Hagee. She will share important principles and stories that, when combined with the information from this book by her husband, Pastor John Hagee, will help you to build an affair-proof marriage that sizzles with joy and excitement every day of your married life.

Strang Communications, the publisher of both Charisma House and *Charisma* magazine, wants to give you 3 FREE ISSUES of our award-winning magazine.

Since its inception in 1975, *Charisma* magazine has helped thousands of Christians stay connected with what God is doing worldwide.

Within its pages you will discover in-depth reports and the latest news from a Christian perspective, biblical health tips, global events in the body of Christ, personality profiles, and so much more. Join the family of *Charisma* readers who enjoy feeding their spirit each month with miracle-filled testimonies and inspiring articles that bring clarity, provoke prayer, and demand answers.

To claim your **3 free issues** of *Charisma,* send your name and address to: Charisma 3 Free Issue Offer, 600 Rinehart Road, Lake Mary, FL 32746. Or you may call 1-800-829-3346 and ask for Offer # 93FREE. This offer is only valid in the USA.

---

www.charismamag.com

WHAT EVERY WOMAN WANTS IN A MAN

DIANA HAGEE

Charisma HOUSE

A STRANG COMPANY

*Dedicated to the only man I ever wanted,
my beloved husband, John Hagee*

Acknowledgments

I want to express my profound gratitude to:

- My King, who has taken me down paths I never thought possible

- My precious children, without whose loving contribution to our lives this book could not have been written. You are a treasure to me.

- Teresa Weaver, my dear friend who encourages me toward my divine destiny

- The members of Cornerstone Church, who have blessed our lives beyond measure

- Dr. Anne Reed, who willingly contributed her experience and hours of her time to this book

"What women want in a man may not be what God wants them to have. What women want in a man is not as easily received as we may think. We have much to do with what we want from others."

DIANA HAGEE

Diana Hagee is the chief of staff for John Hagee Ministries' television ministry. She is the author of *Not by Bread Alone*, a guide to creative ministry through food, and *The King's Daughter*, which received a Retailers Choice Award.

CONTENTS

What Women Want
IN A MAN

> Therefore a man shall leave his father and mother and be joined to his wife, and they shall become one flesh.
>
> —GENESIS 2:24

> What God has joined together, let not man separate.
>
> —MATTHEW 19:6

YOU HAVE OFTEN heard it said that the most important decision you will ever make is whether or not you receive Jesus Christ as Savior. This decision will determine the quality of life you will lead on earth and the eternal life you will have in heaven.

The second most important decision you will make is whom you will marry. This choice will contribute to your future happiness and whether you will be able to serve the Lord to your maximum potential.

The God whom we serve created the world for our benefit. He created marriage for our benefit as well. You and your husband were created in the image of our Creator. He shows us through His infinite mercy and grace the steps we need to take to be all He ordains us to be. We are His children. Our marriages were planned by Him. He shows us what we must do to walk in harmony with our spouse to make our unions the beautiful blessing He has intended.

Most women I know are either looking for a husband, content with the one they have, or wishing they had a better one. When you ask men and women to give the reasons they married, you receive answers such as:

- We fell in love.
- We were physically attracted to each other.

1

- My friends were getting married, so I figured it was time to do the same.
- I needed stability and security in my life.
- Everybody expected us to get married.
- We "had to" get married.
- Our parents did not want us to marry, so we eloped.
- It seemed the right thing to do.

If we as Christians believe that God created marriage and has a purpose for it, then we must conclude that most of the reasons above are not the right reasons for marriage, nor can these reasons sustain a marriage. Christian marriage counselors Randall and Therese Cirner, in their book *10 Weeks to a Better Marriage,* sum up God's reasons for marriage this way:

1. To become one flesh
2. For committed love
3. For mutual service[1]

Rebbetzin Esther Jungreis, internationally acclaimed Orthodox Torah teacher and granddaughter, daughter, wife, and mother of rabbis, in her wonderful book *The Committed Life* states: "Our culture has taught us to equate love with gratification—with getting rather than with giving, with taking rather than sharing, with being our own persons rather than feeling a oneness with our mates. Therefore it's not surprising that people go in and out of relationships, since the returns are bound to fall short of their expectations."[2] In order to have successful relationships, we must stop living by the laws of this world and begin to live by the dictates of the inspired Word of God.

Whatever your marital status, you should be aware of the attack of the enemy on the traditional family in our society. From the beginning, the serpent attacked the covenant God the Father had with His people. Today is no different. When the church competes with the world in the divorce rate, *something is not right*. When the Word of God commissions the church to be in the world but not of the world, yet we mirror the world, *something is not right*.

Things are not right because we use the world and its standards as our life guidelines. We have failed to follow the guidelines set before us

by the Potter who made us, the Savior who died for us, the Spirit who is there to guide us.

What are these *things*?

Scientists are being heralded because they devised a camera that shows a twelve-week-old baby in his mother's womb smile, walk, and yawn, yet our society demands stem cell research using the brain cells of these very babies. "Something is not right!"

There is an increase in sexually transmitted diseases because the "safe sex" purposed by the world is not! Fifteen million new cases are diagnosed each year with an annual cost for treatment of nearly $10 billion![3] When prescription drug usage is on the rise merely because our society would rather turn to a chemically induced euphoria than to lead a righteous lifestyle that produces an inward joy, "something is not right."

When the father is absent from the home and the child is looking for a leader in the gangs of the street...when the Supreme Court of the land rules that to regulate child pornography is an infringement on the freedom of speech...when we, as a people, must petition our government to issue a constitutional amendment that only recognizes a marriage between a man and a woman..."something is not right."

The divorce rate soars in America because our word is no longer our bond, and "covenant" is something we find in a homeowners association contract but not within our marriages. It is no wonder that women in our church come to me requesting prayer for their marriages, asking, "Please pray for my marriage...'something is not right.'"

In the following pages of this book we will examine the relationships between the sexes. My prayer is that if you are a female reader, you will be able to glean what is necessary to choose a godly man, learn how to meet the needs of your husband, and benefit from a beautiful, long-lasting marriage.

If you are a male reader, I pray that you will learn how to attract a godly woman, learn more about giving a woman what she wants and needs, and learn to create a satisfying, lifelong marriage covenant.

I want this book to help you "make things right."

My husband, Pastor John Hagee, surveyed our congregation of several thousand people and asked the questions, "What do men want in a woman?" and "What do women want in a man?" Before I discuss the results of this survey showing these desires from a woman's point of view, allow me to share some research of my own.

WHAT I WANT IN A MAN
(WOMEN SURVEYED—AGE 25)

1. Handsome
2. Full of charisma
3. Financially successful
4. A caring listener
5. Great sense of humor
6. Physically fit
7. Fashionable dresser
8. Well mannered, appreciates the finer things
9. Full of thoughtful surprises
10. An imaginative, romantic lover

WHAT I WANT IN A MAN
(WOMEN SURVEYED—AGE 40)

1. Nice looking (hair is preferred on his head)
2. Opens car doors, holds chairs
3. Has enough money for a nice dinner
4. Listens more than he talks
5. Laughs at my jokes
6. Carries bags of groceries with ease
7. Owns at least one tie
8. Appreciates a good home-cooked meal
9. Remembers birthdays and anniversaries
10. Seeks romance at least once a week

WHAT I WANT IN A MAN
(WOMEN SURVEYED—AGE 55)

1. Not too ugly (bald head is acceptable)
2. Doesn't drive off until I am in the car
3. Works steady, splurges on dinner occasionally
4. Nods head when I am talking
5. Usually remembers punch lines of jokes
6. In good enough shape to play cards

7. Wears a T-shirt that covers his stomach
8. Wants more than nachos for our romantic night out on the town
9. Remembers to put the toilet seat down
10. Shaves most weekends

WHAT I WANT IN A MAN
(WOMEN SURVEYED—AGE 65)

1. Keeps hair in nose and ears trimmed
2. Doesn't belch or scratch in public
3. Doesn't borrow money too often
4. Doesn't nod off to sleep while I am venting
5. Doesn't retell the same joke too many times
6. Is in good enough shape to get off the couch on weekends
7. Usually wears matching socks and fresh underwear
8. Appreciates a good TV dinner
9. Remembers my name on occasion
10. Shaves some weekends

WHAT I WANT IN A MAN
(WOMEN SURVEYED—AGE 75)

1. Doesn't scare small children
2. Remembers where the bathroom is
3. Doesn't require much money for upkeep
4. Only snores lightly when asleep
5. Remembers why he is laughing
6. Is in good enough shape to stand up by himself
7. Usually wears some clothes
8. Likes soft foods
9. Remembers where he left his teeth
10. Remembers that it is the weekend

WHAT I WANT IN A MAN
(WOMEN SURVEYED—AGE 85)

1. Breathing
2. Doesn't miss the toilet[4]

This is obviously written to make you laugh, but sadly there is truth in the fact that the older the woman, the less she expects from her marriage. The graph I plotted from the responses we received to my husband's survey shows that the longer a woman is married the less she expects positive changes to occur in her marriage.

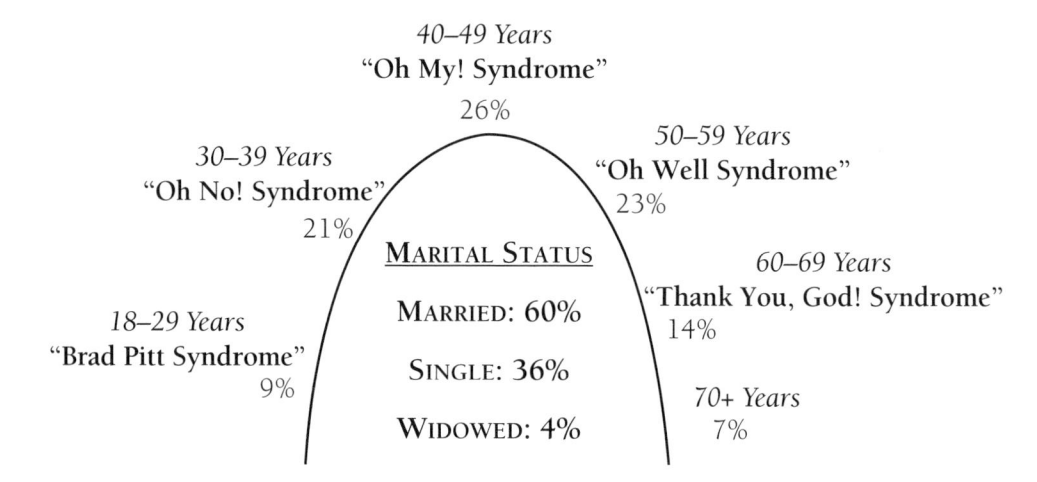

40–49 Years
"Oh My! Syndrome"
26%

30–39 Years
"Oh No! Syndrome"
21%

50–59 Years
"Oh Well Syndrome"
23%

18–29 Years
"Brad Pitt Syndrome"
9%

<u>MARITAL STATUS</u>

MARRIED: **60%**

SINGLE: **36%**

WIDOWED: **4%**

60–69 Years
"Thank You, God! Syndrome"
14%

70+ Years
7%

In the eighteen to twenty-nine age bracket, women have what I call the "Brad Pitt Syndrome." They are looking for beauty, passion, and illusion. Women thirty to thirty-nine years of age are wondering what they have gotten themselves into. I call this the "Oh No! Syndrome." Women ages forty to forty-nine are realizing what they feared at thirty has now come to pass. I call this the "Oh My! Syndrome." At ages fifty to fifty-nine, women resign themselves to the belief that their spouse will never change, or the "Oh Well Syndrome."

Finally, we have the age group of sixty and above. These women have learned to bring out the best in their spouses. They have learned that

their word is their bond. They have learned to follow the voice of the Holy Spirit within their relationships. They realized that it is not their jobs to change their husbands. They have empowered themselves with the strength of God to defuse situations that were designed by the enemy to destroy their marriages. These women have surrendered to the Lord and allowed Him to lead them in wisdom and discernment. They are not victims; they are victorious! I call this the "Thank You, God! Syndrome."

Whatever age group you are in, I want this book to provide hope for you as only the Word of God can. I want you to be excited about what the Potter can do in your marriage. If the Lord can hold the heart of a king in the palm of His hand and turn the king's heart like rivers of water, then He can turn your marriage into something that resembles heaven on earth!

My section of this book should be entitled, "What Women Think They Want in a Man, and How to Get It!" My husband tells the story of a wealthy father who employed a nanny to care for his strong-willed child. As he sat in his study, he heard his son cry out. Immediately he called out to the nanny and asked what was wrong. The nanny calmly replied, "Oh, nothing, sir; your son is simply crying for something he wants that I am not willing to give him."

"I demand that you give my child what he wants!" the father commanded.

"Very well," replied the nanny.

Suddenly, another cry came from the son, much stronger and more intense than the first. Irritated, the father screamed from the study as he ran toward the nanny and his son. "What in heaven's name did he want?"

"A wasp," replied the nanny.

What women want in a man may not be what God wants them to have. What women want in a man is not as easily attained as we may think. We have much to do with what we want from others. This section will try to equip women to receive from others exactly what they need to receive in order to be the best women, wives, and mothers our Creator intended them to be.

The chapters of this book are based on the answers we gathered from my husband's survey regarding "What Women Want in a Man." Each chapter discusses one of the responses, prioritized from the least important quality listed to the most important quality in the survey answers. I have saved the quality most desired by women for last.

Each chapter will also contain a special section for men titled, "Hints for Him." These hints will aid a man to give a woman what she needs.

I will also include a section, "From Dr. Anne," in each chapter. Let me introduce Dr. Anne Reed to you. I am not a licensed marriage counselor. I can speak to you from personal experiences covering nearly twenty-nine years of marriage and my experience as a pastor's wife in a congregation of 18,000 members, including the research I have done for this book. Dr. Anne Reed will contribute additional information from a professional viewpoint. Dr. Anne is a vibrant and dedicated woman of God who counsels according to the Word of God. She received her bachelor of science in education and masters of business administration from Angelo State University in Texas. She did doctorate study at the University of Texas and received her PhD in counseling from the University of Amsterdam.

She has extensive experience in corporate as well as family counseling. Teaching, lecturing, and seminar development have been major scopes and missions for her ministry. Dr. Reed is presently a pastoral care counselor for Cornerstone Church in San Antonio, Texas, under the leadership of my husband and myself. Dr. Anne is dedicated to family reconciliation through healthy Christian spiritual values.

John and I entrust the sheep of our church to Dr. Anne with her skills and her knowledge of marriage relationships. This same trust is extended to the reader as you glean from her wisdom and advice. She will comment on each topic as if you were sitting on her counseling couch.

Scattered throughout each chapter will be a parallel thought from my husband's section of this book, titled, *What Every Man Wants in a Woman*. You will find similar comments from me scattered through the pages of his section of the book. These comments will be called "He Says…" in this section of the book and "She Says…" in my husband's section. As you read these parallel ideas, you will recognize clearly the differences in the way a man thinks from the way a woman thinks. They demonstrate the essence of this book—and these clearly recognizable differences are the reason why we thought it was important to write the book together.

Lastly and most importantly, each topic will end with a prayer of repentance for the things we have done wrong within our marriages and a prayer of new beginnings to enable us to start fresh in our quest to be the best we can be in our relationships with our loved ones and with our Father in heaven.

Repentance is the key to our salvation. Repentance is the key to growing in God. Repentance is a road we should walk often as we strive to be all we can be in Christ. Sadly, repentance is often the road less traveled by the men and women who enter into covenant with one another. It is my desire that by the time you finish reading this book, repentance will be second nature to you and that you will be longing for the good things of God.

Welcome to *What Every Woman Wants in a Man*. After you read this portion of the book written by me from my female point of view, be sure you flip over to my husband's portion, *What Every Man Wants in a Woman*.

The Scriptures dictate for us to put on the helmet of salvation so we can protect our minds from the fiery darts of the evil one. First Thessalonians tells us that the helmet of salvation is also the helmet of hope. The mind is the place where hope abides. Hope is a treasured gift of God. Hope is what enables us to face tomorrow with anticipation and joy. The Word of God states that Jesus Christ is our "blessed hope" (Titus 2:13). I want you to put on the helmet of hope every day and know that the One who holds your tomorrow also holds your marriage. To abide in Jesus Christ and in His Word, which are the manifestations of hope in this world, will make your marriage a sanctuary of heaven on earth, for as long as there is life there is hope.

Want Number Ten:
FAITHFULNESS

Most men will proclaim each his own goodness,
But who can find a faithful man?
The righteous man walks in his integrity;
His children are blessed after him.
—PROVERBS 20:6–7

EVERY WOMAN WANTS to know, without a shadow of a doubt, that her boyfriend, fiancé, or spouse is completely loyal to her in thought and deed. One of the many reasons we, as believers, can have such unconditional trust in our Savior is because of His true faithfulness.

Therefore know that the LORD your God, He is God, the faithful God who keeps covenant and mercy for a thousand generations with those who love Him and keep His commandments.
—DEUTERONOMY 7:9

The adjectives that describe a faithful person are *steadfast in affection or allegiance* or *loyal*. This man is firm in adherence to promises or in observance of duty or *conscientious*. A faithful individual is one who is given to assurance or one who is *bound by promise*.

If a woman says that she wants a faithful man, what she is really asking for is a man who will not have an affair and who will be loyally committed to her for life. She wants to trust him completely. That sounds simple enough. However, where two people are involved within a marriage relationship, there are several complex issues.

Nationally acclaimed clinical psychologist Dr. Willard F. Harley Jr., in his book *His Needs, Her Needs: Building an Affair-Proof Marriage,* refers to the high expectations men and women have for their marriages.[1] Both want their needs met, yet seldom do they communicate those needs to their spouse or take the time to know the needs of the other.

Dr. Harley states: "The main reason needs are often not met within the union of marriage is not selfish unwillingness to be considerate, but true ignorance of each other's needs."[2]

I have found that many individuals try to learn to "do without" having their needs met. They would rather do without than attempt to convey to their mate their true needs. There is no greater fear on earth than to stand emotionally naked before the one you love most in life, fearing that person will laugh at your desires or refuse to give you what you desperately want.

For example, a man who lists sexual fulfillment as one of his needs, and whose wife fulfills this need, makes his wife a continual source of intense pleasure, and his love for her grows stronger.

However, if this need is not met, he begins to associate her with frustration. Eventually, he will decide she "doesn't like sex." One of three things will happen: he will grin and bear it, or he will live a sexually frustrated life, or he will be unfaithful.

Adultery does not occur overnight. The man usually begins by conversing with a close female friend, someone at the office, or a neighbor. The "conversation only" friendship then develops into a deeper relationship of trust and desire. One step at a time the marriage is compromised by deeper feelings of trust and emotional dependence in the third party, and if he does not stop himself, adultery will result.

> **HE SAYS . . .**
>
> **When you buy a car, the car payment is the amount due. When you get married, sex is the payment of what is due.**

Not every man who is unfaithful in his marriage has a wife who does not fulfill his sexual or emotional needs. The rise of pornography and the casual attitude for marriage within the world have contributed greatly to the decline of fidelity within marriage. The word *vow* means little.

Former pastor Bob Moeller, in his book *For Better, For Worse, For Keeps,* makes the clever yet true statement: "If you keep your vows, they will keep your marriage."[3] A vow is a solemn promise made to

God—a promise of fidelity and love for the spouse you have chosen.

We as women need to understand the warning signs of a frustrated partner and turn to the Lord to make us all we can be within our marriage commitment.

We must ask ourselves these questions: What are my husband's needs? What am I doing to meet his needs? What am I doing to create frustration in him? Have I communicated to him what my sexual desires and needs are? What does the Word of God say about our sexual relationships? How can I change and be a better spouse?

There are certain biblical facts about sex that should be acknowledged:

1. Sex is God-given. Satan cannot offer anything in this realm other than distortion and emptiness. Sex was created by God to allow a husband and wife to express oneness through intimate and exclusive love. Our Creator designed sex to be pleasurable. Read Song of Solomon 4:1–16.

2. God created sex to be both a physical and a spiritual bond. He made two people out of one, and the two are not complete until they become one again through the sexual union within marriage.

And Adam said: "This is bone of my bones and flesh of my flesh; she shall be called Woman, because she was taken out of Man." Therefore a man shall leave his father and mother and be joined to his wife, and they shall become one flesh. And they were both naked, the man and his wife, and were not ashamed.

—GENESIS 2:23–24

3. God created sex to have purposeful boundaries. Anything outside of this total and exclusive covenant between husband and wife is destructive.

… "For this reason a man shall leave his father and mother and be joined to his wife, and the two shall become one flesh"? So then, they are no longer two but one flesh. Therefore what God has joined together, let not man separate.

—MATTHEW 19:5–6

4. The God-given purposes for sexual intimacy are these:

   a. *Unity*—"Man shall . . . be joined to his wife" (Gen. 2:24).

   b. *Comfort*—"Isaac . . . took Rebekah and she became his wife, and he loved her. So Isaac was comforted after his mother's death" (Gen. 24:67).

   c. *Procreation*—"Then God blessed them, and God said to them, 'Be fruitful and multiply'" (Gen. 1:28).

   d. *A defense against temptation*—"Nevertheless, because of sexual immorality, let each man have his own wife, and let each woman have her own husband. . . . Do not deprive one another except with consent for a time . . . so that Satan does not tempt you because of your lack of self control" (1 Cor. 7:2, 5).

     A husband is commanded to find satisfaction (Prov. 5:19) and joy (Eccles. 9:9) with his wife and to concern himself with meeting her unique needs (Deut. 24:5; 1 Pet. 3:7). A wife is responsible for availability (1 Cor. 7:3–5), preparation and planning (Song of Sol. 4:9), interest (Song of Sol. 4:16; 5:2), and sensitivity to her husband's needs (Gen. 24:67).[4]

When was the last time you created a romantic atmosphere for you and your husband? When was the last time you chose to meet his sexual desires? Have you even tried to meet them?

A man likes to be courted. He needs to be wanted. A phone call during the day that lets him know you are thinking of him in an intimate way will do wonders. He wants to know he is your hero. Buy, and wear, I might add, flattering nightgowns, and create a romantic atmosphere as often as possible.

When you and your husband find yourselves in an intimate moment, let him know exactly what you need and want from him within the confines of your bedroom. I know some of you are shaking your heads right now and thinking that your husband would probably have a heart attack if you did this. You have to start sometime, and the time is now!

What if you know what your husband's needs are, and you either refuse or can't meet his needs? What then?

To the woman who knows her husband's needs but refuses to meet them, Scripture states in 1 Corinthians 7:2–5:

> Nevertheless, because of sexual immorality, let each man have his own wife, and let each woman have her own husband. Let the husband render to his wife affection due her, and likewise also the wife to her husband. The wife does not have authority over her own body, but the husband does. And likewise the husband does not have authority over his own body, but the wife does. Do not deprive one another except with consent for a time, that you may give yourselves to fasting and prayer; and come together again so that Satan does not tempt you because of your lack of self-control.

The apostle Paul speaks about the importance of the sexual relationship between a man and his wife. This relationship is more than a biological requirement for reproducing. Marriage is the only location where God ordains sex. Within the confines of marriage the sexual union is a blessing. Outside, it is a cause for judgment.

Some of you may simply use sex within your marriage as a tool of manipulation. Manipulation is a sin and will destroy your marriage. When you send verbal and nonverbal signals to your husband that dictate to him what he will or will not receive based on what you get in return, you are practicing manipulation. I instruct you in one clear word, *STOP*! First of all, you are compromising a beautiful gift that God has made provision for within the sacrament of marriage. Second, you are riding for a fall. God is not a respecter of persons, and sooner or later you will pay the consequence for this action.

Some of you may have inhibitions regarding this intimate part of your marriage. In order to fulfill this requirement of marriage, you should seek direction from a professional Christian

HE SAYS . . .

God created Eve and brought her on His arm down the grassy slopes of the Garden of Eden. She was a perfect ten. She was absolutely naked and totally stunning. Adam started singing that well-known song "I Just Feel Like Something Good Is About to Happen."

counselor. You owe this to yourself, your husband, and your marriage.

If you have a medical condition that prohibits you from providing a conventional sexual relationship for your husband, first seek medical advice, and then come into agreement with your husband as to how you can meet his physical needs. My husband and I highly recommend a book written by a Christian gynecologist, Dr. Scott Farhart, titled *Intimate and Unashamed*, which covers sexual topics from a clinical and biblical perspective.[5] You must learn to utilize all the godly tools available in order to have the best marriage relationship you can have.

Bob Moeller makes reference to "three true aphrodisiacs" of marriage. Moeller declares that no matter how beautiful or unattractive, old or young, every individual can possess love stimulants within their marriage.[6]

The first is *forgiveness*. When used, this ingredient can even change the chemical makeup of an individual. Why is there a sudden burst of sexual attraction when a couple has a fight and then reconciles? Our oneness established by our Creator has been restored, and we want to express this restoration through intimacy.

My husband often asks our congregation this question: "Do you want to be right or reconciled?" Ultimately, each individual must make this decision. Forgiveness is not a feeling we achieve but a choice we make. Granting forgiveness is not always easy. At times it is the hardest thing we will ever do.

To forgive someone we don't want to forgive, or to forgive someone who has not asked for forgiveness and has no repentant spirit, is not easy. We would rather bite our tongue in half. Many of my arguments with my husband have turned into arguments with the Lord.

"Lord, did You hear what he said to me?" "I can't believe he could even think that way about me!" "Me! The person who has always stood by him! Me! The person who is always trying to please him!"

"I'll tell you what, Lord; I'll forgive him if he admits he's been wrong *first*." "Lord, I don't want him to simply say he is sorry and think everything is all right! I want blood!"

The Lord then softly rebukes me and reminds me that it is not always about "me"! I have to listen to His voice and do what He asks and do it when He asks. Even when I don't want to, or don't feel that I should. Forgiveness is not conditional to our feelings but is determined by our

obedience. When we extend forgiveness, we emulate our Savior. When we act like our Savior, it brings a smile to the face of God.

There were two couples in our church whose families had become close friends. Through circumstances not ordained by God, the husband of one family and the wife of the other began a torrid sexual affair. Once discovered, we immediately put both couples into counseling, each one proclaiming a desire for reconciliation. Time passed, and healing seemed to occur. More time passed, and the two resumed their affair. Discouraged, yet still hopeful because the offended parties desired to forgive, we led the two couples through counseling once again. However, this time we asked one of the families to leave the church in order to give both families a chance to survive.

The couple that stayed in the church began their road to recovery. The offended party had every biblical right to a divorce but chose for the life and not the death of the marriage. The road was long and steep. The road was often tiresome and tedious. But the path of repentance led to healing. This couple is now a prime example of true forgiveness and restoration, and now offers help to those who find themselves in similar situations. This couple is able to give back to others what God has given them—grace, mercy, and restoration.

The couple that left our church continued down the path of destruction with a pattern of infidelity and forgiveness, infidelity and forgiveness. The Word of God sets before us life and death, blessings and curses. We must choose. Sadly, both husband and wife enabled the other to continue the path of death for their marriage.

My husband tells our sheep that to "extend forgiveness without demanding change makes the grace of God an accomplice to evil." Change is a condition that makes forgiveness a divine tool in the hands of the believer.

To make mistakes is part of our human nature, but to institutionalize those mistakes and make them part of our personality and character is to deny the image of Jesus Christ in which we were created. Asking forgiveness cancels out the past because of the blood covering of our Lord and Savior. This is one of the pillars of our faith through which we can begin anew and free ourselves from the bondage of our past. If we can ask for forgiveness, then we must extend forgiveness.

Moeller states that forgiveness is an act of our will that releases others from the moral debt they owe us.[7] Forgiveness is not given because it is

earned or deserved, but because it's needed. Forgiveness is mercy, not justice. We must learn to extend forgiveness as our Creator extended it to us. His whole nature is forgiving.

The second aphrodisiac is *surrender*. Because of cultural, moral, and generational differences, we all bring fears, insecurities, and inhibitions into our marriages. Moeller states that the level of intimacy and vulnerability that our Creator designed into the sexual union forces these hidden feelings to surface.[8] My husband often tells his congregation that legalism dictates, "If it feels good, then it must be sin!" This doctrine has caused many Christians to believe that enjoying sex is wrong.

God intended the sexual union within marriage to be a source of blessing, enjoyment, and joy for the husband and the wife. When we surrender our lives to God, we miraculously get our lives back to do His will and accomplish all He purposes for us. This action also applies to our marriages. To surrender all is frightening, but it is the only way to maximize our return.

The feminist movement equates surrender with losing one's identity. Nothing could be further from the truth. We do not become a slave to our partner when we surrender to him, and we do not give away our individualism, uniqueness, or dignity.

Surrender within marriage simply means voluntarily yielding ourselves to one another in love. Surrender is letting go of the fears and inhibitions of the past that have caused walls to come between you and your husband, and yielding to the concept that God has ordained the two of you to "become one flesh." Surrender is not weakness. Surrender takes strength and character.

The third aphrodisiac is *unselfishness*. *Making love* is much more than the sexual act. Romance is a great part of the sexual union. Dr. Farhart details the biological differences of men and women in the sexual realm. He discusses the human anatomy and the miraculous way it was constructed by the Creator and why it is we respond so differently to sexual intercourse.[9] It is important for us to have this knowledge, for it is not simply the truth that will set us free but the "knowledge" of the truth that will set us free from the bondages of crass locker-room talk and old wives' tales.

Moeller describes simply the sexual differences between a man and a woman by comparing them to a race car and a freight train. The race car is revved and ready to go. It gets to the goal fast and stops abruptly.

The freight train begins slow, yet eventually and powerfully it gets to its destination and slowly comes to a stop.[10]

It is evident that both partners must be sensitive to each other's needs and be willing to give unselfishly of themselves in order to fulfill the desires of the other. Even the simplest rules, like agreeing not to use the marriage bed to talk about family or business, can add pleasure to your time together. Communicate to your husband that there is nothing more important than your time of intimacy with him.

The world has kept the believer in "secular darkness" long enough. We must let the "Light of the world," Jesus Christ, bring enlightenment to every part of our lives, including our sexual relationships with our spouse.

Women read romance novels and love to go to *chick flicks* because of the tender affection that is shown the heroine. Lovemaking for the woman begins with holding hands and hugs, love pats and compliments. It doesn't begin when the lights go out and the door is locked.

For the man, true lovemaking and satisfaction also include knowing that he is wanted and needed. Your husband's satisfaction and desire are multiplied when he knows he is a hero in your life. Learn to give of yourself unselfishly. There is no greater satisfaction within the sexual act than to know that you have pleased the one you love.

Intimacy is not a formula—it's a way of life.

HINTS FOR HIM

Yearn to be faithful. Strive to be faithful. Be faithful in thought and deed. This is not only a character trait that a woman wants in a man, but it is also a trait that God wants in His people. He rewards faithfulness. (See Proverbs 28:20; Matthew 25:14–30.) Faithfulness is part of a solid foundation for every successful marriage.

A woman wants a man who will commit to his marriage for the long haul. She wants a man who wants to be a loyal husband and values this loyalty as a cornerstone for a healthy marriage.

Listen. A woman wants more than what you are hearing coming from her mouth. Learn to listen to all of her.

Let her know that she is what you want in life and that there is no one else who could satisfy you as she does. Hold her, and tell her you love her.

Finally, learn to communicate your needs and desires to your wife so she has the opportunity to meet every need you have. Make your intimate time together precious and pure.

FROM DR. ANNE

A faithful husband is a blessing from God. How can you have that blessing, and what do we really mean by the term *faithful*? Faithfulness comes when you have a relationship that is truly blessed and a marriage that is consecrated and holy. There is never a doubt of loyalty in that atmosphere. Your husband will be worthy of being believed in word and deed. He will consider you a blessing. He will be steadfast in the covenant he has made with you. You'll never have a need for suspicion or mistrust in an atmosphere of faithfulness.

Here comes the problem. The man I have just described deserves to have a woman with those same qualities. In fact, unless you have those attributes, I can promise you that anything you say to influence your husband will fall on deaf ears.

This is not a book for the rebellious woman who has no intention of changing. Submission to God's Word is required for you to enjoy the blessings that you say you want. You get what you give. God says that He will use the same measuring cup we use to give to others to give back to us (Matt. 7:2). Your degree of faithfulness and loving submission will influence the faithfulness of your husband.

How can you be faithful? Are you faithful to remember the very simple things that you want your husband to be faithful to? Do you remember birthdays, anniversaries, and milestones in your relationship? Do you follow through with the commitment to do what you have agreed to do?

Take a serious look at how you act and how much your mind is subjected to the Holy Spirit. Do you have thoughts about other men? Do you dress, act, or talk in a seductive way? Do you remain faithful to the plans and hopes that you have made with your husband? Do you embellish or lie when the truth is required? How many times have you told a half-truth to justify something to your husband? How many times have you colored your actions because you knew he would disapprove?

Have you considered how your husband would react if he found out that you were talking to or contacting an old boyfriend? What about chat rooms? What about e-mail? How important is it that you please another person more than your husband? How faithful are you?

Are you the wife that can be "faithful" to administer comfort and nurture your husband in times of need? Give what you want to receive.

Your hope for all things is in prayer alone. I pray that you are not involved in any of these things. If you are, *stop it!* Learn to pray for your husband to your Father God. Don't pray *at him*. Learn to pray blessings on your husband. Speak love and encouragement. You don't have to tattle to God about what your husband is doing. God already knows.

CLOSING PRAYERS

Our Creator is the source of our blessings, and as you turn to Him and His Word for direction, you will find Him ever faithful. Forgiveness, surrender, and unselfishness are three powerful traits given to you by God. These ingredients are ordained by Him to create deep, intimate, and loving relationships. When you offer these three elements to your mate in love and sincerity, they become the foundation to irresistible love.

PRAYER OF REPENTANCE

Father, forgive me. As David, I have sinned before You and You alone. I come to You with a repentant heart. Forgive me for the times I have been unfaithful to my husband in my thoughts and in my actions toward him. Forgive me for the times I have rejected him when he was trying to share his inner thoughts and desires with me. Forgive me, Lord, for knowing what he needed and wanted and intentionally not providing. Forgive me for giving my best to others while taking my husband for granted. I have flirted with ideas that would hurt my husband deeply. In hurting him, I have hurt You, and I am truly sorry and ask Your forgiveness.

Prayer of New Beginnings

Precious Father God, I am so thankful that You gave me Your Son, Jesus. He is the greatest example of faithfulness. He never swerved in His loyalty to You. He never looked aside from the plan You had set before Him.

Father, I thank You for the life You have given me with my husband. I thank You that we are both committed to You and to our marriage. I will be faithful to him in everything I say and do. I will not be tempted to open the door of disloyalty. With Your help I will strive to bless my husband daily and do all I can to make our home heaven on earth. Our children will see our marriage and want what we have. I will live my life and think my thoughts according to Your Word. I don't want to grieve the Holy Spirit with disobedience, thereby displeasing my Creator and Savior. Thank You, Lord, for being a God of new beginnings. Thank You for giving to me the man You want me to have so we may serve You all the days of our lives. Amen.

Want Number Nine:
LEADERSHIP

> For the husband is head of the wife, as also Christ
> is head of the church; and He is the Savior of the
> body.
>
> —EPHESIANS 5:23

A WOMAN WANTS A man to know who he is, to know where he is going, and to know how he is going to get there. She wants a man with confidence in himself, in her, and in their relationship. She wants him to lead her and her children with kindness and understanding. She wants him to be firm, yet gentle. She wants him to consult the Lord and her before any major decision is made to insure that he makes the right decision at all times.

Wow! Who can find such a man? His worth is more than all the riches of the world! Actually, this man is probably living with you right now. The question is not *Who can find him?* but *How can I, as his wife, help him to become this leader?*

My husband often says, "For every crooked pot there is a crooked lid!" In observing a diversity of relationships, I have sadly come to the conclusion that some pots don't have lids that fit. In my prayer time for these sheep, I often find myself trying to make a deal with God: "Lord, wouldn't it be perfect if this lid went with that pot?" Or, "How nice it would be for that lid to go with this pot. Life would be more fair and much nicer."

Then, of course, I come to my senses and realize that perfection is attained *in the world to come*—not in this life. In this world, we must walk by the law of God's Word and by the grace of His cross. Only the

Master Potter can mold each of us into the design He wants and make every lid fit perfectly with every pot. To have a "perfect fit" we must let Him work His plan.

There is a perfect plan designed by our Creator. God has placed divinely ordained traits within each one of us that, if activated, will allow His plan to work. However, so often in our human quest for power over our natural world, we forget God's design. Therefore we erect barriers that prevent His plan from transforming our marriage relationships into God's design.

Our quest for power often causes power struggles in our marriages. Noted anthropologist Margaret Mead asked a very important question regarding our society and the role reversal of the sexes: "Have we over-domesticated men? . . . Have we cut women off from their natural closeness to their children, taught them to look for a job instead of the touch of a child's hand? . . . All this in the name of equality?"[1]

The struggle for power has existed long before the desire for equality between man and woman. From the time in the garden, woman has tried to override man's leadership. Eve did not force Adam to take the apple; it happened more like this:

> The night is cool and beautiful by the light of the full moon. You can hear the owls serenade the evening as the wind rustles gently through the lush green leaves of the majestic trees set on the horizon. The sweet fragrance of honeysuckle fills the air. Life is good.
>
> Eve is adorned in nothing but a soft smile and anticipation as she awaits her husband's arrival from a stroll in the garden. Adam has been taking inventory over his entire domain. He sees his wife dressed in desire. The table is set with a splendid meal. Breathless, he admires her incomparable beauty. (So whom could he compare her to?) Oh, what a night this will be.
>
> There is a new recipe on the menu: fruit salad. This dish has a new ingredient: apples. She would not have been so bold as to make such a forbidden course if a slithering traveling salesman had not come calling while Adam was out. He peddled his wares, and Eve bought them. "To have knowledge and wisdom is to have power," the serpent convincingly persuaded her. Dinner is served.

You know the rest of the story. We ate ourselves out of paradise. Today is no different.

One day my husband came home from work and was rather frustrated. It had been a very bad day for him. Little was accomplished, and he was aggravated beyond words when he walked through the door. I have learned to read him well. His eyes were glazed, his jaw set, and his tongue rolled in his mouth. I was making dinner, and there was little I could say that would calm him down from the day's disappointments.

"Adam was so stupid! He listened to that silly woman and ate that dumb apple! If it wasn't for him, we would still be in paradise and not have to work for a living and put up with all this nonsense!" he ranted.

I tried to get a word in edgewise, but nothing would do. Finally, a bit perturbed at him by now, I continued to carefully peel the beautiful red apple I was holding. As I listened to his litany of complaints, I methodically sliced the apple and gently enticed him to open his mouth. Without thinking, he paused momentarily to bite down on the sweet-tasting offering I held in my hand. I watched him as he chewed with satisfaction and swallowed my tasty trap.

"There, if it had not been Adam, it would have been you!" I proudly announced, having proven my point. With that said, he almost threw up my illustrated sermon. He did not appreciate my object lesson. It was a long night.

In order to be a leader, you must have someone to lead. A woman wants her husband to lead; however, we must remember that it is our responsibility to submit to his leadership. And there, my friends, lies the rub.

As I was praying for direction on a topic for a Bible study for our women's class, I felt the Lord leading me to teach on submission. I knew it had to be the Lord's direction, because this was not a topic I was passionate about. I announced the class, and very few women signed up. Later, at the prodding of my peers, I renamed the class, "Submission, and How I Conquered It!" Surprisingly, the class immediately filled, and I began to teach the "S" word.

One of the first questions I asked the women was: "How many of you have no trouble submitting to your husband?" Several women raised their hands. Much to their dismay, I responded to their raised hands with this statement: "If you have no trouble submitting, then you have never truly submitted."

Submission is one of the most difficult actions you will ever undertake as a Christian woman. It is a difficult task. And if not done under

God's empowerment, it is downright impossible! True submission occurs when you follow your spiritual authority's lead, even when every fiber in you feels it's the wrong path to take. And you must do this in a willing and respectful way. Comedienne Rita Rudner gave her opinion on submission: "When I eventually met *Mr. Right*, I had no idea his first name was *Always*."

Submission is a *mandate*, not a suggestion.

> In like manner, you married women, be submissive to your husbands [subordinate yourselves as being secondary to and dependent on them, and adapt yourselves to them], so that even if any do not obey the Word [of God], they may be won over not by discussion but by the [godly] lives of their wives. When they observe the pure and modest way in which you conduct yourselves, together with your reverence [for your husband; you are to feel for him all that reverence includes: to respect, defer to, revere him—to honor, esteem, appreciate, prize, and, in the human sense, to adore him, that is, to admire, praise, be devoted to, deeply love, and enjoy your husband]. Let not yours be the [merely] external adorning with [elaborate] interweaving and knotting of the hair, the wearing of jewelry, or changes of clothes; but let it be the inward adorning and beauty of the hidden person of the heart, with the incorruptible and unfading charm of a gentle and peaceful spirit, which [is not anxious or wrought up, but] is very precious in the sight of God.
>
> —1 PETER 3:1–4, AMP

This scripture lists three main reasons why wives should submit to their husbands:

1. In obedience to the Word of God
2. To bring the lost to the saving knowledge of Jesus Christ
3. To be precious in the eyes of God

These should be sufficient reasons to submit, and to do so in a sweet spirit.

Not hardly! By the very nature of the word, *submission* means "to capitulate to another's desires, to surrender one's will, to give in, to acquiesce to someone else's lead." The antonym of submission is *resistance*. I

find that the "R" word is something women practice much more than the "S" word.

SUBMISSION SECRETS

There are a couple of *submission secrets* I will share with you in order to give you a fair opportunity to successfully accomplish this God-ordained mandate.

Submission is not an act of the will; it is a condition of the heart.

It is fruitless to try and submit your carnal will to that of your husband's. It is the nature of man to win. To attempt to submit "flesh to flesh" is like getting a root canal without an anesthetic. It makes an awful noise and is so painful you don't want to do it often.

Love does not measure success by strong will—tallying who gets his or her way. To the contrary, to love as Christ loves is to give—to give of yourself to the other in such a way that pleases the Creator and the person with whom you have decided to spend the rest of your life. If you live to please a man, you will never please your Father in heaven. In contrast, if you live to please your Father in heaven, then you can please the man you marry.

You must submit to God before you can submit to any man.

I compare this action to that of a satellite uplink. Imagine your husband asking you to follow his direction. You think about it. *Nope! Over my dead body!* is your first thought.

Having wisely decided not to voice your instinctive opinion, you ask God for help. In desperation you look upward. You "link" to Him in the heavenlies.

His Spirit becomes your spirit. Somehow, you suddenly have a change of thought. You realize that if you do your part as the Master Potter mandates, then He will cover you and honor your obedient action.

But wait a minute; there's more. Your second instinct is to say something like, "Well, OK, but I want you to know that I am only doing this your way because the Lord wants me to, and since I am such a 'spirrrritual' person I will do as you ask. Even though I feel

this is the most stupid decision you have ever made!"

Wrong! Satisfying, but wrong. You look up again and ask the Father to renew your mind and create in you a willing and sweet spirit. This task takes a little longer to accomplish, usually determined by the hormonal readings of the moment. I might warn you at this point…since I am in the sisterhood of women, submission never comes at the right time.

The uplink is complete. Now for the downlink. You look at your husband and assure him that you love him. "I know that leading me and our children takes great wisdom and responsibility," you tell him. "I will follow your lead as I pray for God to give you direction and discernment."

It's now complete. The mandate is accomplished. The Lord is pleased. Your husband is shocked. And you will be blessed no matter what the outcome.

We all have heard the phrase "a woman's place." Our Creator has a special place for us. When God puts a woman *in her place*, it is a place of honor, a high and lofty place. When this carnal world puts a woman in her place, it is usually a demeaning place far lower than what our Lord has destined for us to have.

In order to be right where God wants you to be, you must be obedient to His Word. Deuteronomy 28:1–2 tells us that if we heed His voice and obey His commandments, He will cause His blessings to overtake us. I love the sound of that. He will cause His blessings to "overtake us." This means that whether we think we deserve it or not, He will bless us. But first we must obey.

In his book *Spiritual Authority,* Watchman Nee states that to be filled with Christ is to be filled with obedience. Since the Lord initiated obedience, the Father has become the head of Christ. Since God has instituted both authority and obedience, it is natural for those who know God and Christ to obey. Those who know not God and Christ know neither authority nor obedience. Christ is the principle of obedience. Therefore a person who is filled with Christ must be filled with obedience.[2]

God sets up His authority in the home. Throughout His Word we see the pattern of familial authority. To rebel against this divinely appointed authority is to rebel against the kingdom ordained by God Himself. God has set the husband as the delegated authority of Christ, with the wife as representative of the church. It is difficult for the wife to be subject to her husband if she does not realize that the real issue is *God's authority*, not her husband's:

> That they may encourage the young women to love their husbands,
> to love their children, to be sensible, pure, workers at home, kind,
> being subject to their own husbands, that the word of God may
> not be dishonored.
>
> —TITUS 2:4–5, NAS

My position on this subject is simple: I want God's blessing on my life! I don't want to be guilty of blaspheming God's Word! What must I do to qualify for His blessing? The answer is *to obey*!

As you learn to obey God's instruction to be submissive to your husband, you can help him to become an effective and godly leader. The following ten things will help you to do that:

1. *Respect him.* Show honor and reverence to him in your home
   and to your friends and family. "Likewise, their wives must
   be reverent, not slanderers, temperate, faithful in all things"
   (1 Tim. 3:11).

2. *Acknowledge his calling as the high priest of your home.*
   Don't try to override his authority with your children in
   the spirit of Absalom. "Oh, that I were made judge in the
   land...I would give him justice" (2 Sam. 15:4).

3. *Respond to his leadership.* Don't tell him you will follow him
   and then do your own thing. You may deceive your husband
   for a season, but you won't fool the Lord for a second. "For
   the word of God is living and powerful, and sharper than
   any two-edged sword, piercing even to the division of soul
   and spirit, and of joints and marrow, and is a discerner of the
   thoughts and intents of the heart" (Heb. 4:12).

4. *Praise him.* Women do not realize that a man needs praise
   just as often as a woman needs it. Praise your husband
   for providing for your home and family and for leading
   you in the ways of the Lord. "...and let the wife see that
   she respects and reverences her husband [that she notices
   him, regards him, honors him, prefers him, venerates, and

esteems him; and that she defers to him, praises him, and loves and admires him exceedingly]" (Eph. 5:33, AMP).

5. *Be unified with him in purpose and in will.* When you come together as one in your goals and your supplications, God acknowledges your unity, and He grants your petitions. "Can two walk together, except they be agreed?" (Amos 3:3, KJV).

6. *Be his helpmate.* Don't compete with your husband. Learn to complement him. "Now the Lord God said, It is not good (sufficient, satisfactory) that the man should be alone; I will make him a helper meet (suitable, adapted, complementary) for him" (Gen. 2:19, AMP).

7. *Listen to him.* Don't be the mouth of the body when God is calling you to be the ear and heart of the body. The ancient prophet prayed, "Give unto me, O Lord, a hearing heart." Proverbs 4:4 says, "He taught me and said to me, Let your heart hold fast my words; keep my commandments and live" (AMP).

8. *Pray with him and for him.* It is so important that God hear your petitions for your husband. Cover him in prayer daily, praying that discernment and wisdom will guide him. "And pray in the Spirit on all occasions with all kinds of prayers and requests. With this in mind, be alert and always keep on praying for all the saints" (Eph. 6:18, NIV).

9. *Bless him.* I try to bless my husband every day before he leaves our home. There is a battlefield outside of the doors of our home, and he needs all the help he can get. The power of the blessing provides a blanket of protection and favor. "The LORD bless thee, and keep thee: The LORD make his face shine upon thee, and be gracious unto thee: The LORD lift up his countenance upon thee, and give thee peace. And they shall put my name upon the children of Israel; and I will bless them" (Num. 6:24–27, KJV).

10. *Be thankful for him.* So many women do not realize the gift
their husband truly is until they lose him. Thank the Lord
every day for your husband, and call out in him the traits
that God wants in him to be the man He has destined him
to be. "I thank my God always concerning you for the grace
of God which was given to you by Christ Jesus, that you
were enriched in everything by Him in all utterance and all
knowledge, even as the testimony of Christ was confirmed
in you, so that you come short in no gift, eagerly waiting for
the revelation of our Lord Jesus Christ, who will also confirm
you to the end, that you may be blameless in the day of our
Lord Jesus Christ" (1 Cor. 1:4–8).

THE IMPORTANCE OF TRUSTING

I want to talk to you about trust for a moment. It is critical for you to
know, without question, that you can trust God with your life, with
your husband's life, and with the lives of your family members. Make
the decision once and for all that you will trust that God loves you and
wants only what is best for you.

God *IS* trustworthy. Everything about Him is trustworthy. He is
enough for every problem, and His power and wisdom will care for
your every concern. Your trust in God is *your strength*.

This trust brings out the best in you as a woman, as a wife, and as a
mother.

Once a woman puts her trust in God, then she can put her trust in
her husband, but not until then. Without this trust, unity within marriage will not be possible. In their book *10 Weeks to a Better Marriage*,
Randall and Therese Cirner refer to a friend of theirs who told them,
"God I can trust! He's perfect. But my husband . . . that's another story! I
know he makes mistakes!"[3]

They list the following reasons women give for not trusting their
husbands:

1. "He is not spiritual enough," *or* "I have been a Christian
longer than he has."

2. "He still has faults," *or* "I'll trust him when he is perfect."

3. "He has made mistakes with our life in the past," *or* "How can I ever trust him again?"

4. "I'm better at decision making than he is," *or* "I know that I am right and he is wrong."

5. "I've been hurt so many times before in my past that I can't open myself to trust anyone again," *or* "Both my father and my husband disappointed me; I can never trust men again."[4]

What are the reasons you give for not trusting God or for not trusting your husband? Are they really reasons, or are they just *excuses*? Be aware that we sometimes try to avoid doing what is right by giving excuses for why we can't do what is expected of us in God's Word. Is that true of you? How can you change this cycle?

Most women have a very strong drive to lead. We like control because it gives us security. When my husband and I fly around the country, I always seem to worry about our safety. John always assures me that it safer to fly in a plane than to drive a car. But I always tell him that when I am in the air I am not in charge, but when I am driving the car I feel that I have more control of my life. I feel more self-assured when I am driving. It's all about control.

On one occasion we were flying by private charter on a plane that required a pilot and a copilot. I was reading a book when I realized the pilot was right in front of me, asking if all was well. Startled, I looked at the empty captain's seat and loudly asked the question, "Excuse me! But who is flying this plane?"

"The copilot is watching the instruments, and we are on autopilot. Everything is under control," the captain answered as he tried to assure me.

After I *assured* him that I did not like an empty pilot's seat, he took his rightful place. And I had to *trust* that he was in control.

> **HE SAYS...**
>
> **How sad that we spend so many years training for a career and so little time preparing for marriage.**

God is our pilot. He is in control. He instructs our husbands in the copilot's seat. Then there is the Holy Spirit, the autopilot, who makes

sure everything is in complete harmony and balance.

As wives, we simply must trust. We must let go. We must let go of being right, let go of being more spiritual, let go of being hurt, let go of analyzing our husband's faults. We must let go of trying to be in total control of every situation and let God have His sovereign way in our lives and in our marriages.

HINTS FOR HIM

My husband often tells the men of our church, "It's hard to follow a parked car!" A woman wants her husband to take the lead of their household. This can be harmonious only when the husband is also submitted to the Lord as his Savior.

Watchman Nee states that while the Bible teaches that wives should be subject to their husbands, it also instructs that husbands should exercise authority with a condition. Husbands are called upon to love their wives as they love themselves three different times in Ephesians 5. Undoubtedly there is authority in the family. However, those in authority need to fulfill God's requirement. The love of Christ for the church sets the example for the love that a husband ought to give to his own wife. The love of a husband ought to be the same as the love of Christ for His church. If husbands wish to represent God's authority, they must love their wives so much that they are willing to die for them.

Another wise thought my husband gives both men and women regarding the topics of leadership and submission is this: "Wives, follow your husband's lead, and husbands, meet your wife's need." It is the responsibility of the husband to know what his wife's true needs are and to meet those needs to the best of his ability with joy and kindness.

You will never be a successful husband and father if you do not submit yourself to the authority of God the Father and of Jesus Christ His Son. If you are a man who is reading this book, I encourage you to live according to the Word of God. Ask God for direction and wisdom in the leadership role He has assigned to you. Remember this truth: God will equip you to do those things He has ordained you to do.

FROM DR. ANNE

Security and freedom belong to the woman who has a husband who is willing, able, and capable of taking the lead in the relationship she has with him. This godly man uses wisdom to lead his family, *not muscle*. Ideally, a woman wants her husband to lead with compassion and kindness, and he leads with a flexibility and desirability that is pleasing to the wife and brings smiles to the faces of his beloved children. In other words, he does exactly what the rest of the family wants and what agrees with the flow of the moment.

But it's not that simple! The ultimate security a woman desires in her marriage, *more than any other thing in marriage*, is rewarded to her *only* when she is supportive of her husband. Her confidence in his ability to make good decisions will reflect her confidence in him as a husband, father, and, ultimately, as a man. You have great power in your hands, either to encourage God's perfect will or to crush your husband's self-esteem and self-worth. Use this power wisely.

In the Christian home the family should follow the leader willingly. The Christian father and husband should not find it necessary to *force* his family to be obedient. A godly leader exhibits a stillness, maturity, and determination to follow the will of God for himself—and for his family. He must hear God clearly and follow God fully. If he can be dissuaded from the decision that God has made clear to him, then he lacks the consistency and obedience that God requires.

Do not be a woman who wants to take this leadership from your husband. I would be quick to tell you that there is a price to be paid. What good is a leader without anyone to lead? What if those he has been put in charge of refuse to be led? If a leader is not able to lead, out of frustration he will lose motivation and finally stop attempting to lead.

Your input is needed for your husband to make an educated move. How can any leader make an educated, wise decision without all the facts? However, your input is required only once! Continued input is otherwise known by the term *nagging*.

When a decision that your husband made turns out to be one that doesn't work very well, don't humiliate him by reminding him as often as possible that he really "blew it." Proverbs 14:1 says, "The

wise woman builds her house, but the foolish pulls it down with her hands." Don't embarrass him by sharing his decision—and the outcome—with your children and his co-workers and church friends.

God is such a wise instructor. In a very simple way, He will show you how to add strength and honor to your husband as he stands erect and tall in his role. Words of encouragement roll off the tongue so much easier than bitterness. Support can make a situation that is less than ideal easier to live with.

Join your husband in oneness, and make a solid stand together. Ask his opinions. Include him in your family discussions so he can have input that will help the process of leadership. Pray for your husband daily—continually! Prayer is the best support you can give to your husband and to your family. Through prayer, your husband will have the wisdom God wants him to use as he makes his decisions. Prayer never fails, because our God *NEVER* fails.

CLOSING PRAYERS

God created women to give life to those with whom we come in contact! In this chapter, I have helped you to recognize your importance in bringing life to your husband and family by your godly support and prayers. The life you give is *God's life*. If your husband is not yet a Christian, through your submissive attitude you have the power to give eternal life to him by leading him to Christ "without a word" (1 Pet. 3:2).

You have also learned that you can give life to your marriage by submitting to your husband as Christ your Savior submitted to His Father on the cross. By obeying the Word of God in submission, you will give your marriage new breath. Your marriage relationship will become an eternal blessing—one that you begin experiencing *right now!*

PRAYER OF REPENTANCE

Father, in the name of Your Son, Jesus, I ask You to forgive me for insisting on being right at the expense of my husband's dignity and self-respect. I repent sorrowfully. I am truly ashamed of my actions. Father God, in Jesus' name, I ask that You forgive me for undermining my husband's authority. I am so sorry for going behind his back and allowing our children to disobey their father's instructions. I am

grieved that I didn't listen to his advice and did my own thing. My heart is truly heavy. I repent of the times I have used manipulation, domination, and intimidation to get my way. I know that I have sinned against my husband and grieved the Holy Spirit. I ask for Your forgiveness and Your mercy.

PRAYER OF NEW BEGINNINGS

My precious Father, I thank You for all the gifts that You have given me. I am truly blessed of You. I dedicate myself, my husband, and our children to You with the same love You showed us when you gave us Your only Son. I thank You for giving me a husband who loves me as Christ loves His church. I thank You for giving me a husband who shows compassion and understanding as he instructs our children. I accept the blessings that are mine as I walk in submission to You and to my husband. My husband grows in wisdom daily, and we are of one spirit. I want Your blessings and Your favor, which come from hearing Your voice and obeying Your Word. Amen.

Want Number Eight:
RESPECT

Come, you children, listen to me; I will teach you to revere and worshipfully fear the Lord. What man is he who desires life and longs for many days, that he may see good? Keep your tongue from evil and your lips from speaking deceit. Depart from evil and do good; seek, inquire for, and crave peace and pursue (go after) it!

—PSALM 34:11–14, AMP

However, let each man of you [without exception] love his wife as [being in a sense] his very own self; and let the wife see that she respects and reverences her husband [that she notices him, regards him, honors him, prefers him, venerates, and esteems him; and that she defers to him, praises him, and loves and admires him exceedingly].

—EPHESIANS 5:33, AMP

THE DEFINITION OF *respect* is, "to feel or show honor for; to think highly of; to look up to; to have polite regard and to be thoughtful and show kind consideration and concern for another individual." Every human being—man or woman—desires respect.

There is an element of dignity that is linked to the measure of respect we receive from others. The whole world around us can show an ultimate measure of respect for us, but if the person whom we love the most does not give us respect, we suffer from the lack of it.

Respect comes in two forms. The first form of respect is a form of regard that is shown for *the position* held by an individual. As wives we should respect the position of husband, father, and priest. As a husband, he should show respect for the position of woman, wife, and mother.

The Word of God is very clear that wives should show their respect for their husbands through submission to their authority. We are to respect our husband's role as father by not usurping his headship over the family.

36

We are to respect his role as the spiritual head of our household by holding him up in prayer and by having high regard for his leadership.

The Word of God is equally clear that the husband is to respect his wife. Our Creator places woman on a lofty pedestal. Christ says that a husband should love and respect his wife and the mother who brings his children into the world as Christ loves and respects His church. This we do in obedience to the Lord and His Word.

The second form of respect is much more valuable. This form of respect is linked to more than obedience. This form of respect is linked to *the person* and is expressed with love, trust, and gratitude.

Respect at this level is earned. A cardinal rule to follow when desiring this treasured form of respect is to give equal amounts of it away. As wives, before we can ask for respect from our husbands, we must first give respect to our husbands. I have found that some women demand respect for the positions they hold, but they are not as concerned about receiving respect from the hearts of the men who love them most, which is so much more valuable.

> **HE SAYS...**
>
> **Remember that your husband has a God-given role as leader of your home. Allow the Holy Spirit to help you willingly submit to his loving, godly leadership.**

This second level of respect, which is a beautiful expression of love and devotion, is the form of respect I will be referring to in the following pages. Before you can show any form of gratitude to your husband, you must first show it to the Lord, who gives you every perfect gift that comes from above.

> Enter into His gates with thanksgiving and a thank offering and into His courts with praise! Be thankful and say so to Him, bless and affectionately praise His name!
>
> —PSALM 100:4, AMP

THE COMPONENT OF GRATITUDE

Rebbetzin Jungreis describes one of the main components of respect. It's called *gratitude*. Gratitude is one of the pillars of Judaism and Christianity. For believers of Judaism, from the moment they wake in

the morning to the time they go to sleep at night, they are called upon to declare praise and thanksgiving unto God. Rebbetzin says, "Our first words must be a proclamation of appreciation to the Almighty for having returned our souls and given us yet another day. No aspect of life is to be taken for granted—a glass of water, a tree in bloom, the rainbow in the sky must all be acknowledged with a blessing to God."[1]

The Jews proclaim praise unto God because they are commanded to praise Him. As Christians we must do the same, but we must also go one step further because of the cross of Christ and what our Savior did for us on that cross. We should praise Him out of relationship. We should praise Him out of love. When we exercise this form of praise for our Creator, then there is no time for complaints, murmuring, or depression. We will have less chance to take His bountiful blessings for granted.

When is the last time you said *thank you* to the Lord? At times you may feel you have nothing to be thankful for, but this is simply not the case. Everything that is good comes from God. Everything that is of value, like the breath in your lungs and the sight for your eyes, all the beauty that surrounds you comes from God. You should thank Him every moment that you can. To know that the God who created the universe is the same God who inhabits the praises of His people is reason enough to praise Him.

Not to have gratitude for the things of God is the beginning of self-destruction in your walk with God. You have a choice—to focus on the things you lack, or to give praises unto God for the constant blessings that are upon you every day. When you focus on the things you lack, you will always want for more, even when you receive what you want. You will see God through a "What have You done for me lately?" attitude. When you focus on the blessings of God with an *attitude of gratitude,* then your life begins to reach for the destiny He has ordained for you.

Once you learn to express your gratitude to the almighty God who created you, to His Son who died for you, and to His Holy Spirit who guides you, then you can express your gratitude to your husband. Begin this expression of gratitude with two very important words: "Thank you."

Rebbetzin breaks down the word *modim* or *thank you* in Hebrew to give us a greater understanding of what this phrase should mean in our lives. *Modim* or *thank you* has two connotations. *Thank you* also means, "to admit." In essence, "thank you" is an admission that you

are in need, that you are vulnerable, that you cannot do it alone—and that admission is something that most of us do not like to concede. We hate feeling indebted, especially if the favor extended to us was significant. Therefore the greater the kindness and the closer the relationship, then the greater our reluctance to reveal our weakness by pronouncing those two little words. People who have no problem saying "Thank you" to a waiter in a restaurant, a telephone operator, or a salesperson have difficulty saying those same words to the people who are nearest and dearest because "Thank you" to them would be an admission of need.[2]

When is the last time you said "Thank you" to your husband? "For what?" you might ask. *For much*. He chose you as that special person with whom he passionately desires to spend the rest of his life. He helps to provide for you. The children whom you cherish are products of the love you share with him. Together, you go to the throne of God in prayer to give thanks and to petition the King of kings and the Lord of lords for your needs. Thank him often for being in your life.

I can't thank him, you may be thinking right now. *I don't have the kind of husband you just described.* Remember that faith is the assurance or confirmation of the things you hope for, being the proof of things you do not see, and the conviction of their reality. I know that you want the husband I described. You need to begin to thank the Lord for him, and thank your husband. Then watch him as he begins to change for the good. I believe it is your husband's ultimate desire to please you and his Savior, but often he lacks the knowledge of how to do so. You can begin to show him the way by showing respect and gratitude for the husband God has given you. Let God do the rest.

The first cousin of "I can't" is "I don't want to." Perhaps the inability to express your gratitude to your husband is one of the reasons you have a bitter attitude toward him and your marriage. Rebbetzin Jungreis says:

> People who cannot acknowledge kindness always find something or someone to criticize. They make miserable marriage partners, tyrannical parents, and selfish friends. They are convinced that everything is coming to them, that they are entitled to all the goodies in life simply because they are alive. No matter how much they are indulged, they are never satisfied. They just keep taking without feeling a need to give back.[3]

The Jewish sages define a *rich person* as the man or woman who is content with what they have. We as women must learn to take inventory of our possessions. We must learn to be thankful for all of them. This includes our spouses. Be grateful to the Lord for the husband He has given you, and be thankful and respectful to your husband who desires to be needed and wanted.

One of the greatest services a woman can perform for her husband is to respect him in thought, in word, and in action. All three are necessary, because they are interrelated. "Nevertheless let each one of you in particular so love his own wife as himself, and let the wife see that she respects her husband" (Eph. 5:33).

What you think affects what you say, and what you say affects how you act. No matter what shortcomings your husband may have, no matter how many changes he needs to make, always speak and act in a respectful way. The way you speak of him and act around him influences the way your children will perceive their father. It also influences the way other men and women think and behave toward your husband. Most importantly, it will deeply influence the disposition of your heart toward your husband.

> **HE SAYS...**
>
> **Love is not what you feel. Love is what you do.** *Works...* **not words...are proof of your love.**

A portion of the gift of life that a woman is privileged to give to her husband is her encouragement and support. Your husband needs someone who believes in him. He does not need someone who believes he is perfect. He needs someone who knows him intimately—his good points and his failings—and who still believes in him.[4]

I encourage you to put respect into action. Don't just agree that you *should* show respect. *Actually begin to act and speak and think with respect toward your husband.* Showing gratitude and respect to your husband will help him feel important in your life. As a result he will strive to become the man God wants him to be.

HOW TO AVOID THE DEATH OF YOUR MARRIAGE

What happens when you berate, disrespect, and take your husband for granted?

Psychologist John Gottman, PhD, has studied two thousand married

couples, and he says that a minimum of five positive interactions for every negative interaction is essential to marital happiness. Dr. Gottman encourages plenty of touching, complimenting, smiling, and laughing, while warning against criticism, contempt, and defensiveness.[5] Some wives have a lot of "making up" to do.

Rebbetzin Jungreis states that there are fourteen positive commandments and seventeen negative commandments in Judaism concerned with speech. She goes on to say:

> God did not give us laws that are beyond our reach. Even our psychological makeup is designed to guard our tongues. Just consider— every organ in our body is either external or internal; for example, the eyes and nose are external; the heart and kidneys are internal. The tongue, however, is both internal and external and is protected by two gates—the mouth and the teeth, teaching us that before we use it, we must act with discretion, for the tongue is a most powerful instrument, and with it we can either kill or impart blessing.[6]

The Word of God says, "Death and life are in the power of the tongue, and those who love it will eat its fruit" (Prov. 18:21). When you berate your husband, you initiate the death of your marriage.

More than six million Jewish people died as a result of the evil reign of Adolf Hitler. However, Hitler did not murder these people with his own hands—he killed them with his tongue! He poisoned the German people to believe that Jews were subhuman creatures, and he convinced his killers that the Jews deserved to be eradicated from the earth. The power of life and death are in the tongue.

Remember this: what you don't say today can always be said tomorrow. But once you allow words to come out of your mouth, you cannot take them back. Scripture tells us that "out of the abundance of the heart the mouth speaks" (Matt. 12:34). Check the condition of your heart before you allow your mouth to speak. Ask yourself the question, "Am I honoring my husband with my speech, or am I tearing him down?" We can choose to uplift our husbands or to demean them with our speech.

If you have an argument with your husband, don't share that argument with your parents. It will be nearly impossible for them to forgive your husband for inflicting hurt on you, their daughter. It could take much

longer than you desire for your husband to regain respect in the eyes of your parents.

Remember this rule of marriage: when your spouse offends you, God, in His infinite mercy, gives you a measure of grace to overcome the offense. However, when you share that offense with your parents, or others that love you, that same measure of grace is not afforded to them. Ultimately it will hinder them from the best relationship possible with your husband. Respect the private moments you have with your husband—good or bad—between just the two of you and the Lord. You will not regret it.

If you are a young woman who has not yet married the man of your dreams, take the time to carefully observe the man you are dating. How does he treat other people in his life? If you marry him, eventually this is the same way he will treat you.

My husband warns our young people about dating, "Be careful! Anyone can be good for four hours. But the real person is at home in a cage waiting to get out as soon as you say 'I do!'"

YOUR HUSBAND HAS GREAT VALUE

Your husband has true value in the eyes of God, just as you do. It is unfair to treat him as anything but royalty. Why are you surprised that he has lost that "loving feeling," if you spend hours demeaning him and pointing out his faults, constantly dwelling on his imperfections? You should live together in love.

Bob Moeller asks us to practice "cognitive dissonance," which occurs when our minds won't allow our feelings to exist contrary to our behavior.[7] When you feel that you have lost the feelings of love in your marriage, he suggests that for two or three days you treat your husband as if he is of enormous value to you.

> Go out of your way to show true respect, to listen with real intensity and without interrupting, and to compliment sincerely his strong traits. Keep your critical thoughts to yourself, and, instead, showcase his strengths to your friends and family. Anticipate his needs and put them first. If we treat someone with love, honor, and respect we are going to begin feeling it.[8]

Criticism causes men to become defensive, but admiration motivates and energizes them. A man expects and needs his wife to be his most enthusiastic fan. He draws confidence from her support and can usually achieve far more with her encouragement.[9]

It may be that you feel as though you do not know how to praise your husband. You may be thinking, *I only heard criticism when I was young. I never heard my parents praise each other. The only time they had long conversations with each other was when they argued.*

Sadly, I know far too many men and women who relate to this kind of thinking. However, today is the first day of the rest of your life! Ask the Lord today to break any generational curses over your life. Begin today to praise the Lord for His goodness. Begin to praise your husband and your children, and ultimately you will gain respect for them—and for yourself!

The Jewish *Mishna* is a commentary on the Torah, or the Word of God. In it, Jewish sages take the Word and interpret the wisdom within its pages to their congregants. One phrase found within the *Mishna* says this: "Who is mighty? He who masters control over himself." You too can become mighty. You can master what you say to yourself, to your husband, and to those you love. You can do this through the Lord's help in your life, for the Word tells us we can do all things through Christ who strengthens us (Phil. 4:13)!

Satan seduced Eve with his lying tongue and used it for evil. But you can allow the Holy Spirit of the living God to take your tongue, your thoughts, and your attitude and bring them under the control of His power, using your tongue and attitude for good. When you do, you will see great and mighty things come about as a result. You will have a husband who strives to develop to his fullest potential. Your children will be filled with confidence and hope for the future.

HINTS FOR HIM

I know you are probably tired of hearing that you are to love your wife as Christ loved the church, willing to die for her. But what can I say? This is the Word of the living God! You are to be obedient!

Every woman needs respect in order to function. Your wife will find it impossible to be the best wife she can be without your respect. Treat your wife as if she has value to you. She will then

make sure she becomes invaluable to you. Accept her as she is, and soon she will want to improve anything about herself in order to bring you more pleasure.

Ask her opinion, and soon she will not make decisions until she makes sure you and she are in one accord. Let her know you understand how she feels, and soon she will strive to see the world through your eyes as well as her own. Let her know how proud you are of her, and soon she will see her full potential in Christ. Hug her often, for no reason other than the fact that you adore her, and soon she will be the woman who will make your home a sanctuary of joy and peace.

FROM DR. ANNE

Remember that you get what you give. This is never more true than in the area of giving and receiving respect. How you react to situations in your relationship will determine the extent that you will earn the consideration, courtesy, caring, and respect that you most desire. You will need to show him appreciation for his strength of character. Only God can develop this in you as you grow in spiritual obedience and maturity. Ask God to develop in you the ability to show the same measure of respect to your husband as you want him to show to you.

Respect is holding confidences. So many husbands have attempted to share their opinions, dreams, weaknesses, and vulnerabilities, only to have them disrespected by a loose-tongued wife who uses that knowledge as a weapon or to entertain her friends. He may take you into his confidence once . . . maybe he will be foolish enough to make another attempt . . . then he will close up, shut down, and the wall between you will be thick and high. He will have lost respect for you, and your weakness will be your loss!

Don't make what you believe to be the insensitivities of your husband your favorite topic of conversation with your friends. Instead, be willing to praise and support the authority God has placed over you. The words of your mouth are powerful and can impact the attributes, characteristics, and motivations of your husband.

If you recognize that this is a mistake you have made, God's grace and mercy are sufficient to build back a bridge of trust with

your husband and to heal the wounds that may have resulted from your own insensitivity to his needs. When you come to God with a repentant heart, "He is faithful and just to forgive us our sins and to cleanse us from all unrighteousness" (1 John 1:9). Respect can be earned in direct proportion to the willingness with which you give it. With time, you will earn your husband's trust.

Don't ever forget that the role of nurturer and provider for you is not the only role your husband has to fulfill. Encourage your husband to be all that God wants and needs him to be. Be the supportive woman who will make it easier for your husband to hear and obey the voice of his Master.

Don't do anything to discount or sabotage your husband's efforts to do what God has asked of him. Be your husband's helpmate. Give him encouragement, not discouragement. Allow him to grow into the taller, larger role that God has for him.

Wait on the Lord. Renew your strength in Him. The man you have is the man God can use. Prayer will strengthen and develop the qualities that God wants—and that you want also. Prayer will perfect in him the respect and confidence he needs. When the woman of Proverbs 31:10 is diligent in the things that promote her family, her husband and children rise up and call her blessed, and her husband praises her. Isn't that the respect you really want? You can, just like Abraham, have all that you can see. The bottom line is prayer.

CLOSING PRAYERS

In this chapter, Dr. Anne and I have given you the tools to help you get out of the valley of despair. With God's help you can begin to experience a marriage filled with joy and expectation, one that will allow you and your husband to stand on mountains and view eternity.

PRAYER OF REPENTANCE

My Lord, forgive me for the foolish and hurtful things I have thought and said about my husband. I have not only hurt him, but I have disobeyed and disappointed You. I am so sorry. I have given approval to the disrespect of men and husbands by laughing at jokes that make them look weak and silly. My husband didn't deserve that. I

also ask forgiveness for being discouraging and unsupportive when my husband has made an attempt to step out into the role You have ordained for him. I ask that You redeem the time that I have lost as an encourager while I have been looking at his faults and seeing my husband as inept and incapable. Please forgive me, Lord; I will change my ways and my confession.

PRAYER OF NEW BEGINNINGS

Dear God, You have truly blessed me by giving me the husband that I have. He is a good man, and the words of my mouth will say so! I will tell him often that I love him and appreciate him for all he means in my life. Help me to let him know how valuable he is to me. I will compliment him to others and refuse to partake in idle talk that is insulting to him or grievous to Your heart. I will stand up for my husband in the role You have for him to fulfill. Help me to be obedient to Your Word and the role You have created for me to fulfill. My God, guard my tongue from evil and my lips from speaking deceitfully. Without Your constant help and strength I can't do it. I know that You will renew my mind and help me uplift my husband with the love and respect I have for him. Amen.

Train up a child in the way he should go,
And when he is old he will not depart from it.
—PROVERBS 22:6

RAISING A FAMILY takes hard work. Raising a family that loves the Lord takes a three-way partnership—you, your husband, and the Lord. Your children need the kind of father they can trust and the kind of father who trusts the Lord.

The Word of God instructs us to give honor to whom honor is due (Rom. 13:7). I would be remiss if I did not honor my husband for being a godly father. In this chapter it is my desire to *show* you the characteristics of a godly family man by allowing you to witness the interactions of my husband with his family.

I have seen this man weep at the birth of his children, spend hours with them while they needed training, smile with pride at their accomplishments, discipline them when discipline was earned, and fast and pray for them as we stood in the gap for their future. My children are blessed with a great father. I am richly blessed to have a husband who is devoted to his family.

From the moment we were married we wanted children, and God granted our desire. We have five beautiful children and, at the time of this writing, have four wonderful "in-loves" (otherwise know as "in-laws"). My husband and I feel that we now have nine children instead of five, and we are currently praying number ten into our fold. Our quiver is full.

47

I can truthfully say that every stage of their lives has been a joy to us. Even when trials come we can see the hand of God guide our children to the purposes He has for their lives. I give Him daily praise and thanks for the bountiful blessing He has so graciously bestowed on our family.

THE BIRTHS OF OUR CHILDREN

From the moment of conception for each child, we became a team in receiving and raising our children. Our roles have been different, yet as we combined our efforts and our prayers, parenthood has been a joy.

During my pregnancies, I remember my husband patting my belly every night as we prepared for bed. Lovingly, he called each child by name and said, "Though I haven't yet held you in my arms, I love you so much." He prayed a blessing over each child every night as we awaited their births. He wanted me to hold him close, putting my full body against his back so he could feel the kick of our precious children within my womb.

He often tells of the pride that he felt when he saw his firstborn, Tish, in the window of the nursery. He could hardly contain his joy as he watched this beautiful baby girl, full of life and hope.

Chris was very attached to his daddy and often wanted to be carried—even when he was no longer the baby of the family. No matter . . . Daddy carried him wherever he wanted to be carried, telling me, "He's not heavy—he's my little boy!"

Tina and I almost lost our lives at the time of her birth due to unexpected complications. I remember my husband's strong voice of support and his words of supplication as he laid hands on me and prayed the prayer of faith for a safe delivery for our baby and me. The morning after her delivery, he brought a yellow rose to present to his new baby daughter, saying, "I want to be the first man that gives flowers to this precious little girl."

When Matthew was born, the doctor asked if I wanted to hold him right after his birth. Glancing at my husband, I could see the look of awe on his face. "Will you please give our son to my husband first?" I asked the doctor. My husband reached for our son as if he was receiving a precious gift from God. As he welcomed Matthew to this world, Matthew's eyes opened, searching for the familiar voice he had heard so often while he was in his mother's womb. Once he placed his sight

on this man who loved him so much, he smiled his first smile.

Our youngest daughter, Sandy, was born three weeks early, and she developed blood poisoning, which threatened her life. The first time we saw her after her birth, she was hooked up to every wire you could imagine. Tears ran down my husband's face as he put his massive hand in the incubation crib and placed it on her tiny chest as it struggled for breath. "Father, I ask that You breathe life into our baby girl and give her the fighting spirit to win this battle," he prayed. The Lord did exactly as my husband asked, and she still has that very same bold spirit to this day.

RAISING FIVE CHILDREN

I remember my "moments" of raising five children under twelve. They may have been trying moments at times, but they were never alone moments. My husband has always been there to partner with them and me.

When Tish was a Brownie in the Girl Scouts, she came home one day with one hundred boxes of cookies and announced she was going to win the badge for most cookies sold. "Great!" her daddy proclaimed.

"Daddy, you need to sell these boxes for me so I can get my badge!" Tish announced with equal conviction.

"Oh, great," my husband responded with a sigh. But he carried her door to door and sold cookies to friends, relatives, and church members until together they got their badge. The memory our daughter has of that experience is far greater than any badge; it is a precious gift to be treasured always.

Chris loved T-ball and was so excited to begin his new adventure. No matter how busy my husband's schedule became, he was at all the practices and all the games, ready to cheer Chris on. He spent hours in the back yard with Chris, helping him learn the game. As I prepared dinner in the kitchen, I could hear his encouraging words: "You can do it, son. You can do it!"

Through T-ball, Little League, Pop Warner, and varsity football . . . through elementary school, junior high, and high school, the ritual was always the same: "You can do it, son! You can do it!" Chris is no longer playing school sports, but to this day, when Chris is talking to his father about very important business decisions, I can hear my husband's careful instruction as he teaches his son all that he knows.

He continues to encourage Chris, "You can do it, son." He is so proud when his son teaches him things he doesn't know. He is never jealous, always proud.

Tina has always been the quiet one of the family, the tender one. She always did what was asked of her, yet always looked for her daddy's approval. I can still picture her running races in the backyard with her brothers and sisters, her long hair tied in a ponytail, flowing in the wind. She ran like a gazelle. "Look at me, Daddy! Look at me!" she called to her father as she ran.

Even when her voice was drowned by the clamor of the other children's voices vying for their father's attention, you could hear my husband's voice answer her with, "I see you, baby, and you are doing great! I am so proud of you! You're the fastest in the bunch!" As Tina heard his voice, she smiled that confident smile I now recognize in her own baby girl. She would run a little harder, never failing to keep an eye out for her daddy to make sure he was watching. He always was.

One Saturday night when our son Matt was nine years old, he asked to speak to his father after we had put him to bed. Thinking this was simply another ploy to stay up a little longer, I reminded Matt that his father had already prayed with him and was now studying his sermon for Sunday morning, a Saturday night ritual that he still follows.

"Mom, I need to talk to Dad. It's important." I noticed a very pensive look on his face as he lay on his folded arms looking toward the ceiling.

"Can I help you, Matt?" I asked him.

"No, Mamma. I need to talk to Daddy. This is very serious," he replied.

Worried, I thought, *What could it be?* I ran downstairs and interrupted my husband, who was deep in study. "Honey, Matt needs to talk to you! He tells me it is very important and can't wait for morning."

Seeing my concern, my husband left his study and began his walk up the stairs for the very important, mysterious meeting. I followed behind him, ready to enter Matthew's room. Turning to face me, he asked what, at the time, I felt was an unfair question: "Did Matt ask to see you as well?"

My response was quick, "No, but..."

He did not let me complete my sentence. "Then I will go into his room alone, and you can wait here." He gave me no choice but to have an attitude adjustment and wait at the foot of the stairs, praying that the Lord would give my husband wisdom for the *secret* Matt was about to share with him.

After what seemed to be hours, my husband came out of Matthew's room with tears in his eyes and a tender smile on his face. Comforted by the smile, yet concerned by the tears, I quickly asked him what had transpired.

"Matthew wanted me to pray a prayer of repentance with him, for he felt that he said things that offended the Holy Spirit today. He did not want to go to sleep with the offense on his heart," my husband told me, with tears freely flowing from his face.

I too joined in the tears. Mine were more for relief. Then I asked my husband this question: "Well, what did Matt say that offended the Holy Spirit?"

"I don't know. I didn't ask him," he replied.

"What? You didn't ask him! Why not?" I asked in disbelief.

"What is important is that we have taught our son to be sensitive to the Holy Spirit and to repent when he has done those things that have offended God. That, Diana, is the only thing that matters."

I was convicted. We held each other at the bottom of the stairs and had a good cry, thanking the Lord for the good things He had done and would do in our son's life.

One year, my husband and I were invited to speak in San Francisco at the International Full Gospel Business Men's Fellowship Conference, under the leadership of Demos Shakarian. Because of the nature of the invitation, my husband did not realize he accepted a date that would conflict with Sandy's tenth birthday. We had broken a huge rule: never be away for one of our children's birthdays! What to do?

My husband decided we would use his honorarium to pay for the children to come with us. We needed the funds to take care of other things and had to add more money to take care of their airfare, but we knew it was the only choice we had. There we were…the Hagee clan on the road to San Francisco.

Our schedule was hectic, as one can imagine.

One morning I was scheduled to speak at a women's prayer breakfast, and Daddy and Sandy had a date. Sandy knew this date was extra special. First, she was alone with her father. Second, her dad was scheduled to speak that evening before tens of thousands, and he was spending time with her instead of studying his sermon. This was very special. She walked tall as she left the room with her hand in the hand of the most important man in her life.

When my session was over, I went to our room to discover that Sandy and her father had not returned from their walk. It seems that Sandy, ever the most ambitious one, had asked the concierge for directions to a toy store near by. Wouldn't you know, our hotel was located just five blocks down from an FAO Schwarz store—the biggest toy store in the world? Sandy had hit the mother lode.

Several hours passed, and father and daughter returned to the room. By the look on both their faces, I could tell that Sandy had been triumphant, and Daddy had been...well...Daddy had been Daddy. "What did you get for your birthday, Sandy?" I asked, almost afraid to know.

With orchestrated pride, she stood in the middle of the room and boldly announced: "An elephant!"

"An elephant?" I asked as I turned to make careful eye contact with my husband. He looked up, and he looked down, but he never met with my glaring stare.

"Daddy said I could have one toy. Any toy I wanted." Part of her statement was our standard agreement with our kids: "Choose one." The second part, "any toy I wanted," was a new clause, one only Sandy could lobby for. As she ran to boldly announce to her brothers and sisters what she had received for her birthday, her father began to tell me what had occurred.

He had never been to an FAO Schwarz store. As he walked into this palace of toy wonder, he was amazed at the size of the store, the amount of toys to choose from, and, of course, the prices of the toys. But a promise was a promise. He let Sandy choose one toy, whichever one she wanted.

Sandy chose an elephant that was so big my husband could not carry it back to the hotel. So big that we would have had to buy an airline seat for it to come home with us. So big that he had to ship it home in a crate. So big that to this day I do not know how much it cost. He and Sandy share that secret, and I have convinced myself I am better off for not knowing.

HE SAYS...

When you see your wife and loved ones at the end of the day, do you find ways to share joy and laughter? Or have you become so obsessed with work and toil that you have forgotten to develop the sound of laughter in your home?

Our daughter is about to move into her new home with her husband, and she has a very special place for her elephant. There is only

one thing that is bigger than that massive gray trophy, and that is the love and respect for the man who has never broken a promise—her daddy. A promise is a promise.

QUALITY TIME

A family man spends quality time with the whole family as well as with each child who has been given to him by God. Our meal times were, and still are, some of my most treasured moments in my life. We all gather around the table and share what the day has brought. My husband asks the children questions about their dreams, the answers of which usually conclude in waves of hysterical laughter.

When the children were young, we had few funds with which to do much. But it doesn't cost much to make precious memories. One weekend we would go to the movies, another weekend to the zoo, and then we would have a picnic the next weekend. Needing to purchase seven entrance tickets for the movie, we never had enough money left to buy the expensive goodies at the movie theater. So I did something I don't want you to tell anyone about! I packed my diaper bag with stuff. Not just any stuff. *Unique stuff.* I am of Hispanic descent, and I love to cook. I am a good cook. Every Saturday morning I make a Mexican breakfast for my family, a well-loved tradition.

When we had a "movie Saturday," I would pack breakfast tacos of beans and cheese, potato and eggs, and Mexican sausage. I wrapped them in foil and carefully packed them in my diaper bag, ready for our catered outing. We sat all five kids in front of us, sitting behind them so we could provide the matinee brunch. I waited for the theater to become dim before we made our move, so as to avoid the "movie Gestapo."

Once the theater was dark, you could see five little hands reach behind them one by one, whispering their desired choice of tacos, and the feast would begin. By the time you counted to ten, the people around us began to sniff out our secret as the aroma of fresh breakfast tacos competed with stale popcorn and shriveled hot dogs. Our children still remind us of the good times at the movies, and we laugh as we remember our little secret.

One year my husband announced that we were going to do something *big* with the children for our family vacation. *Wow,* I thought, knowing our budget could not afford much more than our standard

trip to Grandma Hagee's and our annual visit to the battleship *Texas* at the San Jacinto monument in Houston. I called my dear friend Rachel, a travel agent, who understood our financial circumstances as she began her quest for the "big, yet cost-efficient" vacation.

Soon she called, with great excitement, to inform me that the Flagship Inn of Dallas, located across the street from Six Flags Amusement Park, had a family special: "Children under twelve *stay and eat for free!*" Eureka! God had provided for our "big" vacation!

We packed the kids in the station wagon and began our journey. We had perfected a ritual for staying at motels. My husband would cautiously drop me off at the front entrance to secure a room, asking for a crib for the baby. While I was doing that, he would drive our car to the back of the motel. In this way, management could not count the number of heads in the car.

After I checked in, I reunited with my family, and we quietly made our way to our nonsmoking "double-double" home away from home. We all knew the regimen—Mom and Dad on one bed, the two girls on the other, the baby in the crib, and the two boys in sleeping bags on the floor.

We were much more considerate of restaurants. Due to the nature of our visits—usually laden with drink spills and an overabundance of cracker crumbs on the floor—we usually rotated our visits to favorite restaurants in order to spare the staff any added stress. I remember one Sunday night when my husband asked me if I wanted to go to a certain restaurant. "Oh, not there," I responded. "Not enough time has passed since our last visit!" We chose another restaurant to insure a good reception when we arrived.

Ah, but this *big* vacation was different! We were out of town! We may never see these people again. We were relieved of any pressure. We were going to have fun on our first big vacation. When we woke up after our first night there, we went down to eat breakfast in the motel restaurant. We informed our kids that they could order anything off the menu that they felt they wanted to eat for breakfast. What a treat! These were not their normal choices. They were usually limited to the kid's menu.

Times were good. They were excited. Each day after breakfast we boarded the shuttle that took us into the amusement park and then back to the motel restaurant for lunch. Then it was back on the shuttle to the park, and back to the restaurant for dinner.

Finally, on the third day the manager came to our table. We knew this was too good to last. "Sir, I would like the ages of your children, please," our suspicious host said to my husband. Instantly my husband whistled his trademark alert to the kids, who leaped from their seats immediately and lined up in birth order.

"Give the man your name and age!" was my husband's command.

"Tish... I am eleven."

"I'm Chris, and I am eight."

"Tina... I'm four."

"My name is Matt. I'm this many," he said, holding up one hand with one finger and the second hand with two fingers.

The manager spared our one-year-old from the interrogation as he slowly nodded his head from side to side and walked away in disbelief. My husband ordered the kids back to their chairs and to their "big people's menu." It was a great vacation.

Lest you think I am married to the perfect family man, let me inform you that he doesn't do shots. When we took our children to the doctor for their vaccinations, he refused to hold them as they received their injections. Only when the traumatic ordeal was over would he then take them from me and hold them tight as he comforted them and assured his babies that they would be all right. It took me a while to forgive him of that, for my children associated me with trauma and pain and him with security and soothing comfort for most of their formative years.

A VALUABLE COMMODITY

I believe time to be our most valuable commodity. You and your husband must discipline yourselves to give your children as much of your time as possible, even when it is not convenient. From the time our children were young, we told them often that they would never be an inconvenience to us. If they needed a ride to and from an event, we were the ride. If they needed a place for their friends to gather, our home was that place. If they needed us to attend an event in which they were participating, one or both of us would attend that event. My husband says, "The reason God gave a child two parents is because between the two of them they make one good parent." A child should never feel that he or she is an inconvenience to your life.

As I am trying to meet the deadline of this book, our youngest daughter, Sandy, is beginning law school. The night before her first day she asked me if I remembered what I had done on the first day she attended kindergarten.

"Yes, I followed your bus to school!" I answered, as I recalled that vivid memory. Satisfied that I remembered, she smiled, and with that her father and I prayed a prayer of blessing over her first day at law school.

The next morning as my husband was leaving for the church office he asked if I was going to work on my book. Even though I knew the importance of the deadlines, I answered with what the Lord had confirmed to me would be my day's assignment. "Today I am going to law school." My husband smiled. He knew that what I was about to do was the right thing for Sandy's next big endeavor in life.

I waited for her orientation classes to begin, and then began my journey to another precious memory. I went to her first session. The staff allowed me into her class filled with three hundred students. Sandy was astonished as she spotted her mother proudly waving to her from the back corner of the room. She placed her hands on her hips and mouthed the word, "Why?"

I motioned back and mouthed, "Because I love you!" Even though she knew the answer, she smiled to confirm it once more. I waited in the car for her lunch break. While I waited, I called her new husband to see if he would like to surprise Sandy with a picnic lunch. Excitedly he agreed, and we wrote another wonderful chapter in the life of a very important person in our lives.

HE SAYS ...

Your marriage must learn to endure adversity to reach achievement. Your attitude toward adversity will determine your accomplishments.

LOVE IN THE TOUGH TIMES

You might think that all our times with our children have been beautiful and without trouble, but that is not the case. Many tears have been shed, many meals have been fasted, and many prayers have been prayed on behalf of their lives. We have grieved together as Satan has tried in every one of our children's lives to bait them toward the wrong path. As the mother and father of five children, we have learned this great truth: a parent is only as happy as their saddest child.

Even though my husband has always shown a great amount of love to our children, he has also been their primary disciplinarian. My children filled many of my days with elaborate forms of animated discussions and negotiations as they pleaded, begged, and bargained with me not to tell their father of the wrong they had committed that day.

Not only did they fear his form of punishment—either a spanking or a restriction of some kind—but also they did not want to disappoint the man who loved them so much. I remember the wails coming from the garage where the chastisement would occur, which were followed by silence. When I entered into the room, I witnessed my husband holding our children and explaining why they should never again do what they had just been punished for.

Whether or not that offense he rebuked would be repeated depended on the child who had committed the action. Within our *quiver* you can find a combination of quick learners and strong-willed offspring. However, no matter what the response was to the punishment, one thing they all agreed upon was the fact that although their daddy loved them, he would not tolerate bad behavior or rebellion.

Establish Some Important "Parent Rules"

You and your husband have to partner together in order to make a good family. One of the areas needing your partnership efforts is in the area of family relationships. You may find these "parent rules" that my husband and I followed to be of value to you in your own family.

1. Partner with your husband; don't compete for his leadership over your children.

One Saturday evening when Sandy was about six years of age, she came to me asking if she could do something. I explained to her why she couldn't, and she left the kitchen disappointed. About fifteen minutes later, she came back to me and proudly announced that her father had given her permission to do what I had already said no to.

Confused and upset, I asked her to follow me to her father's study where he was preparing for Sunday. As I have mentioned earlier, studying for Sunday is my husband's ritual to this day. My children learned early in life that Daddy easily agreed to anything on Saturday evenings.

HE SAYS...

Submission does not make a man the "Hitler" of the house. Submission means that he is a loving, compassionate leader who loves his wife as Christ loved the church.

We walked into Daddy's study, and I asked if he had known that I had told Sandy *no* to the very same thing to which he had said *yes*.

"Sandy," he asked firmly as he realized what she had so cleverly maneuvered, "did your mother already say no to you?"

"Yes," she responded firmly.

"You know you are not supposed to come to me with something your mother has already said no to," he admonished.

"Yes, I do, but I have one question for this family!" Then, with her hands on her hips, my future lawyer asked this question passionately, "Who is running this house anyway?" Our children knew the answer to that question. *We both were.* Together, with the Lord's help and guidance, we would make the decisions that would train our children in the way they should go.

2. Set goals for your family, and stay focused on them. Do your best to help your children accomplish their goals.

Recently, my husband and I celebrated reaching one of the major goals we had set for our children and ourselves years earlier. We determined that each of our children should have a college education. As we watched our youngest child graduate from college, we gave thanks to the Lord for providing the resources to enable us to provide a college education for all of our children. Not only had God provided the resources, but He had also given our children the willpower and tenacity to accomplish this very valuable goal we set before them.

We gave them no option. A college degree was a must. Some of them got the revelation of the importance of being educationally prepared for life sooner than others, but eventually they all saw the light. When your children waiver on decisions that should be followed through to the end goal, stand firm with your spouse and be their strength as they are tempted to take the easy way out.

3. Pray daily with your husband for your children.

I know this is often a hard task to accomplish, because some men find it difficult to pray with their wives. I ask that you make it a point

at the proper time of the day or night to ask your husband to pray with you on behalf of your children. I know that he will seldom refuse you if you do it in the right spirit. If he does refuse to pray with you, it will not be long before the Lord will convince him of the importance of the power available when two agree in prayer.

4. Bless your children and your husband daily.

When my husband leaves our home, I pray a prayer of blessing over him. He not only needs the prayer, but he also needs the encouragement that comes as the person he loves and partners with is putting a covering of blessing over his life. Make this your practice also. Then, together, bless your children. I never let my children leave on a trip without praying a prayer of blessing and protection over them. I believe God is waiting for you and your husband to release these prayers over your children. If not you, then who?

5. Pray for your children's spouses early in their lives.

I had such a long list of dos and don'ts for my children's spouses that the prayer was too long to pray, and it concentrated more on traits than the person. God helped me to shorten my prayer to be very powerful and effective. I learned to pray: "Father, my child's spouse is living somewhere in this world. Keep [him or her] safe and pure before You as You lead [him or her] into my child's life. Bring my child the person who will love [him or her] second to Christ. May they serve You together for the rest of their lives."

Some of you reading this book may be thinking that your children are now out of your home and that it is too late for you to learn some of these truths regarding your family. First of all, know and believe that it is never too late to begin to pray for and bless your children. Begin today.

Second, don't forget your grandchildren. Even though you don't have as much influence over them as their parents do, you still have a powerful impact on their lives. Rebbetzin Jungreis applies King Solomon's scripture, "A threefold cord is not quickly broken" (Eccles. 4:12), to a family composed of three generations. Rebbetzin stresses the importance of children hearing their grandparent's stories, basking in their love, and benefiting from their wisdom as precious, nurturing experiences that cannot be duplicated.[1] Even the grave cannot sever grandparent and grandchild relationships, which are based on unconditional love.

My paternal grandmother was someone who showed unconditional love to me. She died when I was only fifteen years old, but my memories of her and her undying love are still vivid and very much invaluable to me at fifty-two years of age. I remember her warm smile and tight hugs. I remember the many sacrifices she made for her grandchildren, whom she adored. I remember the times we spent in her home. She had no air conditioning in her home, and the sweltering heat of the Texas summer nights would take its toll on us. I remember waking in the middle of the night to find her standing over us waving a small hand fan until she made sure we were as comfortable as possible.

In the month of March of my fifteenth year, she gave me a beautiful gold ring with a single pearl surrounded by eight small diamonds. As she placed it on my finger, she said the gift symbolized her love for me. She died in October of that same year. Long after she was in heaven, I would look at that ring and remember the love she had for me, love even death could not diminish.

Instinctively I knew the value of that ring she presented to me. She was not a naturalized citizen and worked in a clothing factory as a seamstress. Early every morning she would dress in her best and walk to the bus stop, which would carry her to her long, tedious day. She saved money for years to present this special gift to her oldest granddaughter. It is one of the most treasured things I own, and it will forever symbolize her unconditional love for me.

I want to be that kind of grandmother. One who will love her grandchildren as the precious gifts from heaven they are. One who will encourage them to be all they can be in their Creator. One who will show them the love of Christ whenever they walk into the door of our home.

HINTS FOR HIM

Deuteronomy 32:7 tells us to "remember the days of old, consider the years of many generations. Ask your father, and he will show you; your elders, and they will tell you."

As a father you should remember the days past that gave you the most pleasure as a child. There may have been many things your parents could not give you financially, but they gave you plenty of time and love. Give that legacy to your children in handfuls.

If your parents did not give you these two invaluable gifts, then don't hesitate to break away from the heartaches of the past and begin new traditions of love and affection with your family. This decision is one you will have to make with God's help, but when you do, you will break generational curses that have kept your family from the blessings He has ordained for you.

Show your children the way they should go. If you demand honesty from them, then show them what an honest man looks like and talks like. If you demand respect from your children, then show respect to others around you, and they will follow in your footsteps. If you want them to have strong marriages, show love for their mother in their presence, which is the greatest training you can give them. If you want them to honor the Lord in their living and in their giving because you know it will bless their lives, then take them to the house of the Lord and let them see you give unto the Lord one-tenth of the resources He has provided for you.

There is a story of a young child who is climbing a mountain with his father. His father warned him to be careful as he climbed behind him. The son answered back, "Don't worry, Dad. I am putting my feet right where you put yours. I will be fine." The path you show your children is the path they will take.

If you are a grandparent, then tell your grandchildren of the love you have for them—and tell them often. Allow that love and the stories you tell them to be part of the legacy you leave them. The Talmud says, "He who loves his wife as himself and honors her more than himself, who guides his sons and daughters in the straight path . . . of him it is said, you shall know that your home is at peace."

FROM DR. ANNE

If we as women really want a man who is a "family man," we must be a part of establishing the environment that will allow the bonding that is a major part of the family. Only when home is placed in a priority position will each family member want to be present in that home. If there is chaos and friction, your husband will find reasons to work late, play more sports, or otherwise stay away. You

really can't blame him. You would probably escape too if you had the chance.

Home must be a place that meets the needs of the family. Home must be a place of peace, security, respect, and harmony. What is needed to make this happen? There are some key issues that need to be addressed in most homes.

Christian lady, is your home a *home* or a *house*? Does your family come home only long enough to change clothes and sleep? When your husband wants to be with his family, what does he have to do to round up the lot of you so he can see all of you at one time? When you are all together, is this a time of joy or a time when problems are being solved? Do your children argue and compete for attention over the roar of the TV? Does everyone watch the clock so they can go about their own separate ways? Is the television actually the sound track of your lives?

If the last few sentences describe your family life, it is time to establish some important priorities. Encourage and reinforce family values, and, if necessary, retrain your family to make home their hub, oasis, and sanctuary. Home needs to be the place where each member is valued and loved. When home and family are comforting and pleasant, each member wants to be there.

Begin by *turning off the TV!* Once you have gone through the pain of separation anxiety, life will be more enjoyable. Be aware that the addiction tendency to media outlets will always be a temptation. *Just say no!* You will be amazed to find that the family is more content with what they have when not subjected to the hard-sell media marketing. Home will become the blessing God intends it to be.

Second, when your husband returns home each evening, make three positive statements to him before you unload the trials and tribulations of your day. First statement: "Hi, honey," "Hello, sweetheart," "Welcome home," or another loving greeting. Second statement: "I am glad you are safely home," "I have missed you," "I hope you had a good day," or "I love you!"

For your third statement, find at least one positive thing that has occurred during your day. If you think hard enough, you can come up with something! How about: "Little Sarah didn't shave *all* of the cat before your razor became dull," "Only *half* of the paper

roll was flushed down the toilet before it stopped up," or "Junior's grades weren't the lowest in the class."

Your husband may wonder who the new you is and question what you did with his wife, but you can be certain he will be glad for the change. You will have the desires of your heart—a family man who enjoys being in the home he shares with the wife and children God has given him.

CLOSING PRAYERS

It was my desire in this chapter to show you the characteristics of a godly family man by letting you sneak into our family life and observe my own husband's demonstrations of love and support to his children. In the Bible are many examples of godly fathers. One example comes from the apostle Paul, who filled the role of *spiritual father* for many first-century Christians. In 1 Corinthians 11:1 he says that he learned from Christ Himself. We can find no better example of how to be a loving parent than by following the example of Christ. In 1 Thessalonians 2:11–12, Paul says this: "For you know that we dealt with each of you as a father deals with his own children, encouraging, comforting and urging you to live lives worthy of God, who calls you into his kingdom and glory" (NIV). Ask God to help you deal this way with your children—whether you are a mother or a father.

PRAYER OF REPENTANCE

Father God, forgive me for not using Your guidelines when preparing my home for my husband and my children. As my heavenly Father, You always have time for me, and You hear my cry when I am in need. I have not always given of myself to my husband and my children as I should have. I have allowed my time to be stolen by the demands and expectations of others. I have busied my life with trivial matters that will make no eternal difference.

I haven't encouraged our children to set the expectation that home is where the best quality time is spent. I have let the model for my family be set by the world and not by Your Word. I have let the expectations You have set before my husband, my children, and me to be lowered. I repent and will change my ways.

I will direct the atmosphere of our home to be nurturing and caring for my husband and children. I acknowledge that I have not consistently helped to create the atmosphere that will enable my husband to be a godly family man. I ask that You forgive me for the times I have usurped his authority with our children. Forgive me for not showing honor or respect toward my husband before my family. I will ask forgiveness from my husband and my children, and I will do all that I can with Your help to create a peaceful and joyful and godly home.

As a single woman, forgive me for dating men that I know are not family men. I cannot change them; only You can. I will look and wait on the man that I know will honor You and Your Word and will be a godly father to the children You will give us. Amen.

PRAYER FOR NEW BEGINNINGS

Precious Jesus, I acknowledge Your generosity and Your blessings to my family. Father God, You established the family and hold it to a high standard. Thank You for the opportunity to guide and influence my family in obedience to Your ways and Your Word. Our home will be a place You will be proud of, a place of peace, comfort, and love. You will know that You are welcome in my home at all times.

My husband will be proud of our home and will love to be there. My husband will enjoy my company, and I will prefer his company to any other friend. I will pray a blessing over my husband and children every day. I will partner with him to be the parents You have destined us to be. Together we will lead our children in the way they should go.

Your ways are the highest ways. Love, restoration, mercy, and grace will be the words over the entrance to our home, and all who enter will know that You are placed in highest regard. Your presence will be honored in our home always. Amen.

If anyone does not provide for his relatives, and especially for his immediate family, he has denied the faith and is worse than an unbeliever.

—1 TIMOTHY 5:8, NIV

Her husband has full confidence in her and lacks nothing of value. She brings him good, not harm, all the days of her life.

—PROVERBS 31:11–12, NIV

SECULAR HUMANISM IS the world's universal religion, and, like all other religions, it has commandments. Commandment number one is, "Take care of *yourself*, or no one else will." When self-centeredness takes front seat, it isn't long before the world becomes a small place—with each person concerned only for those things that encompass his or her own surroundings.

A self-centered way of life is birthed out of immaturity. Self-centered people are like very small children who are preoccupied with only their own needs and wants. The "me first" mentality is contrary to the principles of Christianity. True maturity can only develop when our lives revolve around *others* rather than ourselves. Maturity means growing in awareness of others and the world around us. A decreased concern for your own needs and an increased concern for the well-being of others demonstrate complete human and spiritual maturity.

Unfortunately, sometimes our development in maturity grinds to a halt at midstream. Some people become adults without experiencing a complete transition from a *me-centered* life to an *others-centered* life.

GROW UP FIRST; THEN MARRY

Marriage is for grown-ups. Maturity is a requirement that is often over-looked when choosing a mate. Developmental disturbances, coupled with the me-first mentality of humanistic theology, are destined to bring grief and trouble to any marriage. A man who is not fully mature in this area of his life is not ready for the commitment and the responsibility of marriage. However, a *Christ-centered* man is able to serve his spouse and children unselfishly.[1]

During my college years, a college friend of mine dated a very good-looking college jock for a while. They really made an attractive couple. With her stunning brown eyes and adoring smile, she was beautiful, and his muscular physique and great looks complemented her beauty. All seemed perfect.

However, it soon became evident that he was "too good to be true!" He was always "short on cash," and what little he did manage to get from his affluent family was quickly squandered on "his needs." Most of their dates were Dutch, and my friend often had to cover the whole night's expenses because he was, once again, "short on cash." "I'll make it up later," he always promised. But he did look great in a pair of Wranglers!

My friend would be quick to tell you that her priorities were not quite right when choosing who to date at that point in her life. Remember this ever-simple rule: *you will eventually marry someone you date.* Duh! This may sound a little too obvious, yet you have no idea how many young women tell me, "We're only dating!," when, as their pastor's wife, I question their choice in men. They have a requirement list for their future husband, but none for the men they date.

What does "only dating," mean? It usually means, "I'm only going out with this person because he can fill my weekend." Yet repeatedly these "fill-in" individuals end up filling a woman's lifetime with sadness and strife.

The young man who was dating my friend not only did not provide for her financially during their courting experience, but he did not provide for her emotional needs either. The self-centered person is too preoccu-pied with his or her own needs and is blind to the needs of others.

Immaturity will always consume more than it will produce—both financially and emotionally. The immature man will take this same

philosophy into the marriage relationship, creating a weak foundation that will soon crumble under the pressures of life.

Later in my college friend's life, the Lord brought to her the man He had chosen for her from the beginning of time. Dan had worked his way through college and was working his way through medical school when they met. Their first date was dinner at a local restaurant and a night at the symphony. My friend felt like a queen—as it should be.

Their relationship blossomed and soon led to the marriage altar. At that stage of her life, my friend was not yet looking for financial security in a relationship; what she needed was someone to complement her whole person—spiritually, emotionally, physically, and financially. In fact, after they married she became their sole financial support while her husband completed his residency in obstetrics. She was glad to fill that role because her husband was supplying her emotional, physical, and spiritual needs. They were a team.

> **HE SAYS . . .**
>
> **I asked a beautiful young lady just out of college, "What kind of man would you like to marry?" She joyously responded, "I want a husband who can dance, looks good, and likes what I feed him." "That's great," I responded. "You've just described Trigger."**

Dan has been a great husband and father to my friend and their children. He has provided for them in so many ways, and he is teaching his own children how to provide for their own.

GOD SAYS, "PROVIDE FOR YOUR FAMILY"

The Word of God is very clear on its position for a man who can—but won't—provide for his family. It says, "He has abandoned the faith!" (See 1 Timothy 5:8.) My friend, this is a very serious charge. Our faith is the foundational cornerstone of our being. It is the source of our relationship with our Savior. To be accused by the counsel of God for "abandoning the faith" is far more serious than I can fathom. In this Scripture verse, the Lord continues by describing such a man as "worse than an unbeliever." Why? Because an unbeliever does not know the Word of God or what God expects of him; therefore, he has not abandoned it.

It is not possible to *abandon* something unless you once possessed that thing. Therefore, the man who "abandons the faith" is a man who knows what God expects of Him, yet he *refuses to do those things*, turning his face away from the will of God for his life. According to God, that man is worse than the man who never believed.

Dr. Harley is clear in his statements regarding the research he did about men and women in the area of financial needs. He states that a woman may not marry a man totally for his money, but money certainly has something to do with her choice of the man she decides to marry. Most women not only expect their husbands to work, but they also expect them to earn enough money to take care of their families.[2]

I come from a family with a very strong work ethic. Both my grandmothers worked very hard inside and outside of the home. One, as I mentioned earlier, worked as a seamstress, and the other worked as a maid until she was over seventy years of age.

My father was a truck driver, transporting produce throughout America, when I was born. Later he worked double shifts as a civil service worker in the field of computers. Eventually he owned a very successful produce company and then a restaurant. Recently, he interviewed for—and accepted—a new job at the age of seventy-one!

By the age of thirteen, my mother was working as a waitress to help her family financially and to put herself through private school. She married my father and raised a family at home. She worked by his side in the produce business and in the restaurant they later owned. She is now seventy-two years of age and serves at John Hagee Ministries in the shipping department, working circles around young men one-third her age. She faithfully prays over every package that leaves our ministry.

My father-in-law worked all the days of his life. He worked as a Merchant Marine for Standard Oil during the depression. He served the Lord in the ministry for fifty-three years as a pastor and evangelist. After retiring, he and my mother-in-law managed the mobile home park they built twenty years earlier in anticipation of their retirement. He managed and maintained that park until his passing at seventy-eight years of age.

My mother-in-law began to care for a household of brothers and sisters at the age of nine, and she worked her way through seminary by teaching in the very same school from which she eventaually graduated. She worked tirelessly by her husband's side for fifty-three years. During those years she held many positions, serving at times as head of the

women's ministry, children's church director, Christmas and Easter pageant director, costume designer and maker, organist, and Sunday school teacher. She was a singer and accordion player with her husband and sons during their time in evangelism, as well as being one of the best prayer warriors I have ever had the privilege of knowing. She did all of this while caring for her husband and four boys. After retiring from the ministry, she worked as a cafeteria worker at a local school until she was seventy-five, and just recently, at the age of ninety-one, she turned her management responsibilities for the mobile home park over to her son Jack. She is still a consultant—on full salary, I might add.

My husband works fourteen to sixteen hours a day, and he has done so since he was twelve years of age. His motto: "You can put in a half day's work; I don't care which twelve hours you choose." He has taught our children this same work ethic—a legacy they will leave to their own children.

My family has always accepted work as a necessary part of life and is thankful for the opportunity to put in a full day's labor. Therefore I find it difficult to identify with the man who refuses to work and provide for his family.

I often hear unemployed men say, "I'm waiting for the right job," or "I was trained in a certain field and am waiting for an opportunity in that field." Don't wait—yield. Yield to what the Lord has set before you. Sometimes the hardest decisions you must make require humility and obedience before provision comes. Learn to yield to the voice of God.

> Be anxious for nothing, but in everything by prayer and supplication, with thanksgiving, let your requests be made known to God.
> —Philippians 4:6

There is no alternative for work. The Creator's position is very clear: Don't abandon the faith! Provide for and protect your family.

The Importance of God's Tithe

I must take the subject of financial provision one step further to *tithing*. I minister to many wives who are tormented by the fact their husbands refuse to give back to the Lord one-tenth of what the Provider has allowed them to earn. A man who rejects the principle of tithing

cannot understand the feelings of a woman who believes and trusts in the Word of God regarding prosperity.

She knows that the Lord requires the tithe. She knows that He will provide blessings to those who obey the Lord with their tithe. She knows that the Lord promises to devour the enemies of her family when her family is obedient in the tithe. She knows that when her family brings its tithe into the storehouse of the Lord, He will not allow the fruits of the family member's labor to be destroyed. She knows.

Yet her husband refuses to tithe. When a woman at Cornerstone Church asks me what her alternatives are when she finds herself in this situation, I must tell her that, based on the Word of God, she does not have many options. She must be obedient to her husband's decision. If she is a godly woman of the Word, she knows what the Word teaches will be the outcome of her husband's choice. This knowledge can be tormenting to her.

If you find yourself in the position of being married to a man who will not give the Lord His tithe, you must wait on the Lord to convince your husband of his need to be obedient to God's Word. Wait for your husband to reject the darkness of his choice and embrace the light, yielding fully to the things of God. This is a very difficult position to be in, and hundreds of thousands of believing families are not blessed to their full potential due to their lack of obedience in the tithe.

This is a question that must be settled before the marriage takes place. Find out exactly what your future husband's plans are for the financial security of you and your family. Make sure his plan is a realistic one and that it is in compliance with the Word of God.

Ask him what his position is on the tithe. If you are married, and your husband refuses to tithe, then you must obey his wishes, pray, and wait. Don't argue about your husband's lack of obedience. You, as a wife, must also learn to yield to the Holy Spirit and wait on His time.

WHAT ABOUT THE WOMAN WHO SPENDS TOO MUCH?

Now, what about the woman who has a husband who works hard for his family but can never fully provide for their needs because of the wife's careless spending habits? What does God's Word say about this woman?

Jokes are often made of men and women in this situation. Have you heard the one about men who have pierced ears? They seem to

be better equipped for marriage; they've already experienced pain and are used to buying jewelry.[3]

Part of what contributes to the debt problem in America is our demand for *instant gratification*. We live in a society where instant gratification takes too long. A man and a woman marry, and they instantly want what their parents have taken a lifetime to assemble. This couple never saw the apple crates their parents used for chairs or the mismatched, hand-me-down furniture. *Generation X* is only perpetuating what the *Baby Boomers* began, which is trying to duplicate what the *Greatest Generation* took years to put together.

The Greatest Generation survived the Depression, and they did so debt free. The next generation invented the word *debt*. Debt is now so common to twelve-year-olds that they carry credit cards instead of cash. A twelve-year-old, however, doesn't pay the bill at the end of the month. The two most frequent causes for divorce are *sexual dysfunction* and *financial problems*. Both of these problems are rooted in something deeper than the way in which they are manifested.

> **HE SAYS...**
>
> **Don't let your marriage be destroyed by your inability to control your financial spending.**

As a woman, you will be held accountable for how you help your husband maintain financial order within your marriage. Your husband should be able to have *full confidence* in you and should "lack nothing of value" because of your management of the household budget. (See Proverbs 31:11–12.)

Many women who manage the checkbook at home fail to keep precise records, allowing the account to be in such disarray that they don't know where they stand financially. With their out-of-control spending habits, they refuse to let the balance in their checking account determine what they will spend. Instead, they charge up to the maximum limit on their credit cards, stressing their budget and creating debt. Satan has them trapped.

What to do? Stop! Stop now! Repent! Acknowledge that you have done wrong, and make up your mind that, with the help of the Lord, you will establish a spending plan that will help you and your family get out of debt—and stay out!

A spending plan is a "necessary good." If you are a woman who is tempted often to buy more than your income can afford, a spending

plan can help you set priorities for a quality of life you can truly enjoy.

During my college days, I had a very special friend who was from the south. She was one of a long line of *steel magnolias*. She met and married a very conservative young man from England. Oh, what a pair they made. One day after they had moved away from our city and back to my girlfriend's southern hometown, she called me, rather frustrated. "I'm so mad at my husband," she told me in her charming southern drawl, which had dramatically increased since she moved back home. "He is not playing fair!"

"What do you mean?" I asked her.

She explained to me that she had asked her husband to purchase a kitchen gadget for her that was outside their budget. Instead of acknowledging the request to be out of their spending plan, he put the ball in her court and asked her this question: "How dear is it to you?"

To say the least, this was an unfair question. My friend realized that her desire for that gadget had little value when put into a financial perspective. Regardless of her desire for that gadget, the point was settled . . . no purchase.

THE IMPORTANCE OF A BUDGET

Dr. Harley recommends three kinds of budgets—a *needs* budget, a *wants* budget, and an *affordable* budget.[4]

A *needs budget* should include the monthly costs of meeting the necessities of your family's life. It should include those things you and your family would be uncomfortable without.

The *wants* budget should include the cost of meeting all your needs *and* your desires. Your desires, or wants, are things that bring special pleasures to your life. These should be within reason, of course.

In order to make positive lifetime changes in your spending plan, it is important to be realistic. A *needs budget* begins when a man comes to his wife and requests that they put a budget together. "Let's start with the basic necessities—food, shelter, and clothing. Choose any two," he demands.

The *wants budget* is established when his wife responds by handing him her "Wants List." However, that wants list should not include weekly visits to the spa by chauffeured limousine.

Now we come to the *affordable budget*. This realistic list is established by subtracting the items on that *needs list* from the amount of

income your family has. Then what is left can be applied for some of the items on your *wants list*. This will help you to define "how dear" your wants are to you. Eventually you will learn to determine how many wants you will be able to include in your budget, based on the money you have left after your needs have been met.[5]

Remember this rule: you will seldom find something as much fun to own as it is to *look forward to owning*.[6]

Life is more than wants. Don't make the mistake of always making your wants your goals. As want after want is attained, they will become your idols, and you will discover that the attainment of wants does not bring satisfaction. Satisfaction is still nowhere to be found. If you continue down this haphazard path, you will discover that the balance between financial provision and emotional, physical, and spiritual provision is nonexistent.

Husband and wife drift apart as they try to meet their own desires; the children receive the residual of their time and affection. The "self-gratification" parents take care of themselves first and hope their children will benefit.[7]

THE LORD PROVIDES THE BALANCE IN YOUR BUDGET

Support one another as you stay within the spending plan you and your husband agree on. Don't create any unnecessary stress or conflict for your marriage. Be satisfied with your spending plan, and set goals for your future that will help build a strong marriage and an example for your children to follow in their own lives.

Ask your husband to forgive you for the bad spending habits you have developed that have kept you and your family in debt. Ask him to agree with you in prayer that you will turn from spending, no longer using spending as a placebo to keep you from dealing with the real emotional issues that may be troubling you.

You may find that you need to turn over the control of the family budget to your husband, or at least come into mutual agreement before anything

HE SAYS…

The less able you are to experience inner peace, the more you will require material symbols like a bigger house, faster car, bigger boat, or larger salary to satisfy your thirst for happiness.

is spent outside your agreed-upon spending plan. It may be difficult in the beginning to surrender your control, but it will be much easier than picking up the pieces of a broken marriage.

Thank your husband often for providing for you and your family. It is difficult to go to a job day after day that may be full of conflict or where unbelievers surround him continually. Let him know often that you don't take his sacrifice lightly.

As he walks out of the door each morning, bless him with favor, wisdom, and discernment for his job. You will be amazed at what the spoken Word of God can do when proclaimed over your husband every day.

Support your husband in the tithe. Teach your children early about the importance of giving to God a portion of what He has so graciously allowed you to produce. Know that when you obey the Lord and hearken to His voice, He will cause His blessings to overtake you!

> "Bring all the tithes into the storehouse,
> That there may be food in My house,
> And try Me now in this,"
> Says the LORD of hosts,
> "If I will not open for you the windows of heaven
> And pour out for you such blessing
> That there will not be room enough to receive it."
>   —MALACHI 3:10

This portion of Scripture is the only place in the Word of God where God asks His body to test Him.

When you give the Lord His portion, He will bless what you have left and cause it to multiply, bringing you provision beyond what you could ever think possible. Be ready for His blessings, because our God is faithful!

HINTS FOR HIM

You must accept the truth that there is no option but to provide for your family. If you have had a difficult transition from the "me-centered" life to the "others-centered" life, then take certain steps to correct your attitude.

1. *Identify the problem.* There is some self-concern in all of us. But if this concern has prevented you from providing for your wife physically, emotionally, spiritually, or financially, then it must be identified and addressed.

2. *Rely on the grace of God.* Your Creator will never reveal your sin to you, convict you of your sin, and then not provide a full measure of grace necessary for the change He *expects* of you.[8]

3. *Communicate.* Your spouse has been praying for change in your marriage, especially about the attitude you have regarding provision. Let her know that your lives will be different from now on, and that together you can make a positive difference in your relationship.

4. *Take action.* The Word of God tells us to "write the vision and make it plain" for all to understand (Hab. 2:2). It is important to follow through with the "provision plan" you put in place, using the Scriptures as your guide. The Lord is faithful, and He will show you how to provide for your wife and children spiritually, emotionally, physically, and financially. Be patient, and trust that your plan will be fulfilled with your dedication and God's help.

5. *Have compassion.* Your family has suffered for your lack of obedience to the Word of God. They have seen someone they love not blessed because of disobedience. Learn to put yourself in their place in order to understand the difficult journey they have walked with you. It will help your own road to recovery.

Provision comes in different forms. Even though financial provision is a very important form—physical, emotional, and spiritual provision are equally as important. The main essence of provision is to give to others what has been given to you by your Father in heaven—unconditional love.

Charles Spurgeon told the story, "Once, while riding in the country, I saw on a farmer's barn a weather vane on which was inscribed these words: 'God is love.' I turned in at the gate and

asked the farmer, 'What do you mean by that? Do you think God's love is changeable, that it veers about as the arrow turns in the wind?' The farmer said, 'Oh, no! I mean that whichever way the wind blows, God is still love.'"[9]

> Jesus answered and said to him, "If anyone loves Me, he will keep My word; and My Father will love him, and We will come to him and make Our home with him."
>
> —JOHN 14:23

FROM DR. ANNE

During my years of counseling, I have found that security, on all levels, is the thing that a woman needs most. She may mask that need in a number of ways, but security is the basic issue. God made us this way, and He provided for our needs to be met by defining the roles of men and women as He did in His Word.

It is important that you are able to make your husband feel needed. A man who doesn't feel needed is not going to provide. If you are so independent that you don't need your husband, is it any wonder that you are not happy? He probably wonders why you keep him around. If you don't show satisfaction and appreciation for the effort that is made for you, why should he try to satisfy you further?

There are three kinds of women who will never have the provider they may say that they want:

1. *The over-achieving woman who discounts her husband's ability to provide.* The wife who makes it clear that she doesn't need anything from her husband that she can't provide for herself will have a husband who provides little or nothing.

2. *The woman who clings too tightly, draining the energies from her husband.* The wife who holds so tightly to her husband's time that she doesn't want him to work and spend time away from her will get him fired very quickly.

3. *The woman who has so many whims and wants that her husband can't keep ahead of her expectations.* A wife whose wants are never ending will frustrate her husband. Her wants are always ahead of his provision, so she uses a credit card. She is more interested in keeping a standard that is equal to her friends than the standard that she and her husband can afford. He is burdened under the mountain of debt and still has a dissatisfied wife. He will soon stop trying.

On the other hand, faith and trust in your husband's abilities to be the provider for your family will set the environment for him to gain the strength and self-confidence he requires.

The wife who is a good steward with what her husband earns is the Proverbs woman who is called **blessed** by her husband. A clean, neat appearance and home, a wife with a smiling face, clean, well-behaved children, and a car clear of debris give a husband encouragement. When a man's wife, children, home, and car all look "on their last leg," he starts the day with a failing attitude.

Learn to be creative in the ways you find to have your needs and wants—and those of your family—met. Bargains are everywhere! Garage sales and resale shops have been a blessing to all of us. Get excited over the designer dress or accessory you find in a resale shop for a mere fifty cents. The Holy Spirit will lead you to bargains.

God told men in His Word to provide protection (both emotionally and physically), food, shelter, clothing, spiritual comfort, and teaching. Men are to provide for their families those things that God has made available to everyone. Learn to be the appreciative, supportive helpmate God intended you to be to your husband.

CLOSING PRAYERS

There is a saying in Spanish that translates, "A cage even though it's made of gold is still a cage." Life is much more than possessions. When my husband performs the funeral service of a church member, the family members never comment on the amount of wealth their loved one made or left behind. These family members remember the time and love that were spent with their dearly departed loved one.

Stay within the balance of the Word of God. Your Provider promises to care for you. In turn, you must take care of your loved ones as you hear His voice and obey His commandments.

PRAYER OF REPENTANCE

Father, forgive me, for I have been wasteful with the resources You have given us. I have spent money unwisely; I have been materialistic and purchased things we didn't need with money we didn't have. I have failed to be a good steward of our blessings. I have not been appreciative of the efforts my husband has made to be the provider for our family. I have not participated in his success. I have hindered him in providing for our family and have not taught my children to spend wisely or to give of the tithe unto the storehouse of the Lord. I repent of my actions, and with Your help I will turn from my ways and walk the path You have chosen for me.

PRAYER OF NEW BEGINNINGS

Father God, I acknowledge You as my Provider. You are the source of every good and perfect gift that I receive. You meet all of my needs and the needs of my family. I will thank You for Your provision every day. I declare this day, in Jesus' name, that I will prepare a spending plan with my husband, and I pledge to follow that plan with joy and discipline. We will tithe to You one-tenth of what You have allowed us to produce. I will trust You to provide blessings that we will not be able to contain. I will communicate to my husband that I need him to provide for me emotionally, physically, and spiritually. I will pledge to him that I too will try to meet his needs, so together we can make our marriage a thing of satisfaction and joy. I will thank my husband and appreciate his sacrifice for my family and me as he leaves for work, and I will proclaim a blessing over him each day. Thank You, Lord, for the grace and strength You will provide to make all this possible. Amen.

HONESTY

> Pray for us: for we trust we have a good conscience, in all things willing to live honestly.
> —HEBREWS 13:18, KJV

> Having your conversation honest among the Gentiles: that, whereas they speak against you as evildoers, they may by your good works, which they shall behold, glorify God in the day of visitation.
> —1 PETER 2:12, KJV

TRUTH IS NARROW. What would you do if you were hiking and came to a wide river, and learned that there was only one bridge down the river a mile or two? Would you stomp in anger and complain about bad planning? Would you say that the bridge was too far away and should have been built right where you are standing? I doubt it! To the contrary, you would be thankful that there was a bridge, and you would gladly walk to it and use it to get to the other side.

If you went to the doctor and discovered that you needed a prescription for medication, wouldn't you want *both* the doctor and the pharmacist to get the dosage exactly right before you took the medication home, trusting that all was in order?

When you get on an airplane, do you have faith that the pilot will listen to the traffic control operators, who will in turn follow their instrument panels with complete accuracy as they guide the plane through the skies?

Truthfulness and honesty are absolutes in life, and they must never be compromised. Truth and honesty are like fine china. They can be broken. They can be mended. But they can never be the same again without the restoration of the Lord Jesus Christ.

79

There must be absolutes in life. In a world where men have redefined history, values, and goals, we must look to something and someone to be the same yesterday, today, and forever. We know that someone to be Jesus Christ. He never changes. He never fails. And we are to pattern ourselves after Him.

Honesty is defined as "a refusal to lie, cheat, or deceive in any way." An honest person shows fairness and sincerity. An honest person is genuine.

The Lord clearly speaks to us in the Book of Micah: "He has shown you, O man, what is good; and what does the LORD require of you but to do justly, to love mercy, and to walk humbly with your God?" (Micah 6:8).

Truth and honesty are essentials in life whether you are a man or a woman. One of the things that every woman needs from her marriage is a sense of security. Dr. Harley states, "Security is the bright golden thread woven through all of a woman's five basic needs (affection, conversation, honesty, financial support, family commitment). If a husband does not keep up honest and open communication with his wife, he undermines her trust and eventually destroys her security."[1]

HUSBANDS WHO LIE

It is crucially important for a woman to be able to fully trust the man she marries—before she marries him, every moment of every day, and for every day of her future. She must be able to trust the information her husband gives her about his past, present, and the future. Without trust, she cannot build a solid marriage foundation. If she cannot trust her husband, she will begin to feel isolated from him and will eventually grow further and further away from him, emotionally and physically.

Honesty must be a foundation stone in marriage. According to the survey we conducted, women desire honesty from their husbands above five other qualities that we have discussed in earlier chapters, including faithfulness, leadership, respect, his ability to be a godly family man, and his being a good provider.

However, some men struggle with honesty. Some husbands find it easy to lie to their wives, often about minor things. Others manipulate or control their wives by the lies that they tell. Some men would fit into the category of a "born liar."

This man has continually told lies about the smallest of things even from a young age. He may say he was working when he was really playing cards. He is easily caught in his lies by simple fact-finding, yet he will explain his lies away with jokes or pleading a "poor memory."

This man finds it very difficult to change, because he can't acknowledge he has a problem. He has never come to know the voice of his conscience. Even a child knows the importance of honesty.

A young woman was basking in the tropical sun as she lay on the sandy, white beach. A young boy came up to her carrying a sand bucket and beach towel. He stood awkwardly over her without a word until she acknowledged his presence. "Can I help you?" she asked curiously.

"Do you believe in God?" the little boy blared.

Surprised by his boldness, the woman quickly replied, "Yes."

His next question came quickly: "Do you go to church every Sunday?"

Again she answered, "Yes."

Then he asked, "Do you read your Bible and pray every day?"

Once again she answered, "Yes!"

She was now overtaken by curiosity as he asked his last question. "Great! Would you hold my quarter while I go swimming?"[2]

When a man refuses to acknowledge the importance of honesty in his life, he will make trust within a marriage almost impossible.

Sometimes a man will tell his wife lies because he believes it will keep him out of trouble. It becomes very easy for him to lie to his wife, and he expresses no remorse unless he is caught. Often, because of his lack of true repentance, he will fake remorse to make the offended party quickly "forgive and forget." Unlike the born liar, he usually resorts to lying when he is under pressure.

A young man got twenty-five dollars too much in his pay envelope and said nothing to his employer. As the week progressed, the employer realized his error and docked the young man's next paycheck.

When the young man noticed the shortage, he immediately went to his employer. "Excuse me, sir, but I am twenty-five dollars short this week," he said.

"You didn't complain last week," his boss replied.

Thinking quickly, the young man replied, "No, sir, I don't mind overlooking one mistake. But when it happens twice, then it's time to say something."[3]

When a problem with dishonesty is acknowledged, a man can, with the help of the Lord and his wife, learn to be honest in the marriage relationship. He can learn to avoid the stressful situations that set him up to fail in maintaining truthful communication with his loved ones.

Some men believe that there are some truths that are too hurtful for their wives to handle, so they tell lies to "protect her." This man is truly bothered by his lies. He considers lying a necessary evil, done to protect his wife and family. For example, he may be the person who takes care of the finances, and he needs to borrow money because he is not able to make ends meet. He has a plan to pay back the loan, so he tells his wife everything is fine financially to keep her from worrying.

He is lying to protect her. Even though it bothers him, he feels it is worth it. This creates a false sense of security in the relationship, and as soon as the lie is exposed (and it always will be), his world comes tumbling down around him. His lies will do irreparable damage to his marriage.[4]

It's possible that the widower in the following story would say that he was lying to "protect" the feelings of the woman he met. A widower was entertaining a woman with whom he had gone on a blind date that had been arranged by his matchmaking children. The homely old maid began to confess her feelings of insecurity to the widower, Mr. Thompson. "I am at a low ebb in my life," she told him. "I have no self-worth. I don't feel attractive."

In a very affirmative voice, the kind gentleman replied, "Let me assure you, dear lady, you are a very good-looking woman. My time with you has been delightful."

Obviously perked by his compliments, she responded in a girlish voice, "Oh, Mr. Thompson, is that really the truth?"

The old man sighed and answered flatly, "No. But there will be plenty of time for the truth when you are emotionally stronger to hear it."[5]

If you are dating a man who exhibits one of these lying habits, run. You will not change him. Marriage will not change him. Only the Lord will change him, and then only when he is willing to acknowledge that he has a dishonesty problem.

If you are married to a man who has a problem telling the truth, then seek help. If your security level is shattered for too long, you will begin to want out of your marriage. Take some necessary steps, and ask

yourself some questions about your own truth and trust level. Are you always truthful to your spouse? Is honesty a problem for both of you? Come to the cross. Remember, books, counselors, and therapists are not the answers for your marriage—God is.

Don't be dismayed if you have discovered that either you or your spouse is struggling with one or more of the kinds of lies that I have described in this chapter. It is never too late to make the changes necessary to strengthen the foundation of honesty in your marriage relationship. Many couples struggle with this issue. However, there is no marriage that can survive a continual climate of dishonesty.

Always remember that "honesty is the best marriage insurance policy."

In his book *Love Busters*, Dr. Harley sets forth clearly defined guidelines to keep your relationship pure and honest before your husband and the Lord.[6] Remember that in order *to get* an honest relationship, you *must contribute honesty* to the relationship.

Follow this rule of honesty: Reveal to your husband as much information about yourself as you know: your thoughts, feelings, habits, likes, dislikes, personal history, daily activities, and plans for the future.

BE HONEST ABOUT YOUR EMOTIONS

So many times we hear men tell us that we are so much more "emotional" about the events of our lives than they are. Because of that, it is sometimes easier for a wife to keep her emotions hidden from her husband. But it will be difficult for your husband to give you the emotional support that you want and need from him if you cannot openly express your emotions—positive and negative—to him. Dr. Harley describes this as *emotional honesty*.[7] Because you have not given him your *emotional honesty*, he will disappoint you by his lack of understanding of the emotions you are feeling.

I remember when our first wedding anniversary was approaching, I began to have fantasies of what our celebration would be like. I envisioned a surprise candlelight dinner at a romantic restaurant. Maybe he would surprise me with a trip. That would be great!

I began to dream of all the possible places he could take me. I thought about what I would wear and how I would react to such a fabulous surprise.

Time passed, and nothing was mentioned about a possible celebration. I could hardly stand it. I created my own excitement. Then the day came. My husband walked in the door with a dozen red roses. I looked for the card. "To the most beautiful woman in the world. I love you. Juan."

What! No trip? My husband could tell I was disappointed. "Is something wrong?" he asked, almost afraid of what I would say.

"No, not at all," I responded. "The flowers are beautiful." I was not truthful with my answer. We went to dinner, and a full year passed before I told him what I expected for our first celebration.

The first thing he said to me was, "I didn't know!" How true, because I didn't tell him. I wasn't honest.

Well, baby, that has changed! I am so honest with what I need and want from him now that I write it on the bathroom mirror with lipstick! I leave notes in his briefcase and in the pages of his sermons! Notes are left on his office calendar: "Diana needs a date night—now!"

Satan is present to destroy the works of the Lord in His people. He wants to keep you from communicating honestly with your husband. If you are dishonest, you will be falling right into the evil one's trap to rob, kill, and destroy your marriage.

BE HONEST ABOUT YOUR PAST

After one of my teaching sessions, a beautiful woman requested to speak to me. She waited until the room was almost empty, then she came to me and began to sob uncontrollably. After regaining her composure, she began to tell me about her wonderful ten-year marriage and her great children. As I listened, I could not imagine what the problem was. She finally got the courage to tell me.

Years before she met her husband, she had an affair that resulted in a pregnancy and an abortion. No one knew—including her husband. This event had tormented her for years. Her ultimate fear was that if she told her husband, he would leave her. This form of blackmail is a standard "method of operation" for the devil. I held her until her

sobbing subsided, and I prayed with her until I could feel the peace of the Lord overtake her.

I convinced her to tell her husband the truth about her past. I knew the wonderful husband and father she described to me would also have a compassionate heart. I told her that the church was ready to counsel them after the past had been revealed. If she would do this, no longer would Satan hold her hostage to this secret. She agreed.

Within a few days she came to me once again, radiant. She told her husband. She recounted the event and said that her husband's biggest disappointment was in her not trusting him with this traumatic event in her life before this time.

Time passed, and she came to me once more. She told me that after the initial shock of her secret, and because of her repentant spirit before her husband, their relationship was better than it had ever been before. She felt a freedom from the past that she had thought would never be possible. She had been delivered from her accuser. The only way to stop paying his ransom was to expose him. This woman and her husband now had a marriage that was pure and honest before each other and the Lord. Make *historical honesty* a part of your relationship with your husband.[8]

> **HE SAYS…**
>
> **Every person in every married relationship makes major mistakes despite the best intentions and all the wisdom in the world.**

Remember that it isn't *honesty* that drives a wedge of distance into your marriage—it is *dishonesty.* Be willing to share the things in your past that have happened to you, even the things that you consider to be failures or areas of weakness. And allow him to share his past—good and bad—with you.

BE HONEST ABOUT YOUR PRESENT

How willing are you for your husband to know everything that is happening in your life today? Are there things that you consider "too minor" for him to have to know? Are there things that you have decided he just "doesn't need to know"?

Provide your spouse with a calendar of your activities, giving special emphasis to the things that affect your spouse. Find a time to discuss

your day and to give him a chance to tell you about his. Recalling the events of your day allows you to practice *current honesty*.[9]

This is tough—especially for my husband and me. I am a detail person, and I remember things well. These are two traits that men find hard to live with. A third kicker—I want to know everything, and I want to know it right away! My husband has to deal with all three.

To become informed with my daily schedule is enough to choke a horse! I have five kids, four "in-loves," three grandchildren, and eighteen thousand church members. I coordinate the special events of our church, serve as the chief of staff of the television arm of our ministry, and maintain our home, which hosts many social events through the year—and I want to tell my husband everything!

I know that my husband feels there was some peccadillo that he must have committed as a child that caused him to owe such a great penance! I try to relay to him the day's events as we lie in bed at night. I find this ritual to be the best sleep aid he has, for long before my diatribe is over, I hear the sounds of sleep coming from his side of the bed.

On the other hand—and you know there is always another hand—my husband doesn't flow with information as freely as I do. I often find out what is happening in the church through leaders or assistants. That used to bother me a lot. Now it doesn't bother me as much, but since we are talking about honesty, it still bothers me *a little*. Men are wired totally different than women. They can't help it. Things that I consider important he couldn't care less about, and therefore he forgets to tell me about them.

The most important component is honesty. To forget something is not the same thing as avoiding telling me about something or dishonestly relaying the facts to me. If you learn to understand this, it will save you much grief and keep you from many arguments. The longer you are married, the more you will realize this fact: the fewer arguments you have, the better your life will be.

BE HONEST ABOUT YOUR FUTURE

There is something special in sharing the future with the person you love. To sit on the back porch or lie in bed at night in the privacy of your bedroom and reveal your dreams is some of the most intimate

honesty you will ever experience. Dreams are sacred ground, never to be taken for granted or belittled.

As you learn to reveal this intimacy with your husband, and he with you, your marriage will go to a new level of trust that you never thought possible. Many men and women don't share this deep side of themselves for fear the person they love will reject their dreams, so many of these hopes and aspirations remain unachieved because they were never acknowledged or communicated.

Revealing your thoughts and plans . . . your hopes and dreams . . . and your goals and aspirations allow you and your husband to experience *future honesty*.[10]

Even the Lord Himself shares His plans with you for the future: "'For I know the plans I have for you,' declares the LORD, 'plans to prosper you and not to harm you, plans to give you hope and a future'" (Jer. 29:11, NIV).

CREATE A CLIMATE OF COMPLETE HONESTY

Too many times I have heard the following phrase at luncheons or similar women's gatherings: "What he doesn't know won't hurt him." To the contrary, it will not only hurt him and his future trust in you, but it will also contribute to the demise of your marriage.

This has never been a problem with me. I was a boring child, never doing anything much of consequence . . . always doing as I was told. I have always had a keen sense of conscience.

My mother kept a Ping-Pong paddle behind the living room couch for the purpose of corporal punishment. When I felt that I did something wrong, I would begin to cry, run to the living room, retrieve the paddle, and run to my mother. I would hand her the paddle, and she would spank me, at which point the level of my cries would increase by several decibels. Then I would return the paddle to its rightful place. To this day,

> **HE SAYS . . .**
>
> **Communication happens when you, as husband and wife, can honestly tell each other who you are, what you think, how you feel, what you love, what you honor, what you esteem, what you hate, and what you fear, desire, hope for, believe in, and are committed to without fear of a prolonged argument.**

neither my mother nor I can remember what my offenses were. The important thing is that I was repentant for them.

My method of operation is still the same. When I have done or said something I feel my husband may not approve of (don't get excited, I'm still the same boring individual), I pick up the phone and open my conversation with, "Honey, I just said something I think you should know about." Why do I do this? Not because I am a "goody-two-shoes," and not because I am afraid of my husband. I do it because I don't want to disappoint him. I don't want anything to get between my cherished relationship with my husband and his trust in me.

Not telling the whole truth is the same as telling a lie. To provide partial information that leads your spouse away from the complete truth is deception. To manipulate the facts to create a false impression is dishonest. Build your marriage on the foundation of *complete honesty*.[11]

HINTS FOR HIM

There is no greater compliment than to be known as *an honest man*— a man of integrity, one who always tells the truth, not just to his wife, but also to his children and to those with whom he is associated.

There is no such thing as a little white lie. Not only do these lies add up to create an image not equal to the image of Christ, but they will also eventually entrap you in the end. A lifetime of integrity can be destroyed by one decision to lie.

A relationship of trust can crumble if you choose to be dishonest with your wife. Don't take that chance. The Bible clearly asks you to choose life and blessing. (See Deuteronomy 30:19.) Maintaining an honest lifestyle before the Lord and your loved ones will always result in long life and bountiful blessings.

My husband often tells the story of John Smith, a loyal carpenter who worked for a very successful building contractor for more than twenty-five years. One day his boss called John into his office and said, "John, my wife and I are leaving for a tour of Europe. We will be gone for six months before I come home and retire. I'm putting you in charge of the last house we build. I want you to order all of the finest materials, including the furnishings, and oversee the job from the ground up."

John accepted the assignment with great enthusiasm and excitement. For ten days before ground was broken at the building site, John studied the blueprints. He checked every measurement, every specification. Suddenly he had a thought. *If I am really in charge, why can't I cut a few corners, use less expensive materials, and put a sizable amount of money into my pocket. No one will know the difference. Once it's painted, it will look like all the other houses.*

John set out on a path he had never traveled before, the road to deception. He ordered second-grade lumber, but his reports indicated that it was top-grade. He ordered inexpensive concrete for the foundation, put in cheap wiring, and cut every corner he could. Yet he reported the purchase of the finest materials.

When the home was completed and fully painted, he asked his employer to come and inspect it. "John," the contractor said, "what a magnificent job you have done! You have been such a good, honest, and loyal friend and carpenter all these years that I have decided to show my gratitude by giving you this house you built as a gift for a token of my appreciation!"[12]

The truth will find you out. The Word of God warns that what we do in secret He will shout from the housetops.

> There is nothing concealed that will not be disclosed, or hidden that will not be made known. What you have said in the dark will be heard in the daylight, and what you have whispered in the ear in the inner rooms will be proclaimed from the roofs.
>
> —LUKE 12:2–3, NIV

Remember, the Lord your Creator knows your heart. He records the words of your mouth. To be known as an honest man by your wife, children, and loved ones is the greatest testimony you will have and the greatest legacy you will leave.

FROM DR. ANNE

If there is a single quality that has major impact on the building up, as well as tearing down, of marriage, it is *honesty*. This is a many-sided value that will make or break a marriage.

Honesty is a character strength that women say they want in their husbands, but this strength can be the most frustrating quality their husbands possess. Honesty must be carefully defined—especially from God's point of view.

"Being honest" should never be confused with being brutal and uncompassionate. An honest person does not compromise his or her values by tempering honesty with qualities of care, consideration, and tactfulness. Remember that husbands are to love their wives just as God loves the church. God never abuses.

There isn't a woman alive who hasn't asked her husband, "Does my hair look all right?" or "Does this dress look OK for tonight?"

Hurt feelings will be avoided and your husband will still be honest if he replies, "I think you are so beautiful. You know, you have another style I like better." God shows us mercy and is gracious to us. Shouldn't we be gracious and merciful to each other? This should be particularly true for the mate that God has given us. Find a way to respond to your mate with honesty that is offered with gracious, compassionate, and loving balance.

Honesty is *balanced* by the tact and compassion that we see modeled by Jesus Christ Himself. The love that Jesus had for those to whom He ministered was reflected in His statements and personal position. He never compromised truth, but He didn't purpose to hurt or destroy—only to shed light.

How honest are you as a woman of God? Are you strong enough to receive and accept leadership that is uncompromising and honest? Will you be honest with *yourself* as well as with your husband? Or will you bare your fangs and hiss when his *honesty* doesn't agree with what you wanted to hear?

There are two persons involved in every verbal transaction involving honesty. One is the person who is being honest with you—and the other is *you!* Every marriage will need both people in that marriage to be committed totally to honesty—whether in the position of expressing an honest opinion or statement, or receiving the expression from his or her mate.

A man with honesty is governed by a sense of right and wrong, which is not swayed by a whim, even his wife's whims. He is not easily manipulated by circumstances or ego. When he is away, he isn't subject to corruption by peer pressure or social conformity.

He doesn't lie to his wife or to others. He is correct in his morals and conduct.

Balance in all of the marriage qualities, including honesty, encourages and elevates without compromising the facts. Honesty, combined with the companion characteristics of compassion, encouragement, and support, builds confidence and trust.

Ladies, use wisely every opportunity you have to elevate and support your husband. Your husband *does* care what you think about him. Based on your responses to him, he will go to work feeling like a winner or a loser. Follow the example of Christ, who ministered to each person He met in truth balanced with grace and compassion.

Closing Prayers

Why be held captive to the ways of the world? Embrace the freedom of truth. The Word of God tells us that the knowledge of the truth will set us free—free from the chains of the past and free from the fear of tomorrow. There is nothing so liberating as the truth. Truth must have a covenant with love, and honesty must be intertwined with trust, in order for the union of holy matrimony to succeed.

Prayer of Repentance

Father God, I lied today, and I am so sorry. I have lied a lot lately. I have almost made it a way of life. I make up a story so I can avoid trouble and conflict. I am not straightforward with my husband. Yet I demand honesty from him. I lie by not telling him things he really should be told. I sometimes manipulate the truth by exaggerating or minimizing the facts. I am also guilty of asking questions that I know will cause an argument if he is honest with his answers. I have not been truthful with him about my needs and desires, and I have later accused him of not meeting them. I call on Your forgiveness, Lord. I know that I can begin anew and turn from my past as I repent before You and those I have hurt.

PRAYER OF NEW BEGINNINGS

Lord Jesus, I want to be one with my husband as You are one with the Father. I will not lie to my husband about my feelings, my needs, and my desires. I pledge to be forthright and honest. I will be kind and gentle in my conversation with my husband so he can respond to me in the fashion I long for. I want to share all that I am with him, as I share all that I am with You. I want him to feel secure in being honest with me. Together we can take our needs to You in prayer. I want to grow closer to my husband each day as our lives are a reflection of the example You have set. I want my husband to trust me, and I want to trust him. This will be an example of our love and devotion to You and one another. I praise and honor You, my God. I can't do this without You. I desire to please You. I want the desire of my heart to be pure and to be reflected in the words that come from my lips. Amen.

Want Number Four:
COMMUNICATION

> My son, if your heart is wise, then my heart will be glad; my inmost being will rejoice when your lips speak what is right.
>
> —PROVERBS 23:15–16, NIV

WOMEN OFTEN FALSELY accuse men of not listening. We know they can hear us all right—they are just not paying attention. Actually, this is a gift. A man can follow the moves of a graceful quarterback on the turf while watching TV or track the path of a little white ball on the green until it falls in a shallow hole, all the while nodding and occasionally delivering a "hmmm," while his wife is having a passionate, cathartic, one-sided conversation with him.

I have come to the conclusion that men are truly different. The old adage says, "Thank God for the difference!" As women, it is important to identify the differences *and* acknowledge that *God* created most of these differences. We have no business changing that which God has ordained. But we must learn to adapt to these differences.

When I was newly married, I attended a Bible study taught by an older lady in the church. She told the young group of women that if we wanted to change certain characteristics in our husbands, we should pray. Eventually, God would make the changes we desired.

I was sure what she was saying had to be right on target—after all, she was an older woman! I thought, *Wow! My mother never told me this!* I went directly home, made my "Change Order," and submitted it to God.

I put my wish list in my Bible and prayed over it every day. "Lord, make my husband more spontaneous and less methodical. Make him more flexible and less rigid. Make him want to smell the roses and not trample over them." Every day I prayed and waited for *the change*.

One morning the answer came. Now, I must tell you that I am not a "woo...woo..." kind of person. I don't hear the voice of God audibly. I don't see colorful pictures in my head. Yet I am sensitive to the Holy Spirit who lives inside of me, and I try to listen to His voice when He speaks.

On this morning, as I was praying a thought came to my mind: *Today you will receive the man you have been praying for. I will make the changes in him you have requested.* Because this thought came out of the blue, I knew it was God. I was excited. I thought, *That wasn't difficult at all!* As I was celebrating my answered prayer, another thought came just as unexpectedly as the first. It seemed God wasn't finished: *Today, I will give you the husband you want—but then I can no longer use him.*

My celebration turned to spontaneous humility. I began to weep. I knelt on the floor and asked God to forgive me. My husband no longer used of God? I could hardly stand it! "Because of me! Please, Lord, no!" I prayed fervently. After my time of repentance was complete, the sweet presence of the Holy Spirit comforted me as He began to show me how He used the traits He put in my husband for His purposes.

The methodical approach he has for life is what God molds into the discipline needed for the hours of study and preparation of the Word of God. It enables my husband to present his message to the sheep of His pasture every Sunday. His rigid stance is the strength he must draw from when standing on the uncompromising message of the gospel of Jesus Christ. The determination that drives him is the tenacity the Creator put in him to fight injustice and stand for good, no matter what the cost. I wanted to change that which the Creator put into him for His purposes. I was the one who needed to change.

MEN COMMUNICATE DIFFERENTLY THAN WOMEN

We want our husbands to communicate with us in the same way we communicate with other women. They can't. Bill Cosby said, "Women don't want to hear what you [men] think. Women want to hear what they think, in a deeper voice." Men want women to be content with the quality of communication they have with other men. We won't be.

We all know the stereotypes: men dominate the remote control and relish in the power they have as they surf through the channels, while women enjoy watching the commercials. When men are under pressure, they brood or go to a hockey game and scream for blood. Women eat chocolates and go shopping. A man can go into a room full of people and leave after two hours, not knowing a soul. A woman can go into a public bathroom and make friends with a perfect stranger as they compare the makeup they use. We are different!

> **HE SAYS...**
>
> **Women enjoy the process of reaching a goal. Men want to get to the goal as soon as possible—forget the process.**

My husband finds it hard to remember that when we were courting we would spend several hours on the phone every evening. I, of course, remember it all. It is a sweet, romantic memory of our past. When I ask him to tell me more about himself and what he is thinking, his response is: "I've told you everything there is to know about me! It was different then."

Different, yet the same. The same time, effort, and attention it took for a man to court his wife is the same he needs to keep her feeling secure and happy within the marriage relationship.

Communication is meant to be a blessing in marriage, not a torment. When I hear the jokes about communication between men and women, I conclude that marriage is both: a blessing for the woman and a torment for the man. It doesn't have to be this way. When seen through the eyes of love, communication is the lifeline for any marriage.

COMMUNICATION RULES

An old adage says, "It's better *felt* than *telt!*" There are some communication rules that I want to share with you that demonstrate the truth of learning to communicate *through experience.* Some of the experiences that teach us good communication with our spouses are positive, "right-on" examples of how to do communication the right way. Others are... well, others teach us how to communicate *the next time* in a far better way than we did *the last time.*

As I let you into the life of my husband and me in the following paragraphs, you will see that we too have learned from experience. Perhaps

after sharing this experience with us, you will decide to incorporate these communication rules into your own life. Take it from me...they work!

Communication rule: Communication is not nagging or boasting.

When my husband and I decided to make our first trip to Israel, we were very excited. I was four months pregnant with our son Matthew, but nonetheless eager and ready for the trip. This was going to be a second honeymoon experience for us. I had no idea how long the trip would take. We were not the seasoned travelers we are now. My husband, being the determined man he is, made the decision to go to Israel one Sunday evening. The following Monday morning, he called New York to begin making arrangements for what would be a life-changing experience.

He began his phone conversation with these words: "New York, I want to go to Israel on the next tour out!" We were booked by the end of the day. We began our journey less than one month later by leaving San Antonio and flying to Houston. From Houston we flew to New York, from New York to Amsterdam, from Amsterdam to Athens, Greece, and from Athens to Lanarca, Cyprus. Once in Cyprus, we boarded a Greek liner and began a voyage across the Mediterranean Sea to Port Said, Egypt. After three days in Egypt, we boarded the ship once again and sailed into the beautiful Port of Haifa, Israel.

Are you tired yet? I was. By the time we boarded the ship in Cyprus, we had already been traveling thirty-six hours! I was exhausted. The story gets better.

Communication rule: "If Momma ain't happy, ain't nobody happy!"

We boarded the liner, which was not exactly the *Love Boat,* I might add. We had difficulty finding our room. We asked several crewmembers for directions, but most of them did not speak English. Finally, one of them understood us sufficiently to lead us to the floor above the boiler room. You guessed it; our room was directly over the boiler room. My husband opened the door, and I walked into the room, quickly observing that the place intended for our second honeymoon had no bed.

"John, this room has no bed!" I announced as if it was some brilliant deduction.

"Yes, it does, honey," my husband answered, staring at one of the tiny room's four walls.

"No," I responded, "I see no bed. They must have us in the wrong room!"

With that, John walked to the wall and pulled two straps that were hanging suspiciously from the wall. Suddenly, as if produced from thin air, two bunk beds appeared in the room.

My mouth fell open. He looked at me and made what I thought was a very imprudent remark. "I'll flip you for the top bunk!" I stared holes through him as I held my pregnant belly in such a way to make sure he realized that I was the woman who was carrying his child and that I was not very happy at the moment.

> **HE SAYS...**
> **Conflicting expectations are the source of most unhappiness in marriage.**

"I was only kidding! I'll help you strap into bed," he responded sympathetically, trying to make amends for what he now considered to be a foolish proposal.

Communication rule: Good communication is *quality*, not quantity.

As my husband climbed into the top bunk, I lay there remembering my last encounter on the high seas. It was not a pleasant memory. We had taken what became known as the *infamous Hagee family fishing trip* in the Texas Gulf three years earlier. Unbeknownst to my husband or me, I was also with child at that time. I had never been on the ocean before, and I was not feeling well at all. The nausea I felt was overwhelming. I know I hold the record for the *Guinness Book of World Records* for chumming—at least eight hours! It was not an amusing experience.

Now on this first trip to Israel, I was about to embark on my second high sea voyage. I became worried and was prompted by my fears to ask my husband for help.

I called out to my husband, who had just positioned himself in the narrow berth above me, "Honey, I need you to pray that I will not get seasick."

Rather impatiently, he replied, "You won't get sick. It's all in your mind. Don't think about it, and you will go straight to sleep."

"I don't care where it is!" was my determined comeback. "I need you to pray for it, wherever it is! I want you to pray that I will not get seasick!"

The prayer that came from my husband's mouth was not what I had in mind. "Dear Lord, keep my wife from getting seasick. Amen."

"That's no prayer!" I shouted. "Why, that didn't even clear the ceiling!"

John was aggravated now. "Look, Diana, it had to clear the ceiling, because my nose is touching the ceiling!"

I couldn't leave well enough alone. "John Hagee, I need you to pray a real prayer!" I issued my demand, and, much to my disgust, I could hear the sounds of snoring coming from above. He was asleep! How dare he?

This story is a classic example of the communication differences between a man and a woman. I wanted a bodacious prayer, a long, powerful, bring-the-house-down, Charlton Heston, part-the-Red-Sea kind of prayer! He wanted to be more prudent. A quick and to the point prayer for him was sufficient.

My husband feels God needs no pleading; He just requires faith—imagine that! I was too exhausted to wake him, and to continue the argument over a prayer for healing somehow didn't seem right.

The ship began to rock as it embarked on its journey across the Mediterranean. Bored, I began to purvey the tiny space we were in. I adjusted my eyes to the dim light coming from the miniscule porthole. There was one single dresser in the room, positioned right next to my narrow bed. The other end of the dresser rested against the opposite wall of that little room.

There were two doors to our "stateroom with an ocean view." One led to the hall, and the other to the bathroom. The only other furnishings were the two berths, which pushed up into the wall during the day. We were definitely in tight quarters. Finally, the rocking of the ship, coupled with the serenade of the engine below us and the sounds of slumber coming from my husband, put me sound to sleep, a miracle in its own right.

Communication rule: Don't speak without thinking about the full nature of the consequences.

Suddenly, I was awakened from my deep "miracle sleep" by the thud of my head tapping against the dresser, which was sandwiched between my cot and the wall. From the captain's announcement later, we learned that we were in the roughest storm he had ever experienced in his career. As my mind became clearer, I could hear sounds coming from the "naval latrine." I listened closely, and soon realized that it was the sound of my husband upchucking his dinner.

This is true confession time. When I heard that sound, I thought of what it represented, and I immediately began to feel it was vindication for the halfhearted prayer my husband had offered for me earlier that night. I called out from my bunk, "Honey, are you sick?"

No response.

"John, do you need my help?" No decipherable answer came from the bathroom, just continued gagging.

I went to the door of the room ready to say boastfully, "I told you so!" But instantly I felt compassion for the man lying in front of the metal bowl anchored to the floor. It was not a pretty sight. His legs and arms wrapped around the latrine as if it were his life jacket, his head was positioned deep into the bowl. All I could hear were sounds of muffled gagging interrupted only by his gasps for air. Without thinking I said, "Guess what? Your prayer worked, and I'm not even nauseous!"

You can imagine the look that came from his red face, and I knew that he would later have to repent for his thoughts.

Communication rule: Timing is everything.

I quietly backed out of the small cubbyhole and sat on the narrow bed until the sounds of retching stopped. He came out of the room and began to dress. I was shocked, because it was barely four in the morning of God only knows what time zone we were in. "Where in the world are you going?" I asked.

"I'm going to ask the captain how long before we are off this tub!" was his aggravated response. I sat on the edge of my bunk, which by now gave me a small sense of security, and remained there until his return. As he walked back into the room, I asked him cautiously what the outcome of his visit had been. "Eight more lousy, stinking hours!" he railed.

He took the bedding off the top bunk and laid it on the floor next to my bed. I got into my cot. As he lay there on the floor, he reached for my hand. I

HE SAYS . . .

Through sickness and health, for richer and poorer, marriage requires devotion and a mature ability to commit when it's the last thing you want to do.

took it and held it tightly. Of all the things I felt I had the right to say, and all the things I could have said, I chose to softly whisper, "I love you."

"I love you, too," was his tender response. Our second honeymoon had finally begun.

PRAYER—THE BEST COMMUNICATION TOOL

I could go on and on and recount several books written about communication by qualified counselors, but, if needed, you can read these books on your own. What I do want to share with you is what I have found to be the best form of communication you will ever experience with your spouse. It is the communication you have in prayer with each other and with God.

The Lord uses communication to maintain a lifeline to His people. He uses several forms of communication. One is His written Word. Another is His voice, which is manifested through our conscience. He speaks to us through His people, who are the hands and feet of the living God. We, in turn, communicate to our Father in supplication, in praise, and in worship. Without participation in these forms of communication, the Christian will become distant from God, and his soul will soon dry and wither.

When we come to Him united, in one accord, as husband and wife, and lay our needs at His altar, our Lord makes a promise to us. Jesus is the Promise Keeper of all promise keepers:

> Again I tell you, if two of you on earth agree (harmonize together, make a symphony together) about whatever [anything and everything] they may ask, it will come to pass and be done for them by My Father in heaven.
>
> —MATTHEW 18:19, AMP

Can you imagine? *Anything and everything!* The operative words in this promise are "agree," "harmonize," and "symphony." What beautiful music we must make in the heavenlies when we pray together with our spouses in unity!

When my husband and I pray together, we get answers from heaven. And it is simply not possible to be angry with one another when you pray!

> For this reason I am telling you, whatever you ask for in prayer, believe (trust and be confident) that it is granted to you, and you will [get it]. And whenever you stand praying, if you have anything against anyone, forgive him and let it drop (leave it, let it go), in

order that your Father Who is in heaven may also forgive you your [own] failings and shortcomings and let them drop.

—MARK 11:24–25, AMP

Find a private time and place for prayer. Satan will make sure that the phone will ring, your children will scream for you, or the doorbell will ring. My husband and I like to have our prayer time while we walk. We are away from intrusions and able to call on the Lord in freedom. I am sure you and your husband can find a place and time on which you can agree.

Make a prayer list. My husband and I have prayed together for almost thirty years; therefore, it is engraved in our minds. First, we come into a time of repentance, asking forgiveness for anything we have said, done, or thought that has grieved the Holy Spirit. Our list then begins: We pray for our children by name, their spouses, and our grandchildren—those already here and those to come. We pray for the protection, direction, and prosperity of our church, television outreach, and school, and for everyone associated with them. Then we submit any personal petitions we may have. Finally, we pray for the peace of Jerusalem and end in a time of praise for our Lord and His blessings.

Learn to pray in *agreement*, not in competition. There is no sweeter sound in the heavens than the sound of a husband and wife in harmony before the throne of God. There is nothing more powerful.

The more this divine communication occurs, the more you will want to talk to each other about other things. You will find that the "things" you speak about with your spouse will not include gossip or tale bearing. Your conversation will concentrate on the petitions that you put before the Lord and the testimonies associated with those prayers. With your husband you will share the dreams and aspirations each of you has as together you come into agreement. Your children will know that when Mom and Dad pray, things happen. This teaching is far greater than any book or class you will ever enroll them in. Without communication, your marriage will wither and become dry, just like the soul when it has no time with God.

HINTS FOR HIM

In the leadership chapter of this book, I made a statement about a woman submitting to a husband's lead and a man submitting to a wife's need. Both men and women need communication. As the leader of the household, it is important that you understand the importance of communicating to your wife.

HINT #1: There is nothing sweeter than your wife hearing these words coming from you: "Honey, I'm home. I can hardly wait to tell you about my day! How did your day go today?" It sure beats dragging information out of you, which forces your wife into the role of interrogator.

HINT #2: Your wife would love a "just because" telephone call from you. End this call with "I love you, and I bless you in the name of the Lord." When expressions of love are unsolicited, they are invaluable.

HINT #3: Listen. Women need to be listened to just as much as men do. One of the greatest gifts you can give your wife is your undivided attention. I know your time is precious, and she does, too.

HINT #4: Just as with God, communication comes in many forms. Some men find it difficult to express their feelings in conversation. Some of the most beautiful forms of communication are handwritten letters. I keep the letters, cards, and notes my husband has given me through the years in a special drawer, and when I need a special blessing, I go to the file and make a little withdrawal of all the love stored and deposited on those pages. They are priceless to me.

HINT #5: Other forms of communication that women love are what I call "love pats" or "love smiles." This can take place at any time of the day or night. They can be in private or in public. They are simply special personal ways you let each other know you care. Remember, some of the most treasured investments you will make in your wife cost you nothing.

HINT #6: *Let it drop!* Take heed to what the Lord instructs His people. In order to qualify to come to His throne in supplication, you must leave your offenses and let them go! If not, you won't be heard. No exceptions!

As you meet your wife's needs through the communion of your heart with hers, you will help to make your marriage the beautiful union God intended it to be.

From Dr. Anne

Communication is the *sharing* of ideas. This can involve two people or one person gaining knowledge from an outside source. Communication is also *expressing* ideas. True communication is a *dialogue,* not merely a monologue. Communication happens when one person is speaking and the other person is listening.

Some women have a habit of talking incessantly, hardly pausing for breath or to allow dialogue. They pause only long enough to reload for another assault. Do you want your husband to "communicate"? If you do, it requires your husband giving feedback to your monologue. That's what turns the monologue into dialogue.

Communication is more than an echo of your own opinion. A differing opinion should not spark an argument. Opinions that are different will not shut down communication as long as there are communication rules that are respected by both husband and wife. Allow time for both of you to be heard without interruption. When an argument arises, give each other permission to take a timeout from the discussion. Set a time when both of you will return to the conversation. Determine that during the timeout, neither of you will attempt to discuss the subject about which you were in disagreement.

When I am counseling couples about the issue of communication, I give each person the following list of rules:

- No name calling.
- Never attack the person—only the subject.
- Never use violence.
- Always give the opportunity to rephrase the last statement.
- Always pay attention.
- Never interrupt.
- Stick to the subject.
- Set an appointment for a subject requiring serious discussion (this avoids distractions).

- If the discussion goes too long, set a time several days later to continue the discussion.

How much conversation, information, and talk are enough? When is the best time to share quality time? When you have both had a challenging day, when you are shifting gears from the day's work, and you enter the common place you share (probably your home), that is NOT a good time to unload problems or demand answers.

Both of you need to use wisdom and allow the other to have "reentry time." A quiet environment is unbelievably calming. Decompression won't take long if you both cooperate. Children should see this time as calm family time, not as a contest for attention from both parents.

Genuine love and communication are not defined by an emotional experience. An emotional experience cannot seal your relationship with your husband or with your Father in heaven. If the Word of God doesn't have lordship in your life, then God is not the Lord of your life.

Our desire for an intimate relationship with our spouses is a God-given desire. It can't be accomplished without knowing the motivations, thoughts, or ways of your spouse. Jesus said, "I and My Father are one" (John 10:30). His Father's thoughts and ways had been communicated to Him. Jesus spent time in sweet communion and communication with God. Jesus spoke to God. God spoke to Jesus. They shared a common heart, vision, and love.

Do you place a priority on the time you spend with God? With your husband? Do you value the time you spend with your husband? Make this your goal, and see if your communication with your husband doesn't drastically improve.

CLOSING PRAYERS

It is no coincidence that the word *communicate* derives from the word *commune*, which means "to converse intimately, to give and receive or have Holy Communion." To give of each other by sharing each other's thoughts and dreams in an unselfish manner, looking for no gain in return other than a closer relationship with the one you love, is one of the most precious expressions of love you can give to your spouse.

PRAYER OF REPENTANCE

Lord, I get very lonely sometimes. I forget that You too get lonely for my voice as well. Forgive me for not talking to You more. I know if I repent before You, it will cancel those things I have done that have brought disappointment to You. Forgive me, Lord. I ask also that You forgive me for the times I have spoken to my husband in critical, nagging, and accusing tones that I know will not edify him, strengthen our relationship, or be a good example of my relationship with You. I have also been guilty of not listening to him when he is trying to talk to me about his needs or desires. I ask for Your forgiveness. I want my own needs met, and I am not sensitive to hearing his thoughts and needs. Help me, Lord, to calm my thinking and to communicate my feelings without the cloud of my emotions. I need to talk with my husband about good things, those things that are beautiful, and bring hope to our future. Help me to make this happen. Amen.

PRAYER OF NEW BEGINNINGS

First of all, Lord, allow me to give You praise for the opportunity of beginning anew. A fresh start is what I need. I have read in Your Word, my Father God, and I know that it reflects Your desire to communicate with me. You want to hear my petitions, and You want me to listen as You answer my prayers. I am so grateful. Help me, Lord, to apply the rules that define my communication with You and my communication with my husband. I vow to be still and know without a doubt that You are my God. I vow to be still and listen to the words and thoughts my husband is conveying to me. I will apply his words to the knowledge I have of him and his ways. I know You and Your ways. Help me to understand my husband's communication to me. I know he is trying, and together, with Your help, we will start fresh and have a new attitude about our communication with each other. I will, with Your help, forgive him for hurting me. I will "drop it" and come to You with a pure heart. I will pray with my husband in one accord, as together we approach Your throne in harmony. I thank You, Father, for being there for me and mine whenever we call upon Your name. You are so precious to me. Amen.

Want Number Three:
SENSE OF HUMOR

A happy heart is good medicine and a cheerful mind works healing, but a broken spirit dries up the bones.

—PROVERBS 17:22, AMP

HUMOR IS DEFINED in various ways. Humor can describe anything from a person's temperament, mood, and state of mind to a person's ability to express or appreciate what is funny or amusing.

Life is too short not to be filled with laughter and good times. Then again, laughter and good times are many things to many people. In his book titled *Being Happy in an Unhappy World*, my husband describes many things that happiness is not.[1]

I know that women are not looking for the eternal comedian. I have been around men who are actually extremely gifted at making other people laugh. However, a little goes a long way, and after a while, you are ready for serious and meaningful conversation. You can often look deep into the eyes of individuals who have to be the life of the party and see a sadness that does not fit with their outward façade. It is very difficult to have a great sense of humor without being a happy person.

Some people just don't have a talent for humor. I, for example, have a quick wit, but I couldn't tell a joke successfully if you paid me. On the other hand, my husband has both talents. Our children all have quick minds and a great sense of humor, and our times together are often hilarious. However, I know from visiting in other households that not all families have this in common.

Humor is not laughing at someone else's expense. I've been in social gatherings where the husband or wife is making fun of his or her spouse in some sort of demeaning way. The one making the jokes may be the center of attraction for the moment, but I always look at the person who is the target of the humor. That person may be laughing on the outside, but often he or she is trying to keep from crying.

> **HE SAYS . . .**
>
> **It's important to laugh together, not *at* each other, but *with* each other.**

A HAPPY PERSON DEFINED

Who is a happy person? I know that women, and men, are looking for a person with whom they can enjoy life, a mate who will look at the bright side of things even when the circumstances are not exactly conducive to laughter. In His Word, the Lord gives us the answer to this question by listing at least nine kinds of people who are happy. (See Matthew 5:1–12.)

1. Happy are the humble.

When my mother-in-law married my father-in-law, she was an accomplished Bible teacher and conference speaker. She had speaking engagements booked for years in advance. She loved to teach the Word of God, and she did so with a power and anointing that was electrifying.

My in-laws made the decision to begin a church in Channelview, Texas. She fulfilled the engagements she had for the rest of the calendar year and humbly canceled those for subsequent years.

As she pastored the church with her husband, she realized that her talent for speaking drew larger crowds than her husband. She made the decision to retire from the pulpit to see her husband's ministerial potential realized.

After my father-in-law had gone to heaven, she shared with me the blessings of answered prayer she had received regarding her decision to retire from teaching the Word of God, something I knew she loved. Her decision to stop teaching had not been an easy one. When she came to the conclusion to bring that part of her life to a close, she had a long conversation with the Lord. She shared with Him her desire.

"Lord, as I lay down my ministry to help develop my husband's, I want you to give me a son who will take up the banner of the gospel. I want him to preach to this nation and the nations of the world. I want to have the privilege of witnessing this in my lifetime."

My mother-in-law has a very unique relationship with the Lord. When she speaks, He listens. He knows her heart. He knows her love for Him. He knows the dedication she has for the things of God.

Over sixty-four years later, at ninety-one years of age, she is witnessing the life of her son, my husband, as he preaches the good news of Jesus Christ to this nation and the nations of the world. This winter, with God's help, he will be going to Nigeria, where he will preach for more than two million people each night. Who would have thought!

Vada Hagee would have thought. She humbly laid down her gift. She humbly forfeited her desire to preach the Word of God. She humbly made a request of her God. She had faith in a God who never fails.

She received the desire of her heart. She is oh, so happy as she listens to her son and her grandson Matthew preach the gospel of Jesus Christ as she eagerly awaits the Lord's angels to escort her to her heavenly home. God granted her a double portion.

2. Happy are those who mourn.

Who are those who mourn? Does that only describe those who grieve for the passing of a loved one? We know that our Savior gives peace that surpasses understanding to those who grieve.

No, mourning means more than expressing grief over death or other human tragedy. It refers to those who express sorrow for sin. In short, those who mourn are those who repent before the Lord with tears of brokenness.

Years ago in America, the altar was called "the mourner's bench." It was there, Sunday after Sunday, that those who heard the gospel of Jesus Christ would kneel and confess their sins. That wooden altar was stained from one end to the other with tears worth their weight in gold.

To repent you must take an honest look at yourself and admit that you did wrong. You must feel remorse for your actions and resolve never to repeat those actions again.

To repent before God is one of the most beautiful acts of submission you will ever commit. Rebbetzin Jungreis tells a story of a man

described in the Talmud by the name of Eleazar.

He was known as the most immoral man of all time. One day in the company of a prostitute, he experienced a moment of truth when she accused him of being beyond hope, saying he would surely spend eternity in hell.

He was shocked! If a woman of such ill repute accused him of immorality, then he must find help. He ran from her home and called on the hills and the mountains to plead on his behalf. But there was only silence.

He called on heaven and earth for mercy, and there was only silence. He turned to the stars and constellations, begging them to intercede on his behalf, but they too were silent.

Eleazar finally determined that the matter rested entirely with him. He was the only one who could plead his cause, and he repented before his Creator. Suddenly, a heavenly voice was heard, "Eleazar, repentance is accepted!"[2]

Rebbetzin Jungreis goes on to explain the symbolism of the story. The hills and the mountains were Eleazar's parents. He tried to shift the blame for his corruption and his immoral acts to his parents, but the heavenly courts would not accept his rationalization.

Next he blamed the heavens and the earth—which symbolized his environment, his school, and his friends, but that too was rejected. Finally, he turned to the stars and the constellations, which symbolized the bad fate that life had dealt him. His pleading was met with no response.

He finally found the courage and the strength of character to repent before the Lord as King David did: "Father, I have sinned before You and You alone! I must accept full responsibility for my actions!" Repentance was granted, and Eleazar was a happy man.[3]

For the man or woman who has sinned before God, no amount of good humor or tasteless jokes can substitute for the happiness we feel when we mourn for our wrong actions and repent before the Lord.

The Lord describes this happiness as being the result of experiencing God's favor and especially conditioned by the revelation of His matchless grace.[4] This makes for true happiness, my friends.

3. Happy are the patient.

Bishop Charles Blake of West Angeles Church of God in Christ tells the story of the mule that had served his master for years. The mule was now old, and one day the mule fell into a deep pit. The selfish,

evil master felt the mule was not worth the feed to sustain him or the bullet it would take to kill him, so the farmer decided to pile garbage over the mule, hoping he would soon be buried in an avalanche of trash and die.

The mule, refusing to yield to the fate of his evil master, shook off the garbage as it was piled upon his back. Then he would stomp on it, pack it down, and wait patiently.

Every day the evil taskmaster would pour more and more garbage on the mule. Every day the faithful mule would shake off the garbage, stomp on the debris, and wait patiently.

Finally the farmer told his neighbors to dump all their garbage in the pit, hoping this would be the demise of the stubborn mule. No matter the amount of garbage that was tossed his way, the mule was methodical in his response. He would shake off the garbage, stomp on it, pack it down, and wait patiently.

One day the farmer and his friends threw one too many loads of garbage! The persistent mule shook off the garbage, stomped on it, and used the debris for an escalator to the top. The trash became his door-way to freedom!

Life is not always fair. Many times we find ourselves in the deepest pits of despair, but as Corrie ten Boom so eloquently stated, "There is no pit so deep that Jesus is not deeper still."

Patience is a virtue, and to wait on God and His provision for our needs will never be without reward. Scripture describes happiness for the patient man or woman as joyous and spiritually prosperous. It brings life filled with joy and satisfaction in God's favor and salvation, regardless of the outward conditions.[5]

4. Happy are those who desire righteousness.

Righteousness is only attained through the blood of Jesus Christ. It's by His sacrifice that His white robe of purity is put over every sinner at the cross. We cannot earn our righteousness; it is freely given. Happy are those who "hunger" for righteousness.

Hungering to do those things that please God is something I believe He acknowledges from His throne in the heavenlies. When we are obedi-ent to His Word, it brings Him pleasure. In His Word He has promised that "gladness and joy will overtake" us if we obey His commandments (Isa. 51:11, NIV).

We may not always be successful in our efforts to please Him, but the sincerity with which we try must be pure.

There is a story about a Jewish family that was deported to the ghettos of Poland in World War II during the regime of Nazi Germany. Of all the lack they suffered, they missed the teaching of the Word of God the most. The father of the family, along with the community leaders, managed to continue teaching the Torah to their children. Desiring to be obedient to the commandment of the Lord to care for the widows and the orphans, the mother did her best to feed all those she could from the meager rations the family received.

Finally they were deported to the Bergen-Belsen concentration camp. Under the most brutalizing conditions, the father continued to teach the Torah to his children. As Rosh Hashanah approached, the rabbis of the camp gathered the people who hungered for the Word of God and amassed three hundred cigarettes, which carried an enormous amount of value in the black market. They did not buy food to celebrate the holiday; instead, they purchased a holiday prayer book and a shofar.

The sound of the shofar brought all that recognized the call to worship near the barbed-wire fence that bordered the camp. The Nazis came running. When they reached the young men who were blowing the ancient horn, they beat them without mercy. As they were being beaten, the men cried unto God: "Blessed art thou, our God, who has commanded us to listen to the sound of the shofar."[6]

These young men were not entirely successful at calling the righteous to prayer, but their desire to obey God's commandments was pure.

In the modern church, pastors are forced to cancel evening services because their members don't attend. Weekend services are added to their worship times, not to accommodate the masses but in hopes of drawing them to the house of God at a more convenient time. This is not hungering for righteousness.

The Scripture promises that those who hunger and thirst for righteousness will be spiritually prosperous in the state in which the born-again child of God enjoys His favor and His salvation. They shall be completely satisfied as they yearn to be right standing with God.[7]

> **HE SAYS...**
>
> **Ask yourself this question: "Am I truly happy?" If not, why not? The answer lies within yourself.**

5. Happy are those who show mercy.

To have mercy is to show kindness and to forgive. A young man secretly misappropriated several hundreds of dollars from the firm for which he was working. When the action was discovered, the young man was asked to report to the office of the CEO of the company.

As he neared the office of the senior member of the firm, the young man was heavy hearted. He was certain he was about to lose his job. He feared legal action against him. His whole world was collapsing around him, as he was about to receive what he justly deserved.

Once in the office, the CEO questioned the young man about the whole incident.

"Are you guilty of the accusation?" the senior officer asked in a very straightforward manner.

"Yes, sir, I am. I take full responsibility, and I am very sorry for my actions," the young man answered in as strong a voice as he could produce.

Suddenly the executive asked a question that totally shocked the repentant young man. "If I decide to keep you in your present position, do you think I can trust you in the future?"

Shocked, yet without hesitation, the young man lit up with hope and said, "Yes, sir, most definitely; I have learned my lesson!"

The executive continued to share more about his decision. "I have decided not to press charges, and you can keep your job in your present position."

He ended his meeting by telling the young man something that would change his life forever. "I think you ought to know, however, that you are the second man in this firm who succumbed to temptations and was shown leniency. I was the first. What you have done, I did. The mercy you are receiving, I received. It is only the grace of God that can keep us both."[8]

There is a mercy bank in all of our lives. The more you deposit mercy into your bank, the more you will receive when you need to make a withdrawal.

6. Happy are those with a pure heart.

The psalmist asks the question:

Who shall go up into the mountain of the Lord? Or who shall stand in His Holy Place? He who has clean hands and a pure heart, who has not lifted himself up to falsehood or to what is false, nor sworn deceitfully. He shall receive blessing from the Lord and righteousness from the God of his salvation.

—PSALM 24:3–5, AMP

There is nothing so pure as truth and honesty coming from a child. Oh, to keep that kind of purity through our lifetimes. Several years ago we had the privilege of having a "giant" of the evangelical world spend the night in our home. Oral Roberts was spending time with my husband, and we were privileged to have him stay in our guest room. What treasured memories I have of this humble servant of God in my kitchen, commenting on the wonderful aroma of the pot of beans I was cooking for supper. It was a great visit.

I remember, as if it were yesterday, that just before his departure, Dr. Roberts gathered my husband, the children who were home, and myself around him for a prayer of blessing. We assembled in a circle and held hands, bowed our heads, and closed our eyes. I was overflowing with anticipation.

He prayed as only Oral Roberts can pray—powerfully! When the prayer was finished, my eyes were filled with tears, and the peace of God filled our home. Without warning he turned to our daughter Christina, who was twelve at the time and standing to his right, and asked, "Sweetheart, did you feel the power of the Lord flow out of my hand into yours?"

Time stood still. What would she say? A myriad of thoughts filled my mind in a millisecond. *This is Oral Roberts, for heaven's sake! Maybe I should tell him the power arced and reached me! After all, I was moved to tears!* I thanked the Lord that our youngest daughter, Sandy, was not there, for God only knows what she would have said. *O Lord, please intervene!* I thought.

Christina looked at me, she looked at her father, and then she looked directly at Brother Roberts and answered, "No, sir."

I held my breath and dared not look at anyone but my daughter, who needed the reassurance from me that all was good. I smiled at her to signal all was well. But what about Brother Roberts?

Being the man of God he is, he bent down and put his arms around

our Tina and hugged her tightly, kissing her on the forehead. He told her that she was a brave girl to tell the truth and that he loved her for it.

She saw the Spirit of the Lord coming from him. I released the air from my lungs and repented of my fear. Christina was happy.

Happy are those who tell the truth and maintain purity in their hearts, for they shall see God!

7. Happy are the peacemakers.

We all want peace, but few of us are willing to do what is necessary to bring peace to the nations of the world or the world around us. When Christ was born, the angel declared to the frightened shepherds, "Glory to God in the highest, and on earth peace to people of good will." (See Luke 2:14.)

Yet the world has seen very few years of peace since Christ our Prince of Peace came. There is a story of a conversation between a dove and a sparrow. "Tell me the weight of a snowflake," a sparrow asked a wild dove.

"Nothing more than nothing," was the answer.

"In that case, I must tell you a marvelous story," the sparrow said. "I sat on the branch of a fir, close to its trunk, when it began to snow—not heavily, not in a raging blizzard—no, just like a dream, without a sound, and without any violence. Since I did not have anything better to do, I counted the snowflakes settling on the twigs and needles of my branch. Their number was exactly 3,742,952. When the 3,742,953rd flake dropped onto the branch, the branch broke off the tree."

Having said that, the sparrow flew away. The dove, since Noah's time an authority on the matter, thought about the story for a while and finally said to herself, "Perhaps only one person's voice is lacking for peace to come to the world."[9]

Perhaps only one voice is lacking for peace in your household. Perhaps only one voice is lacking for peace within your heart. Perhaps that voice is yours.

8. Happy are the persecuted for doing right.

The first four rules of happiness deal with what God wants to do in us. The next three reveal what comes out of us because of what God has done within us. The next two deal with how the world responds

to us. Cyprian, a third-century martyr, wrote this powerful letter to his friend Donatus.

> This is a cheerful world as I see it from my garden under the shadows of my vines. But if I were to ascend some high mountain and look out over the wide lands, you know very well what I should see: brigands on the highways, pirates on the sea, armies fighting, cities burning; in the amphitheaters, men murdered to please applauding crowds; selfishness and cruelty and misery and despair under all roofs. It is a bad world, Donatus, an incredibly bad world. But I have discovered in the midst of it a quiet and holy people who have learned a great secret. They are despised and persecuted, but they care not. They are master of their souls. They have overcome the world. These people, Donatus, are the Christians—and I am one of them.[10]

Cyprian lived in a day when being persecuted for doing right was almost an art form! Yet today, good people are still being persecuted for doing right—sometimes even in a marriage relationship. This beatitude tells us that "happy are the persecuted for doing right." Our reward, our happiness for doing right, does not come from external circumstances—it comes from within. It is because of what God has done within us that we can maintain our joy even when others respond to us with some form of persecution.

> These things I have spoken to you, that My joy may remain in you, and that your joy may be full.
>
> —JOHN 15:11

9. Happy are the criticized.

The Lord is very clear about how we should respond to those who speak ill of us:

> But I tell you, Love your enemies and pray for those who persecute you, to show that you are the children of your Father Who is in heaven; for He makes His sun rise on the wicked and on the good, and makes the rain fall upon the upright and the wrongdoers [alike].
>
> —MATTHEW 5:44–45, AMP

We are to bless those who curse us.

What do we do when criticisms are true?

My husband describes the difference between *constructive criticism* and *destructive criticism* very clearly. Constructive criticism takes place when you criticize an individual, but when another person criticizes you, then that is destructive criticism.

Jamie Buckingham was a good friend of ours. His honesty and candor were so refreshing you could listen to him for hours. One day my husband and I were in his home visiting with him and his wife, Jackie, a sweet and precious partner to his dynamic ministry.

One of the many books Jamie wrote was *Daughter of Destiny*, a biographical account of the life of Kathryn Kuhlman. After listening to several stories about her ministry, I asked Jamie if he knew why she always wore her long signature dress with the flowing sleeves.

> **HE SAYS . . .**
>
> **Your attitude is never content until it's expressed. It determines your success or your failure.**

He told me that one day she received a letter from a gentleman who was very gracious and kind about his comments regarding her television program. However, he did have one criticism. He told her he was distracted by her constant pulling at her dress to maintain it below her knees. He suggested she wear a long dress.

Kathryn, who was very sensitive to criticism, read the letter and acknowledged that he was right. She wore long dresses from that day forward.

Jamie later wrote an article about her response:

> A lesser person would have responded with anger, or passed it off as just another senseless remark. But she was not that sort of lesser person. She heard. She coped. She let it help her toward her goal of communicating. All of which was possible because there was no root of bitterness to give a bad taste to everything that came into her life, which presented another viewpoint.[11]

Norman Vincent Peale once said, "The trouble with most of us is that we would rather be ruined by praise than saved by criticism."[12]

Our attitude is everything. A man who has a healthy attitude about himself will do exactly what the Bible says. He will bless his enemies when they attack him and will listen to his conscience and discern

when he should change his path. As a result, this man will experience the kingdom of heaven.

The man who blesses his enemies and discerns when he must change will be a person who is happy with himself and happy with the world around him. Ultimately he will reflect the God who lives within him.

HINTS FOR HIM

True laughter is an outward expression of the joy that lies within. Strive for happiness in your life.

HINT: You can't become a comedian when you aren't one. So don't try.

HINT: Don't use your wife as the brunt of your jokes. It won't honor her, and God will not honor you!

HINT: Learn to laugh at yourself. Sometimes you are the greatest source of humor you will find.

HINT: Allow laughter to diffuse anger.

Pastor Hagee and I are blessed with a wonderful church family. Over the course of thirty-eight years of pastoring, we can honestly say that many people have blessed us...some by staying in our church and some by leaving. If you are a pastor or a pastor's wife, you know exactly what I'm talking about.

One day a former church member said something very cruel about our congregation. They were making it known that the reason they left our church was due to its ethnic makeup. My husband became incensed and was determined to "set the record straight" with this wayward soul. He went into his study and began to respond to the insulting remarks in the form of a letter.

There was a challenge, however. There is always a challenge to almost every situation in the ministry. I believe the Lord tosses them in to make sure we stay close to Him and His instruction.

The challenge: the author of the offensive remarks happened to be related to very loyal and precious church members. I reminded my husband of this very important fact, but no matter, his "hot button" had been pressed and there was no turning back. I followed him into the study and began to give him all the reasons why this letter of rebuke should not be written—all to no avail.

"John, the Word says to forgive as you have been forgiven!" I said as I quickly tried to remember scriptures to support my stand.

"I have forgiven them! But I have not forgotten what they said about the righteous!" he irritatingly responded.

"Remember that you are to bless your enemies!" I shouted.

"They don't deserve a blessing!" he shouted back, continuing to type as fast as his fingers could hit the keyboard—and hitting the keyboard they were.

I began to read over his shoulder and hyperventilate at the same time. I am the diplomat of the marriage. Pastor is known as the "tell-it-like-it-is" pastor, and I am known as the "what-he-really-meant-to-say-was…" pastor's wife.

I knew that this letter could not be sent; it would hurt too many people. But my husband was determined. He is a true shepherd to the sheep God has entrusted us with, and in his eyes, a great transgression has been committed when anyone hurts his church members.

The more I read the rebuke, the more I railed, "No! You can't say that!"

"Watch me!" was his heated response.

"You must show mercy!" I pleaded.

"They have been shown mercy; God would have given them leprosy!" he firmly retorted without taking his concentration from the keyboard.

I could see I wasn't getting through to him, and I became desperate. Suddenly, as if someone else was in control of my body, I did something I had never done before. I walked from behind him and stood by his computer keyboard as I pounded on the keyboard with all ten fingers as fast and as hard as I could.

The computer screen abruptly began to blink and groan as icons began appearing everywhere. Question marks, pound signs, asterisks, and exclamation marks took the place of the words of chastisement and reprimand. It was a surreal, out-of-body experience.

My husband tried to retrieve his document of hot coals, but he could not. He stared at the screen as if in a stupor and then looked over at me. The look he gave me was not a good one. I stared at him, and then my glazed gaze went back to the computer screen filled with electronic gibberish.

Silence filled the room as if a vacuum had sucked all the sound waves out of the air. I could not believe what I had done.

Then, what seemed to be eternal quiet was suddenly replaced by the two words that came from my husband's mouth. "You dimwit!" he shouted.

As if someone had snapped his fingers in front of my face, I was awakened from my trance as I heard his reaction to my exploit. I took my eyes from the screen, put my hands on my hips, and looked back at him with a "not-so-good look" as well. When you get a German and a Mexican mad at the same time, the battle lines are drawn and sparks can really fly.

"I am not a dimwit!" I indignantly responded.

The stare-down was on. Neither one of us would retreat from our glares. Then suddenly, as unexpectedly as I had pounded on the keyboard, he began to laugh hysterically. I impulsively joined in. Before long we were both laughing so hard that tears were running down our faces, and we could hardly catch our breath.

I bent down and kissed his forehead as he stood to hug me. Once we stopped laughing and regained our composure, we agreed in prayer that the person making the remarks would be silenced by the Lord and that our congregation would be spared from hearing the evil comments that were meant for harm.

All was satisfied. The Lord had been called to intervene. Our church family would be covered by His protection. My husband released his frustrations on the keyboard of the computer. My diplomatic instincts were satisfied, and the letter of rebuke was lost in electronic eternity.

If we took the time to analyze the moments of anger and frustration toward our spouse, we would most likely find our annoyance was motivated by insignificant incidences that were overreacted to because of stress, anxiety, or something totally unrelated to our husband or wife. We must not leave the door open for the enemy to take our peace or our marriages through anger.

> "Be angry, and do not sin": do not let the sun down on your wrath, nor give place to the devil.
> —EPHESIANS 4:26–27

Allow laughter to defuse anger.

HINT: Be patient. Be patient in marriage; it will help you laugh with your wife when life isn't fair. Be patient with this world; it will give you a longer life.

My husband, by his own confession, is not a very patient man. I have been good for him. Time for me is a gift. I cherish it. I don't waste it, but I don't hurry through it, either. Two o'clock in the afternoon today will soon be two o'clock in the afternoon tomorrow; I simply enjoy the journey. My husband has had to endure my attitude about time and learn about patience.

One Sunday after church we took a plane to Houston to attend the wedding of the son of very dear friends of ours. It was a beautiful Jewish ceremony, and we were now waiting to enter the lavish reception. My husband was tired and couldn't understand why the reception was not underway an hour after the ceremony.

Some friends of ours were patiently waiting with us as my husband began to fidget. He kept looking at his watch and asking me why the doors to the reception room were not open. After I explained to him that it was not my wedding, he went to the men's room; he said he needed to kill time.

Concerned we would not be having a very pleasant evening, I went to those who were serving refreshments and asked them when they thought the reception would officially begin.

They gave me their *guesstimation*—one hour! I thought, *This is it. We are soon heading to the hotel for room service and an early night*. Our friend heard the answer and was amused to see how my husband would respond.

He came out of the men's room and asked if I had an update. "Yes," was my cautious answer.

"Well?" he asked.

"Soon." I responded.

"How soon?" he asked with a little more emphasis, yet cautious not to raise his voice among friends.

Our friends were curiously watching our exchange. "Very soon," I told him, aware that I was skating on thin ice.

Losing what was left of his frail patience, he firmly called my name, "Diana! How long before the reception begins?"

Our friend came to my rescue. "Well, Reverend Hagee, let me put it this way; in terms of eternity...not long."

With that we all burst out laughing and had a wonderful evening. Laughter can change everything. "How long must I be happy?" you might ask. In terms of eternity—forever.

FROM DR. ANNE

In the 1930s and 1940s there was a radio show called *Fibber Magee and Molly*. One line from Molly that worked its way into every episode was, "T'aint funny, Magee!" It came after Fibber laughed at something she had taken quite seriously. She had failed to share his humor.

Marriage can be a lot of fun—if you don't take it too seriously. Life is so much easier to manage when we see how ridiculous many problems in our lives really are. Humor can diffuse tension. When you are able to identify quickly and consistently an interaction that leads to a recurring argument between you and your spouse, you can prevent family disruption. You can even choose to use this knowledge to establish an inside joke, between you and your husband, that can alleviate the tension when this issue rears its head again. Many couples who have been married ten-plus years have one-liners that prompt a squeeze of the hand and a knowing smile.

Humor requires that two people see the same thing as *funny*. A one-sided joke is insensitive, cruel, and rude. There is a line between humor and humiliation that, if not sensitively recognized, can destroy confidence and trust. A compassionate spouse learns that line quickly and generalizes the information and skills to other situations. Having fun and sharing humorous experiences and thoughts can be like a mini-vacation offering relief to the seriousness of everyday life. Knowing the appropriate time, place, and subject requires wisdom and maturity. After a quarrel, a wife said to her husband, "You know, I was a fool when I married you."

The husband replied, "Yes, dear, but I was in love and didn't notice it."

Let God show you how your spouse can enrich your life, not reflect it. Your spouse is not a reflective image of yourself. You are a reflection of God, and so is he. Knowing when to make light of

your differences is the way to grow. We are able to be different and still be safe. We don't have to feel abandoned and alone because we have differences.

Don't make light of marriage intimacy. Be sensitive to subjects your husband considers uncompromisingly serious. Be of one mind and one accord. A marriage without a sense of humor is like a pebble in your shoe that feels like a boulder the longer you walk on it. Laughter removes the pebble.

There isn't a lot that happens in life that doesn't have a light side. Even the serious things don't have to have serious lasting effects. Laughter's importance can be observed in tense situations. It can be used to defuse potentially explosive situations. Remembering is good. Learning is good. Not having to have scars from wounds is better. Properly applied, humor can deflate a tense argument. It gives you a different perspective.

Lighten up, and let your family breathe and develop a perspective that encourages humor. Tomorrow's memories are being made today. Let them be good ones. Smile quickly, and laugh a lot!

CLOSING PRAYERS

We are in this world, not of it. We are not rewarded for being able to live with one foot in the world and the other in the church. No, we are rewarded for being and doing right despite the outward conditions and pressures we face. This kind of happiness can only come directly from the throne of the living God.

PRAYER OF REPENTANCE

Father, I have needed to laugh for a long time. I have blamed my lack of joy on my husband. Forgive me. I have not looked inward. I must find my joy in You and within Your Word. I have also been entirely too serious in my dealings with my husband. I have refused to be derailed from my anger. My husband has tried to make peace with me by joking and letting me see how sorry he is for my upset. I have refused to let it go and "drop it," and I have carried the disagreement beyond the stopping place. I will be aware of this in the future and will be willing to sacrifice my need to be angry. Forgive

me, Lord Jesus, for presenting a hostile atmosphere in my home. I have allowed fear and anger to take the place of Your joy and peace in my home. I repent and will make changes according to Your Word. Amen.

PRAYER OF NEW BEGINNINGS

Thank You, Lord, for my marriage, which brings me so much pleasure. You have told us that a merry heart does us good like a medicine. Thank You for taking our burdens and worries so we can see the lighter side of our lives. Thank You for laughter and joy. Your joy is truly my strength. I accept for my own life the promise that You gave to Job, promising to fill my mouth with laughter and my lips with joyful shouting. I will pass that blessing on to my family.

You have taken me from the bondage of negative issues and given me peace and resolution. I will learn to be happy in all things, for You are the source of my joy and my strength. With Your help, I can do anything. I love You, Jesus. Amen.

Want Number Two:
ROMANCE

Set me as a seal upon your heart, as a seal upon your
arm; for love is as strong as death.... Many waters
cannot quench love, nor can the floods drown it.
—SONG OF SOLOMON 8:6–7

EVERY WEEK THE public is bombarded with magazines about the "beautiful people." You know the magazines—if you don't subscribe to them, you catch a glimpse of the covers as you wait to check out at the grocery counter. They contain pictures of half of the world's beautiful people dating the other half of the world's beautiful people. Each person is usually posed with someone of the opposite sex, holding hands or touching in one manner or another. If you read the cover stories, each will probably mention somewhere in the caption that this couple is "romantically involved."

But read a subsequent issue of the same magazine, and you will probably notice that something strange has happened: the two persons you saw linking arms in January are no longer linking arms in March. The caption informs you that January's couple has gone their separate ways, but March has brought a new "romantic interest." Buy next month's issue, and see what happens!

Is it *romance* or *infatuation*? Columnist Ann Landers made a very clear distinction between infatuation and romantic love: "Infatuation is instant desire—one set of glands calling to another. Love is friendship that has caught fire. It takes root and grows, one day at a time."[1]

Infatuation is marked by a feeling of insecurity. You are excited and eager, but not genuinely happy. There are nagging doubts, unanswered questions, little bits and pieces about your beloved that you would just as soon not examine too closely. It might spoil the dream.

Love is quiet understanding and the mature acceptance of imperfection. It is real. It gives you strength and grows beyond you—to bolster your beloved. You are warmed by his presence, even when he is away. Miles do not separate you. You want him nearer. But near or far, you know he is yours, and you can wait.

Infatuation says, "We must get married right away. I can't risk losing him."

Love says, "Be patient. Don't panic. Plan your future with confidence."

Infatuation has an element of sexual excitement. If you are honest, you will admit it is difficult to be in one another's company unless you are sure it will end in intimacy.

Love is the maturation of friendship. You must be friends before you can be lovers.

Infatuation lacks confidence. When he's away, you wonder if he's cheating. Sometimes you even check.

Love means trust. You are calm, secure, and unthreatened. He feels that trust, and it makes him even more trustworthy.

Infatuation might lead you to do things you'll regret later, but love never will. Love is an upper. To love makes you look up. It makes you think up. It makes you a better person than you were before. The woman who feels that way knows true love.

SEVEN WAYS TO ROMANCE YOUR HUSBAND

I must be honest. I purposefully did not read my husband's section of this book so I would not be influenced by its content. However, he and I together sat in our bedroom and created the following seven romantic things a man and a woman can do for one another to generate romance in their marriage.

There is a misconception that men want *only* sex and women want *only* romance. How untrue. This misinformation has contributed to more marriage problems than any of us care to acknowledge.

But before we take a look at the seven ways to romance your husband, please understand that romance is not sex. In all the research I

HE SAYS...

For some women, being romantic means buying her flowers....Whatever spells *romance* **for your wife, all women respond to romance and want more of it.**

did for this book, secular and Christian alike, the common thread was a clear distinction between *romantic love* and *sexual intimacy*.

Romance is so much more. Romance lasts. Romance generates a love so deep that if sex were not possible for whatever reason, love would still grow. Romantic affection creates the necessary environment for a good marriage, and sex is one of the main events. Romance is precious.

Consider these seven ways to romance *your* husband.

1. Tell him you love him.

> Tell me, O you whom my soul loves...
> —SONG OF SOLOMON 1:7, AMP

The old "I told you I loved you when I married you, and if I ever change my mind, I'll tell you" line is not applicable here. A man wants to hear these three little words come from your mouth and your heart often.

A phone call during the day with a simple "I love you" is great. Ladies, don't overdo—remember, quality vs. quantity; you don't want to smother the man!

Love notes in his briefcase, travel bag, or clothes drawer does wonders to confirm your love for him. Sign your note with a kiss, wearing his favorite color lipstick, and spray your perfume on it! An e-mail with a scripture of blessing over your husband, along with a P.S. that says "I love you," will bring a smile to his heart.

Men want to know they are loved.

2. Praise him.

> O my love, how beautiful you are! There is no flaw in you!
> —SONG OF SOLOMON 4:7, AMP

Encouragement is so important. To tell your husband you are proud of him does more for him than you know. A wife's support of her husband

contributes more to his success than any other factor. As the Lord encourages His own, so should a wife encourage her husband and make him aware that she appreciates all he does for her and their family.

We live in an award-conscious society. Why not begin a tradition in your family and award your husband for the good things he has done? Why not ask your children to award their father on special occasions with the "Best Father" trophy, and let them explain why he has earned this prestigious award, before time takes its toll on all of us!

A man stopped at a flower shop to order some flowers to be wired to his mother, who lived two hundred miles away. As he got out of his car, he noticed a young girl sitting outside the flower shop crying. Concerned, he asked her what was wrong. She replied, "I wanted to buy a red rose for my mother, but I only have a dollar, and a rose costs three dollars."

The man, warmed by her desire to bless her mother, said, "Come with me. I'll buy you a rose." The little girl gratefully smiled. The man bought the single rose for the girl and ordered the flowers for his own mother.

As they were leaving the shop, he offered the young girl a ride home. Excited, she responded, "Yes, please! You can take me to my mother!" She directed him to the local cemetery where she lovingly placed the rose on her mother's freshly dug grave.

The man returned to the flower shop, canceled the order, picked up a bouquet of a dozen red roses, and drove the two hundred miles to his mother's home where he presented the flowers in person.[2]

Men want to know they are important; don't take them for granted.

3. Prepare a special meal for him.

> Sustain me with raisins, refresh me with apples, for I am sick with love.
>
> —SONG OF SOLOMON 2:5, AMP

Yes, I really did write that. No, I wasn't forced. When a man offers to take his wife out to dinner, it is a very, very nice gesture that shows she is greatly appreciated. She doesn't have to spend hours in the kitchen cooking and cleaning. She is blessed and feels special.

When she prepares a special meal for her husband, he is aware of the time she put forth in creating it. She has let him know he is important

enough to her that she is willing to sacrifice her time and effort to make this loving gesture.

A woman who hated to cook told her homemaking girlfriend that the quickest way to a man's heart was not his stomach; it was his chest![3] If you don't like to cook, it is even more of a romantic signal to prepare a special meal for him because he knows you are going out of your way to please him.

I love to cook, so I must make this kind of romance a little unique. When my husband comes home in the evening, he walks into the kitchen, gives me a hug and a kiss, and asks how my day went. Then he goes into his study and drops off his briefcase, which is filled with research for Sunday's sermon or the latest book he is writing. From there he goes into our bedroom and watches the evening news until dinner is ready.

If, when he comes through the door, I tell him that he can't go into our bedroom because I have something special planned, he immediately smiles and usually says, "Aw," no matter how tough the day has been. The mood has been set.

When I call him to dinner, he walks into our bedroom with anticipation and sees a small table set with linen and china in front of the fireplace. There are candles on the table and a single red rose in a crystal vase. He loves red. The only light in the room comes from the lit candles and the fire. I then serve a five-course dinner.

Men like to be pampered.

4. Give him gifts.

> The mandrakes give forth fragrance, and over our doors are all manner of choice fruits, new and old, which I have laid up for you, O my beloved!
> —SONG OF SOLOMON 7:13, AMP

How do you feel when your husband buys a present for you? You feel like a queen with all the wealth of the world. Give gifts to your husband, too. The gift doesn't have to be expensive. The fact that you thought of it with him in mind will be more than sufficient.

I give my husband ties. He loves bold, red ties. Sometimes I frame a special picture of the two of us, or one of him with the children or

grandbabies. Think of what would especially bless your husband, *and do it*.

Men love presents.

5. Surprise him.

> Arise, my darling, my beautiful one, and come with me.
> —SONG OF SOLOMON 2:10, NIV

This could be dangerous. The biggest surprise I ever gave my husband was given one Sunday evening during church services twenty-four years ago.

I had something very important to tell him, and he was busy preparing for the evening service and did not want me to bother him. I kept trying to interrupt him in my usual persistent manner, and he kept putting me off: "Just another minute." Time came for service, and he looked up and asked what I needed. I told him it could wait for church to be over.

Well, by now you probably know me—I couldn't stand it, so I wrote a note, folded it in two, and asked an usher to take the note to my husband on the platform during the music portion of our service. John took the piece of paper and opened it. His eyes opened wide, and he made the thumbs-up sign and flashed a big smile my way. What did the note say? It was my announcement to him that we were going to have a baby!

No, you don't have to get pregnant to surprise your husband! There are so many ways to create romance with surprises. My sister surprises her husband with bed-and-breakfast weekends. What about a picnic?

Date nights make for great surprises! Occasionally I call my husband and ask him if he would like to have an exciting date for the evening. I make arrangements for dinner and a movie. (It's always nice to be treated, so make sure the evening is paid for.)

Sometimes I put his favorite chocolate on his pillow so he can find it when he prepares for bed. The anticipation that surprises create is so essential for romance. Men love surprises.

6. The power of your touch

> Let him kiss me with the kisses of his mouth!... For your love is better than wine!
> —SONG OF SOLOMON 1:2, AMP

One of my friends dated a man who never showed her affection when they were out together. I once asked her about it, and she said he did not like to display a "public show of affection." I remember thinking to myself, *I don't believe him.* They eventually broke up, and she married a wonderful young man who believes in holding hands and hugging. They are very happy.

A couple of years later, I saw her former boyfriend with his new girlfriend at a restaurant. I smiled as I saw him affectionately hold the hand of the woman he loved. True romantic love needs an affectionate touch to survive.

> **HE SAYS...**
>
> **When a wife says "Come and hold me" to her husband, he rubs his hands together as his testosterone meter explodes and responds, "All right..." He is ready for raw sex. She simply wants affection.**

It is very important to show affection to your husband every opportunity you get. Take his hand when you are walking together, or pat his shoulder as you pass by him. Kiss him often. Even if it hasn't been part of your past behavior, try beginning anew by giving him what it is you want in return.

One of the most beautiful pictures of romance I have ever seen is one I witness every Sunday morning at Cornerstone Church. On the front row center of the second section sit a wonderful man and his precious wife. They are in their late eighties. They sit so close to each other you couldn't get a sheet of paper between them. Every Sunday they hold each other's hand. These two wrinkled and gnarled hands are clasped tightly, and the other two hands are raised in praise and worship to the Lord.

What a statement they make! The message of romance they send every Sunday is a memorial to the love they have for each other and the love they have for God.

Men love hugs and kisses.

7. Loyalty

I am my beloved's...and my beloved is mine!
—SONG OF SOLOMON 6:3, AMP

I was a little taken by surprise when my husband told me that one of the romantic things about our relationship to him was my loyalty. He said that as a man, there is nothing so special as to know that the woman you love can be trusted and that she will never bring you heartache.

Proverbs 31 describes the perfect woman as being one in whom "her husband safely trusts" (v. 11). Trust is the fabric of every human connection. Without trust there can be no confidence, emotional stability, or hope for the future. Trust is the cornerstone of your marriage relationship.

Remember the sacred vows you made. They are your word and your bond. To know that my Lord made a vow to me at the cross when I repented before Him and received Him as my Savior, and that vow will never be broken, gives me a peace and a comfort that cannot be duplicated.

> **HE SAYS...**
> **May I ask you this question? Is your love loyal?**

Because of the faith I have in a God who never fails, I want to please Him even more. I want Him to know that I will never turn away and serve another god. I may disappoint Him from time to time, but I am His and will never abandon my faith in Him.

HINTS FOR HIM

This is simple. Every "romance rule" I gave to women in this chapter, I equally give to the husband as a "ditto romance rule" for keeping his marriage a fertile ground for romance. To me the most romantic relationships I have ever seen are not the young newlyweds who hopelessly cling to each other, or the new parents who hold the product of their love in their arms. No, the most romantic relationships are between couples who have been married thirty, forty, fifty, sixty years—they know the secret to true romance.

FROM DR. ANNE

An excellent marriage takes effort. You probably liked your husband the first time you met him. You began to enjoy spending time together. You began to understand each other's family history. Over the years, you shared experiences and developed your own history together. Affection grew with the passage of time.

Sometimes we let those romantic feelings grow cool over time. Are you still giving your time to shared experiences and continuing to develop the history that stimulates affection and appreciation?

Our understanding of the relationship God has with His children is a direct correlation to our understanding of the marriage relationship. Without that spiritual understanding, we have absolutely no concept of the sacrifice that is necessary to allow marriage to meet the needs of the two individuals involved and to meet the standards set by God Almighty. In the most challenging times of our lives, God cares for us, comforts us, and reveals His love to us.

In the same way, a woman wants, and needs, to feel the care and comfort of her husband's life. She wants to feel "special" to him. She holds a place in the life of her husband that can't be met by anyone or anything except her. When she walks into the room he lights up. He values her personality. He likes the way she laughs, the way she smiles, the way she presents herself. He understands her when no one else seems to; he forgives her imperfections.

How fabulous to not have to be perfect to be loved! How wonderful to know that when your husband places a gentle hand over yours that you are being reassured of your value.

Wives, don't ever forget that you get what you give. You will be accepted, appreciated, and affectionately acknowledged as you are genuinely willing to accept, appreciate, and acknowledge your husband. Maturity, history, and sharing should increase the love and affection that you have for your husband and that he has for you. Couples who are able to reflect the attributes of trustworthiness and commitment are more able to abandon themselves to a sensual marriage experience. First Corinthians 13:7 reminds us that love is to show no end of its trust.

I believe that we get what we give. I believe in the law of reciprocity as it pertains to relationships. It is no coincidence that mathematics—the language of science—encodes logic into a device called an *equation*, which requires its elements to be equivalent on opposite sides of the argument.

Sir Isaac Newton captured the essence of natural balance when he codified the law of physics, which states that every action precipitates an equal and opposite reaction. Cause and effect: for every up there is a down; you get what you give eventually.

If you want your husband to be "Mr. Right," then you must first see that you are "Mrs. Right." We must each take responsibility for ourselves as well as for the relationship.

Our God loved us when we were yet unlovable, but don't be so foolish as to expect that from your husband. God is God; human beings are human beings, although we are striving to be more God-like. My prayer for you is that God will develop in you the softness and sweetness that He created you to have. May your husband receive the loving affection that you show to him and return it in an overflowing proportion.

Allow the qualities you want in your husband to be found in your own life.

CLOSING PRAYERS

To tell your husband often that you love him—*essential*. To praise him for his accomplishments—*uplifting*. When you prepare a candlelight dinner for him—*romantic*. Surprising him with a special evening—*intimate*. To leave loving notes for him to find—*heartwarming*. Giving him hugs and kisses—*affectionate*. And being loyal to him *always—priceless*.

PRAYER OF REPENTANCE

Lord, I have failed to show my husband the spontaneous affection and appreciation that he really needs. I am sometimes too caught up in my own world of job, children, church, and personal desires, and I have nothing left for my husband. I have been wrong. I have failed to tell him that I love him. I have not tried to uplift him with praise, but I am quick to criticize. I am so busy that I seldom show him I care by preparing a special meal or giving him a small gift as a token of my love for him. I can't remember the last time I surprised him. He needs my romantic attention, and I have failed to give it. I don't provide loving pats or kisses because I fear rejection or am too preoccupied with my own life. I have been disloyal to him, and I need Your forgiveness—and his—to begin anew in my marriage. Forgive me, Lord, for breaking my vows to You and to my husband. I may be loyal to him, but I don't give him much evidence of that loyalty in my actions. I need to confirm my loyalty to him

and let him know that he is the only man I want or need. I desire a new marriage, Lord, one that will fulfill both my husband's and my needs and desires. I have not given of myself, yet I have demanded to receive. I ask for Your forgiveness and for Your strength to try again and to succeed. Amen.

PRAYER OF NEW BEGINNINGS

Lord, I truly want to begin over. I want to be romantically attracted to my husband as I was when our relationship was fresh and exciting. I want him to be attracted to me in the same way. I pray that I will learn to be aware of how I respond to his needs and desires and that I can communicate mine to him. I ask for You to help me to develop an immediate response of love and respect instead of fear and rejection. I will give to my husband as You have given to me. You have been generous with Your grace and mercy toward me and have loved me when I have been unlovable. Thank You, Father. Please help me make my marriage a thing of love, romance, and loyalty. I want us to be one of those couples who hold hands and give hugs and kisses to each other when we are old and gray. I want to keep my sacred covenant to You and to my husband. I want to make him happy that he is married to me. I need Your help, Lord, and I know I will receive it, for You are faithful. I love You. Amen.

ten

Want Number One:
GODLY MAN

> For the grace of God that brings salvation has appeared
> to all men. It teaches us to say "No" to ungodliness
> and worldly passions, and to live self-controlled,
> upright and godly lives in this present age, while we
> wait for the blessed hope—the glorious appearing
> of our great God and Savior, Jesus Christ, who gave
> himself for us to redeem us from all wickedness and
> to purify for himself a people that are his very own,
> eager to do what is good.
>
> —TITUS 2:11–14, NIV

S O YOU WANT a godly man? Perhaps the first question should be,
"Do you know how to recognize a godly man?" In essence, the
characteristics that the women in our church have listed as their
ten "wants" in a man are the characteristics of a godly man. We have
discussed those characteristics in this book.

THE BIBLE'S *GODLY* MEN

When I read these top ten *wants,* from the least to the most desired, I
immediately began to think of some of the heroes of the Bible, the men
in Scripture whom we identify as truly godly men. Have you ever wondered what it might be like to be married to one of them?

Noah

Think of Noah...the Scriptures say he was a "just and righteous
man, blameless in his [evil] generation; Noah walked [in habitual fel-
lowship] with God" (Gen. 6:9, AMP). God knew Noah to be a godly
man. Now, go into the theater of the mind for a moment with me, and
imagine what it would be like to be married to Noah.

He comes home one afternoon with architectural plans in his hands

and tells you he has had a visitation from the Lord Himself. The great I AM has commanded him to do something he has never done before—with no budget and no true understanding of its purpose. Furthermore, God is going to destroy the earth with water from the skies—a phenomenon not witnessed by any human being. So, he quits his job and begins his assignment.

Then he tells you that after his building project is completed, you and he and the children will take a long cruise. However, he doesn't know exactly *where* or for *how long*. And there is one more catch—your part! You must help him gather and care for those who will travel with your family, something about "two by two." You will have a thankless job, but he feels very strongly that he should obey the wishes of the Lord, for Jehovah God has promised to provide.

Would you willingly work by his side?

Abraham

Abraham was commanded by God to leave a very comfortable home and to depart from his family and his country. God loves Abraham so much that He promises Abraham to give him a seven-clause covenant. (See Genesis 17:1–8.)

1. I will make you a great nation.
2. I will bless you.
3. I will make your name great.
4. You shall be a blessing.
5. I will bless those who bless you.
6. I will curse those who curse you.
7. In you, all the families of the earth shall be blessed.

This man has surely found favor with the Lord. What kind of a husband would he make?

Let's examine Abraham a bit further. He comes to you and recounts his visit with God, and he tells you that he doesn't really know where the two of you will be going. However, you must leave the dream house you just built and travel in a caravan. Finally, he persuades you to leave your lavish lifestyle and all that is important to you. He also assures you that Yahweh has promised to bless him with descendents *that will be too many to count.*

Oh, and it gets better, sweetheart! While on your trip to "God only knows where," Abraham convinces you to act *as his sister* for *his* protection. This hurts your feelings, and you feel rejected. Even though this request from Abraham will put *you* in eminent danger, you think about it a bit. Still hurt, you finally agree.

Time passes, and the journey, which has been tough, finds you older now. You have given this man some of the best years of your life. You have a weak moment (all women are allowed their fair measure of weak moments). You determine that at your present age, you probably won't produce an heir for your husband. Therefore, you suggest—only once, I might add—that he go into your handmaiden and produce a child with her. Without hesitation he agrees, *a little too quickly, if you ask me*. To add insult to injury, your favorite handmaiden, now heavy with your husband's child, is flaunting her favored status.

Would you leave your home and go with this man?

Moses

Moses was a man so loved of God that God chose him to lead His people, the apple of His eye, out of bondage. Moses is the man whom God trusted with His law. What would it be like married to Moses? Moses is gone days at a time on spiritual mountain retreats without you. When he is home, he is overwhelmed with his task of leading millions of people *somewhere*, to arrive *sometime*. It seems to you that you are hopelessly stuck in the desert. Moses spends all his daylight hours—and well into the night—in counseling sessions trying to solve the chosen people's problems.

He brings their problems home with him every night. You become so upset that you call your father to take Moses to lunch so he can advise him on how to lessen his workload. The marriage is stressed. When will it end—this endless desert wandering with these complaining travel companions who demand all of your husband's time?

Would you support this man and his ministry?

David

David was a man after God's own heart, a leader among men, a great warrior—and an adulterer and a murderer and a failure as a father. What would it have been like to be married to him?

All these men have something in common. *They were flawed individuals chosen by a flawless God to do His will.* In order to accomplish their purposes, these men had to have a very supportive and godly woman by their side.

Today, we too are like these men—we are all flawed creatures. But there is a remarkable difference: the blood of a faultless Lamb covers us. These men lived under the Law; we live under the grace and mercy of our Savior Jesus Christ. It is His mercy that keeps us from getting what we deserve and His grace that gives us what we do not deserve.

CAN MY HUSBAND BECOME A GODLY MAN?

The question remains. What is a godly man, and how can you help your husband to become one?

A godly man is a reflection of his Savior. He must have the mind of God. He must see what God sees. He must have the heart of God. He must be the hand of God.

Booker T. Washington, in his autobiography *Up From Slavery,* told of a beautiful incident demonstrating his older brother's love. He said that the shirts worn on his plantation by the slaves were made of a tough, bristly, crude flax fiber. As a young boy, the garment was so abrasive to his tender, sensitive skin that it caused him a great deal of pain and discomfort. His older brother, moved by his brother's suffering, would wear Booker's new shirts until they were broken in and smoother to the touch. He would allow his own skin to become raw with irritation. Booker said it was one of the most profound acts of kindness he ever experienced.[1]

We do not know the older brother's name, but we can recognize the spirit that motivated him as Christ's. You may not remember a godly man's name, but you will never forget the name of the God he serves.

Another example of a godly man comes from the story of a godly Salvation Army missionary. Tears glistened in the eyes of the Salvation Army officer as he looked at the three men before him. Dr. Shaw was a medical missionary who had just arrived in India, where he had

been assigned to a leper colony. Before him he saw three men who had iron clasps around their hands and feet, which were cutting into their infected, diseased flesh. Led by compassion, the doctor asked the guard to release the men. The guards protested, telling the doctor that they were not only lepers, but criminals as well.

"I'll be responsible," the doctor said. "They are suffering enough already." He asked for the keys, then knelt and tenderly removed the shackles and treated their open sores.

About two weeks later the doctor had second thoughts about freeing the criminals. It was necessary for him to make an overnight trip—and he had to leave his wife and child alone. His wife insisted that she was not afraid, for God would be with them. With that assurance, the doctor left on his journey.

The next morning the doctor's wife went to the door of her home to find the three men lying on her front steps. One of the men explained to the startled woman, "We know the doctor go. We stay here all night so no harm come to you."[2] These dangerous men responded to the act of love so mercifully given by the kind doctor.

THE MIND OF HIS FATHER

A godly man has the mind of his Father when he sees the hurting and those bound by the ravages of sin. He thinks as God thinks, in terms of love and compassion for the loveless.

One father always ended grace over the family meal with these words: "Come, Lord Jesus, be our guest, and bless what You have provided." One day his little son asked him a very important question.

"Papa, every evening you ask Jesus to come and be our guest, but He never comes."

"My son," replied the father, "we can only wait. But we know that He will not refuse our invitation."

"Well, then," asked the little boy, "if we invite Him to come and have dinner with us, why don't we set a place for Him at the table?" Moved by his son's innocence, the father allowed the boy to set a place at the table for Jesus.

Suddenly, they heard a knock at the door. When they opened it, a poor, helpless, little orphan stood shivering in the cold. The son looked at the hungry young child in the doorway for a moment, and

he turned to his father and said, "I see Jesus couldn't come today, so He sent this boy in His place."

The father said little as his son brought the orphan to the table and sat him at the place reserved for Christ. A godly man must see the world and those around him through the eyes of God.[3]

On one of our many trips to Israel, Pastor Hagee and I were privileged to see one of the most beautiful acts of the heart. While on the flight to the Holy Land, two of the ministry partners with whom we were traveling shared their testimony with Pastor and me.

They had accepted Christ while watching my husband present one of his sermons through television. They told of the homosexual lifestyle they turned away from and the newfound joy that was now theirs. Thrilled with their new life, they were now on the trip of a lifetime.

Sadly, because of their past lifestyle, one of them was suffering from AIDS and was concerned what others on the trip might think. My husband assured them that all would be fine and that they should not be concerned with anything other than enjoying the life-changing journey they were about to experience.

One evening soon after our arrival, while in Tiberius we decided to take a walk after dinner. The young man who was ill was quite weak and frail after the long plane ride and could hardly walk. We provided a wheelchair for him. After much prayer, the young man gave my husband permission to tell the others in our group that he was ill and needed their prayers and assistance.

I remember my husband's prayers that evening as we held hands and asked the Lord to prepare the group for the news regarding our young friend. "Father, give them Your ears as they hear this news, and keep them from fear as they respond to this child of God with Your loving heart."

The next morning during our time of devotion, we told the group of our young friend's need for healing from this dreaded disease. With tears in their eyes, members of the group came up to him one by one and knelt around him as, together, we agreed in prayer for his healing.

From that moment on, the men of the tour would take turns pushing the young man's wheelchair and helping him on and off the bus. We saw them laugh with him and sit with him at meals and share each other's lives. It was a wonderful testimony of God's love.

But the most profound moment for me took place at the Garden Tomb. We had our time of praise and worship where we shared the

Lord's communion with one another, then released the people to enter into the empty tomb. One by one they entered in. One by one they came out in tears as they left the barren, hollowed-out cave.

My husband and I were standing on the upper platform watching these precious pilgrims experience a very solemn moment, when something beautiful happened. The young man was sitting in his chair several yards from the tomb, because the large stones of the Garden made it difficult to maneuver his wheelchair. Two of the men from our group came to him and placed their arms under his body as he anchored his frail arms around their shoulders. These men, never once concerned for their own health, carried their brother toward the tomb.

The people who were gathered around the doorway made a path for the three men to enter the dark mausoleum. All was quiet. All bowed their heads and prayed. The three men walked out of the tomb with tears flowing down their faces.

My husband and I joined in their tears. We felt privileged to be able to see a demonstration of the heart of the living God arising out of that empty tomb.

A small orphaned boy lived with his grandmother. One night their house caught fire. The grandmother, trying to rescue the little boy asleep upstairs, perished in the smoke and flames. A crowd gathered around the burning house. The boy's cries for help were heard above the crackling of the vicious blaze. No one seemed to know what to do, for the front of the house was a mass of flames.

Suddenly a stranger rushed from the crowd and circled to the back. He spotted an iron pipe that reached to an upstairs window. He disappeared for a minute, and then reappeared with the boy in his arms. Amid the cheers of the crowd, he climbed down the hot pipe as the boy hung around his neck.

HE SAYS...

Do you want to do something great for God? Be kind to His children! Kindness is a language that the deaf can hear and the blind can see.

Weeks later, a public hearing was held in the town hall to determine in whose custody the boy would be placed. Each person who wanted the boy was allowed to speak briefly. The first man said, "I have a big farm, and everybody needs the out of doors."

The second man told of the advantages he could provide. "I'm a teacher. I have a large library. The boy would get a good education."

Others spoke. Finally the richest man in the community said, "I'm wealthy, and I could give the boy everything mentioned tonight—a farm, an education, and even more, including money and travel. I'd like him in my home."

The chairman asked if anyone else wanted to say a word. From the back rose a stranger who had slipped in unnoticed. As he walked to the front of the room, deep suffering showed on his face. Slowly the stranger removed his hands from his pockets.

A gasp went up from the crowd. The little boy, whose eyes had been focused on the ground until now, looked up. The man's hands were terribly scarred. Suddenly, looking into the man's face, the boy cried out in recognition. Here was the man who had saved his life. His hands had been scarred from climbing up and down the hot pipe as he salvaged the child from certain death.

With a leap the boy threw himself around the stranger's neck and once more held on for life. The farmer rose and left. The teacher, too. Then the rich man. Everyone departed, leaving the boy in the scarred hands of the man who had won him without a word.

> **HE SAYS . . .**
>
> **Remember: God has no superstars! He only has servants. Servants are willing to be poured out in an endless stream of the love of God.**

The godly man sees the scarred hands of his Savior when reaching out with his own hands to his wife, his children, or to a stranger in good deeds and kindness.

And finally a godly man must learn to say *no* to the world. The world does not recognize the righteousness of the God whom we serve. The world charms its victims with the "feel good" philosophy of our day. The world teaches that there is no right or wrong; it's all *relative*. The world entices with pleasure and rejects self-sacrifice.

The Word of God says that the man who says *no* to the world and *yes* to God is happy, fortunate, and to be envied because he fears, reveres, and worships the Lord. A godly man will walk in the path that God has set before him according to the commandments He has given.

HINTS FOR HIM

A godly man is:

1. Faithful
2. A spiritual leader
3. Respectful
4. A family man
5. A provider
6. Honest
7. A good communicator
8. Happy
9. Loving

FROM DR. ANNE

Women often *think* they know what they want, but, by nature, they are unwilling to allow God to develop in man the qualities and attributes that will ultimately result in God's giving them a man who is the true desire of their heart.

The top ten characteristics from the survey in this book result in obtaining a woman's number one desire, which is for a godly man. Yet all ten are contingent upon the woman allowing God to take over.

So often, manipulation of a man through circumstances and decisions is labeled *cute, funny,* or *a perfect way for a woman to get her way and fool the man into believing the idea was his.* God says that this is witchcraft. Manipulation and control are Satan's way of inserting himself into the relationship.

As women, we are only in charge to the extent that we are submitted to God's perfect will through His Word. Our minds require a renewing and washing with the Word through the direction of the Holy Spirit. How can we as women not thwart or stop God from developing in our husbands the qualities that will answer our prayers? How can we be helpmates to God in the process?

God gave to each of us His own Spirit to guide, build, counsel, and teach. He gives wisdom, understanding, good judgment,

and strength. He ministers truth, reprimands, and gives counsel for correction.

There is absolutely NO passage in the Bible where women are given the mandate or authority to take on the Holy Spirit's role. You are to be only what God requires of you. Becoming your husband's *Holy Spirit* is not a requirement—indeed, it is blasphemy for you to assume that role.

CLOSING PRAYERS

As you pray for a godly man to come into your life, remember that a godly man deserves a godly wife. You must learn to humbly submit yourself in marriage to a godly man and to have a fervent commitment to the Lord as you nurture the next generation. You must learn to hear the voice of God and to take the path He has charted for you to become all you can be. He will give you all that you have desired to have. Live according to His plan, which will bring you blessings untold and a *soul satisfaction* that will be incomparable to anything else.

PRAYER OF REPENTANCE

O Lord, I have allowed myself to be more influenced by the roles that society has laid out for me than by Your infallible, inspired Word. Please forgive me. I am a good woman, Lord. I don't set out intentionally to counter Your will. I become distracted and influenced by the things of this world, not by Your guidance. Help me, Lord God, please. I am asking for a renewed mind so that You can teach me Your ways and precepts. I repent and will make an active effort to please You. I will strive to be the godly woman my husband needs so that he can become the godly man You intended him to be.

PRAYER OF NEW BEGINNINGS

Thank You, Father, for Your love, which gives me and my family another chance to get things right. I will not raise my children or conduct myself as a person of the world, but as a child of God. Help me, Lord God, to say no to this world and yes to You.

I know that You are faithful and will make my family a reflection

of Your very best. As a wife and mother, I have been blessed by You with the opportunity to love and be loved. I will show my love by actively honoring my husband and allowing him to be the head of our household and the priest You have placed over us. I give You praise, honor, and glory for Your goodness and continued blessings. Thank You, Father, for new beginnings.

eleven

THE TORAH WAY

Thus says the Lord: Let not the wise and skillful person glory and boast in his wisdom and skill; let not the mighty and powerful person glory and boast in his strength and power; let not the person who is rich [in physical gratification and earthly wealth] glory and boast in his [temporal satisfactions and earthly] riches; but let him who glories glory in this: that he understands and knows Me [personally and practically, directly discerning and recognizing My character], that I am the Lord, Who practices loving-kindness, judgment, and righteousness in the earth, for in these things I delight, says the Lord.
—JEREMIAH 9:23–24, AMP

YOU HAVE JUST read the Word of the Lord. I encourage you to read the above passage seven times before you continue to read this closing chapter. Seven is the number of perfection, and I believe that once you receive in your mind and in your spirit the message the great I AM is sending us in this Scripture passage, then the rest of life will begin to come into focus.

When reading my many sources for the research in this project, I came across a book by Rebbetzin Jungreis, titled *The Committed Life*.[1] Rebbetzin is the widow of a rabbi, as well as the daughter, granddaughter, and great-granddaughter of a rabbi. She is also the mother and the grandmother of a rabbi. These credentials, and the love she has for the Lord, have qualified her to establish a *Torah Center,* where people of all ages come to hear her teach the inspired Word of God, which is known to the Jews as the *Torah*.

She tells of many counseling sessions she has had through the years, and one of the phrases that impressed me throughout the reading of *The Committed Life* is her advice to those she counsels: "You have done it your way; why not do it the Torah way."

I give this same advice to you now. You have tried to make your marriage work, and you have failed. You have tried to make your spouse be the man or woman you desire, and you have failed. Why not do it the Torah way? Why not do it God's way?

There was once a village that had every type of craftsman and artisan in its midst—tailors, carpenters, shoemakers, silversmiths, and so on. There was only one trade lacking—a watchmaker.

As the years passed, the clocks and watches of the villagers broke down until none showed the correct time, so some of the villagers stopped winding the watches all together. "What's the point?" they asked. "They're not accurate anyway."

> **HE SAYS...**
>
> **Remember this: Your marriage can be a *better* marriage, or it can be a *bitter* marriage. The choice is entirely up to you.**

But a small number of people kept winding their timepieces in the hope that a watchmaker would eventually come to town and set things right. So it was that one day a watchmaker did arrive, and the people lined up to have their clocks repaired. But the watchmaker was able to fix only those that had been kept wound. The others had rusted beyond repair.

Our watches—or our hearts—do not always give us a proper reading. But if we keep winding them, if we keep them going, then eventually when the Watchmaker—God—comes, He will set our hearts right and connect us to Him.[2] It is important to stay linked to His Word and to rely on the gift of faith, for in the final analysis, faith in the God that never fails is the only thing that gives meaning to our lives.

The *Torah*, the Word of God, is greater than all other books in the way that Mount Everest is greater than a grain of sand. The Bible is greater than other books just as Niagara Falls is greater than a dripping faucet. The Bible is greater than other books just as the light from the noonday sun is greater than a single candle. Its contents are not made of mere words on thin sheets of paper; the Bible records the promises of the Great Promise Keeper who created the universe and holds it in the palm of His hand.

In attempting to teach some of the wealth that is within its cover, I have found that every word, every letter, and every punctuation mark has limitless meaning. It has been studied by the great minds of the

ages, yet a child can find comfort in its message. It is God's blueprint for our lives. It is imperative that we stay linked to it.

God tells us in His Word to choose. To choose for life and not for death. To choose for the blessing and not for the curse. Today you should make a conscious choice to choose for the life and success of your marriage, and make a proclamation before the Lord and your spouse as you do so.

TAKE THESE NECESSARY STEPS

To choose for the life and success of your marriage, you must take certain steps that will enable you to have the relationship you desire with your spouse as you walk hand in hand on the journey called *life*.

First, you must stay connected to the Creator who fashioned you in His image. The Book of Psalms promises that God is near to all who call on Him, to all who call on Him in truth.

When you call on the name of God, hope enters your speech, your mind, and your heart. Where there is life, *there is hope*. Jesus Christ is the Living Water and the Blessed Hope. Proclaim to the Lord with your mouth: "I make a choice to stay connected to my source of life and blessings. I will stay connected to the Lord whom I serve and to His Word that gives me strength and guidance." Do it the Torah way.

Second, you must repent before God, whom you have offended. Every time you have shown insult, anger, or disdain for your spouse, you have shown it to God. The act of repentance tells the Lord you have recognized your sin, have shown remorse, and are ready to begin anew.

Repentance is one of the greatest acts of obedience you will ever commit. You can pray these words: "Today, Father, I repent before You and my spouse, whom I have offended with my thoughts, my speech, and my actions." Do it the Torah way.

Choose to keep the covenant. You must make a decision to stay married to your spouse for the rest of your life. Your spouse may have hurt you, but learn to forgive, for those who forgive will be forgiven. Pray: "Today I choose to keep the covenant I made before God and my spouse."

You must choose to love your spouse second only to Christ, your Savior. In order to be committed to any relationship, you must choose to love. Loving as Christ loves is the greatest accomplishment to which you can attain.

You might have to humble yourself to accomplish this; Jesus humbled Himself before His accusers prior to His death. You may have to suppress your ego; Jesus said *no* to self as He knelt before His disciples and washed their feet. Whatever you sacrifice for love, God will restore to you above what you could ever think or imagine. Do it the Torah way.

Choose today to show, without reservation, the love that God has put into your heart for your spouse. The desire you have for romance must be within the confines of the holy sacrament of matrimony. Any temptation to take this desire outside of marriage is an evil inclination that will deceive you and demand instant gratification no matter what the cost.

Subdue any desire outside of the covenant of marriage, and make every effort to show love and romance to the person with whom you made covenant. God's Word will keep you in God's constant presence. Pray: "Lord, today I proclaim that I will love my spouse unconditionally—as You have unconditionally loved me." Do it the Torah way.

Know that God has a great plan for your marriage. Together you will serve Him in the path He has chosen for you. He takes the most painful situations in our lives and makes them testimonials to His power. We are given challenges so that we can learn to overcome—not to give in.

God always has a greater plan. As you and your spouse wait on Him to reveal to you His plan, determine to be patient, learn to persevere, and always trust in a God who will never disappoint you. These choices will change your life forever. Pray these words: "Today we choose to live our lives for You, Father, and to hear Your voice, obey Your commandments, and wait on Your blessings."

> **HE SAYS...**
>
> **Are you willing to do whatever God directs you to do to make your marriage better? If you will make that commitment—and never forget it, your marriage can be like heaven on earth.**

MATTHEW AND KENDAL'S WEDDING CEREMONY

As I bring my section of the book to a close, there is no better way that I know to close this book than to share with you a portion of the marriage ceremony that my husband officiated for our son Matthew and his wife, Kendal, which took place a little over a year ago.

In these words you will find the essence of everything I have tried to teach you in this book.

The ceremony began with this prayer:

> Heavenly Father, we have come into this house of the Lord to unite this man and woman together in holy matrimony, after the covenants of our God, as we have done for all generations past in our family. Today we come to the house of the Lord to honor the Word of God and to continue the blessing that God has given us to carry the gospel of Jesus Christ to the ends of the earth.
>
> May the Holy Spirit fill this room, and may the anointing of God rest upon this ceremony, while we speak into existence the eternal covenant written by the hands of angels in the chronicles of heaven, with pens of iron and points of diamonds, which shall be remembered for the ceaseless ages of time and eternity.
>
> Bless these covenants that they may hold the prosperity and blessing that God gives to those who take them, for God does nothing without the sacredity of covenant. In Jesus' name we pray and ask it. Amen.

Then my husband continued by addressing Matthew and Kendal.

> We have come into the house of the Lord to stand before the Lord Himself, your family, and your friends to express your desire to live together from this day forward as man and wife. You are coming tonight to speak into existence a divine covenant that God has recorded clearly in His Word.
>
> God is the author of marriage. In the genesis of time, God created a man and said it was not good that he should be alone. So God created for that man the perfect partner and brought Eve across the grassy slopes of heaven and presented her to Adam. And because of this divine appointment, we have always felt that a man and a woman in the house of God also come together by divine appointment.
>
> This is a marriage that your mother and I have prayed for since the day you were born, as we have prayed for all of our children, that God would bring them to that special person with whom they would walk down the road of life with the anointing of God on

their lives, because theirs was a marriage made in heaven, declared on earth, and lived in grace.

Marriage is a covenant, which means it is the death of two wills and the birth of one. For the last time in your lives, you have walked into a building as individuals. From this night forward, God sees both of you, or He sees neither of you. From this moment forward, you become a unified whole. For Christ Himself has said, "These two, saith God, shall become one flesh."

The role of the husband is that of a prophet, a priest, and a provider. Matthew, God holds you responsible for this home. He holds you responsible for the spiritual development of your children. And I know that you will train your children in the way of the Lord.

Kendal, as his wife, you are saying tonight in the expression of this covenant that you submit yourself to the leadership of Matthew; that you are going to be the queen of this house, submitted to your husband as Christ is submitted to God the Father.

At this point in the ceremony, my husband began to explain the significance of the Jewish *Chuppah*, the marriage canopy under which Matthew and Kendal had chosen to be married. Three of our five children, including Matthew, have married under the *Chuppah*, or the Jewish marriage canopy. This canopy is a multifaceted symbol: a home, a garment, a spiritual covering. The Chuppah is usually a piece of cloth held by four poles. It is open on four sides to embody the hospitality that the married couple union will exhibit in their home. Visitors will be welcomed as they enter into the home from the north, the south, the east, and the west.

The Chuppah is the symbol of a covering over the bride. By being married under the canopy, the groom is indicating that he accepts the bride as his own.

The Chuppah is a sign of God's presence at the wedding and in the home as it is established under the canopy. *Chuppah* means, "that which covers or floats above." At the weddings of our three children who were married under the Chuppah, my husband placed his *tallit,* or prayer shawl, which symbolizes the name of God, on the top of the marriage canopy. It is said that there is a spiritual presence in the space beneath the tallit because the divine Name floats above it.

Four honored guests hold the poles of the canopy, which symbolize the prayer support the marriage will receive. Those in attendance
pledge to pray for the bride and groom as they begin their new lives
together under the covering of God.

> You are being married tonight beneath a Chuppah. In ancient Israel,
> marriages were performed under a prayer shawl held on poles by
> four men. This custom is rich with spiritual significance. It means,
> first of all, that it is a marriage bound in the name of God.
>
> From the names of God come the five blessings that are in the
> Scripture: *Jehovah Rophi*, our Healer; *Jehovah Shalom*, the God
> of peace; *Jehovah Jireh,* the God who is our provider; *Jehovah
> Rohi*, the Lord who is our Shepherd and Leader; *Jehovah Sham-
> mah*, the God who is there.
>
> As you stand under the Chuppah, which is emblematic of the
> Word of God and the covering of God, so shall all of these blessings
> fall upon you and your children and your children's children.
>
> Marriage beneath the Chuppah is marriage beneath the Word
> of God and His leadership, as evidenced by the 613 knots, repre-
> senting the 613 principles of truth found in the Word of God. As
> the Word of God is eternal, so shall your relationship be eternal.
> As the Word is endurable, so shall your lives and your marriage be
> enduring. As the Word is unshakable, so shall this relationship be
> unshakable.
>
> Your marriage shall go through storms, for Jesus gave in His
> Word the parable of the master builder who builds a house on firm
> foundation. He said, "And when the storms came..." He didn't
> say, "*If* they come..." He said, "*When* they came..." And they will
> come, but because you are building your relationship on the Lord
> and His Word, the gates of hell will not prevail against it.
>
> The Word brings generational blessings. Fifteen years ago
> tonight, my father, and your grandfather, stood on this platform
> and dedicated this church. You are here tonight by the providence
> of God to continue a generational blessing that has been ours for
> centuries, and that is to proclaim the gospel of Jesus Christ.
>
> The Chuppah is a tabernacle built for two, and it implies a mar-
> riage of miracles. When Elijah rolled up his prayer shawl and hit
> the Jordan River with the mantle, the water parted. And the sons

of the prophet, who saw him, said, "God is with him." Because you have honored the Lord as a couple, so will the Lord honor you as a couple from this night forward. You will live beneath a double portion of blessing, which God has given you.

The Chuppah guarantees a marriage protected by prayer. In ancient Israel, the four men who held the prayer shawl by its four poles made covenant to pray for that marriage each and every day. Those who stand with you on this platform tonight give covenant to pray that your marriage will prosper and succeed in God.

Four also speaks of perfection, for heaven is a foursquare city. Your marriage can be a thing of perfection. Never measure it by the people who live across the street or by other people that you know. Measure it by what God says it can be, because your marriage can be as the days of heaven on earth all the days of your life.

The words from my husband to Matthew and Kendal, which follow, are words that bring wisdom that can, and should, be applied to any marriage, *to your marriage,* to strengthen it and make it all that God wants it to be.

You will learn to give to each other the greatest gifts—the gift of love, the gift of peace, the gift of consideration, the gift of affection, and, above all, the gift of forgiveness, because sooner or later one of you will make a mistake. Your capacity to forgive the other will give strength and endurance to this marriage.

From this night forward, as you honor the God of Abraham, Isaac, and Jacob, His blessing shall follow you. His presence shall be with you. His prosperity shall be upon you. His angels will go before you to prepare your way and behind you as your rear guard. No good thing will He withhold from you, because you have made Him the object of your affection.

There are three covenants in the Word of God: the Shoe Covenant, with which Boaz married Ruth; the Salt Covenant, which is a covenant of loyalty; and the Blood Covenant, by which Christ redeemed the church, His bride, on the cross.

The Salt Covenant is a covenant of loyalty. When two people wanted to make an eternal, binding covenant, they would take

salt from the individual pouches that were worn on their belts, exchange it with one another, and recite the contents of the covenant while shaking the contents of the pouch.

The only way the covenant could be broken was for each granule of salt from each pouch to be retrieved, which was an impossibility. This has become perennially and eternally an expression of a covenant that is eternal and unbreakable.

Matthew and Kendal, if you will now exchange salt and repeat with me: "Because the grace of God has brought us together, the grace of God will keep us together, now and forever."

The final covenantal prayer of blessing over Matthew and Kendal can be applied to your marriage also:

Now, may the Lord bless you and keep you. May the Lord make His face to shine upon you. May the Lord be gracious unto you, and may the Lord give you peace. May the Lord bless your going out and your coming in. May the Lord anoint you to fulfill the divine destiny that God has given to you. May everything that is brought against you be crushed by the protection that God Himself shall provide. May you be blessed in your health. May you be blessed in your relationships. May your children and your children's children be blessed, because they are the heritage of the righteous. From this day forward, as you submit yourselves to the Christ of the cross, may your lives be filled with joy that is unspeakable and with peace that surpasses all understanding. May your home, as the Word of God says, be as the days of heaven on earth. In Jesus' name we pray and ask it. Amen.

DO IT THE TORAH WAY

As I was writing the last chapter of this book, our son Matthew and his wife, Kendal, announced to our family the coming birth of their first child, a child to be born on the week of my husband's sixty-fifth birthday. The blessings of our gracious God continue to fall on our family. Thank You, Father, for You are good.

As the world publicizes its prenuptial agreements, which are nothing more than a series of termination clauses, our church gives to each couple

that marries within its walls a *Katuba*, or marriage contract. This contract embodies the holy sacrament of marriage. The Katuba reads as follows:

> We stand before God in the company of our family and friends as we pledge to each other our mutual love, trust, and respect. We promise to be faithful friends and companions, rejoicing together through life's joys and comforting one another through life's sorrows.
>
> We covenant to be open, honest, loyal, and devoted to one another. Our commitment to God the Father and Jesus Christ, His Son, will be woven into the fabric of our lives by the power of the Holy Spirit.
>
> We will be overtaken by His blessings of peace, health, and prosperity as we diligently obey the voice of the Lord our God and observe all of His commandments.
>
> The laughter of children will grace our home as we raise them according to His Word. As we share life's journey together, we will witness our children's children serving the Lord.
>
> Together we pledge to build a Christian home filled with prayer, love, wisdom, and a dedication to one another as we demonstrate the love of Jesus Christ to one and all.
>
> We enter with solemn joy into this covenant with each other and the God of Abraham, Isaac, and Jacob.

Do it the Torah way.

As you contemplate the contents of this book, may the Lord God of Abraham, Isaac, and Jacob, our Savior Jesus Christ, be your peace. For so great is peace that God's name is *Peace*...so great is His peace that all blessings are to be found within it.

NOTES

WHAT WOMEN WANT IN A MAN

1. Randall Cirner, *10 Weeks to a Better Marriage* (Ann Arbor, MI: Servant Publications, 1995).

2. Rebbetzin Esther Jungreis, *The Committed Life* (San Francisco: HarperSanFrancisco, 1999).

3. Scott Farhart, MD, *Intimate and Unashamed* (Lake Mary, FL: Siloam, 2003), 74.

4. These surveys were inspired from the Wilkinson Family Home page, Miscellaneous Humor, "What Women Want in Men" at http://search.atomz.com/search/?sp-a=000312a2-sp00000000&sp-k=Humor&sp-q=what+i+want+in+a+man.

CHAPTER 1
WANT NUMBER TEN: FAITHFULNESS

1. Willard F. Harley Jr., *His Needs, Her Needs: Building an Affair-Proof Marriage* (Grand Rapids, MI: Fleming H. Revell Co., 1986).

2. Ibid.

3. Bob Moeller, *For Better, For Worse, For Keeps* (Sisters, OR: Multnomah, 1994).

4. Adapted from *The Woman's Study Bible*, New International Version, "Sexuality: A Gift From the Creator" (Nashville, TN: Nelson Bibles, 1998), 112.

5. Farhart, *Intimate and Unashamed*.

6. Moeller, *For Better, For Worse, For Keeps*.

7. Ibid.

8. Ibid.

9. Farhart, *Intimate and Unashamed*, chapters 2–4.

10. Moeller, *For Better, For Worse, For Keeps*.

CHAPTER 2
WANT NUMBER NINE: LEADERSHIP

1. Margaret Mead, *Male and Female* (New York: HarperCollins Publishers, 2001).

2. Watchman Nee, *Spiritual Authority* (Richmond, VA: Christian Fellowship Publishers, 1972).

3. Cirner, *10 Weeks to a Better Marriage*, 85.
4. Ibid.

CHAPTER 3
WANT NUMBER EIGHT: RESPECT

1. Jungreis, *The Committed Life*, 191.
2. Ibid., 194.
3. Ibid., 217.
4. Cirner, *10 Weeks to a Better Marriage*, 89–90.
5. Bobbie Yagel, *15 Minutes to Build a Stronger Marriage*, quoted in "What Makes Love Last," *Ladies Home Journal*, LHJ.com, http://msnwomen .lhj.com/lhj/story.jhtml?storyid=/templatedata/lhj/story/data/14115 .xml&catref=cat1950002.
6. Jungreis, *The Committed Life*, 219.
7. Moeller, *For Better, For Worse, For Keeps*, 85.
8. Ibid.
9. Harley, *His Needs, Her Needs*, 185.

CHAPTER 4
WANT NUMBER SEVEN: FAMILY MAN

1. Jungreis, *The Committed Life*, 320.

CHAPTER 5
WANT NUMBER SIX: PROVIDER

1. Cirner, *10 Weeks to a Better Marriage*, 120.
2. Harley, *His Needs, Her Needs*, 125.
3. Rita Rudner, *Reader's Digest*, September 2004, 111.
4. Harley, *His Needs, Her Needs*, 125–126.
5. Ibid.
6. James Hewett, *Illustrations Unlimited* (Chicago, IL: Tyndale House, 1988), 342.
7. Avery Corman, "The New Parent Trap: Can There Be a Good Divorce," *Reader's Digest*, September 2004, 124.
8. Cirner, *10 Weeks to a Better Marriage*, 120.
9. Hewett, *Illustrations Unlimited*, 324.

CHAPTER 6
WANT NUMBER FIVE: HONESTY

1. Harley, *His Needs, Her Needs*, 91.
2. Hewett, *Illustrations Unlimited*.
3. Ibid.
4. Harley, *His Needs, Her Needs*, 93–94
5. Hewett, *Illustrations Unlimited*.
6. Willard F. Harley Jr., *Love Busters: Overcoming Habits That Destroy Romantic Love* (Grand Rapids, MI: Fleming H. Revell, 1992), 89.
7. Ibid., 90.
8. Ibid., 92.
9. Ibid., 96.
10. Ibid., 97.
11. Ibid.
12. Hewett, *Illustrations Unlimited*, 288.

CHAPTER 8
WANT NUMBER THREE: SENSE OF HUMOR

1. John Hagee, *Being Happy in an Unhappy World* (San Antonio, TX: John Hagee Ministries, 1993).
2. Jungreis, *The Committed Life*, 43–44.
3. Ibid.
4. Read Matthew 5:4 in *The Amplified Bible*.
5. Read Matthew 5:5 in *The Amplified Bible*.
6. Jungreis, *The Committed Life*, 179–180.
7. Read Matthew 5:6 in *The Amplified Bible*.
8. Hewett, *Illustrations Unlimited*, 347.
9. Ibid., 404–405.
10. Ibid., 488.
11. Ibid., 135–136.
12. Norman Vincent Peale Quotes, Brainy Quotes, http://www.brainyquote.com/quotes/authors/n/norman_vincent_peale.html.

CHAPTER 9
WANT NUMBER TWO: ROMANCE

1.   Ann Landers, "Is It Love You're Feeling or Just an Infatuation?", Relationships, The Art of Loving, adviceline.com, http://www.artofloving.com/relationships/5loveinfatuation.htm.

2.   Hewett, *Illustrations Unlimited*, 327.

3.   Roseanne Barr, *Reader's Digest*, September 2004, 108.

CHAPTER 10
WANT NUMBER ONE: GODLY MAN

1.   Booker T. Washington, *Up From Slavery* (Laurel, NY: Lightyear Press, 1990).

2.   Hewett, *Illustrations Unlimited*, 118.

3.   Ibid., 116.

CHAPTER 11
THE TORAH WAY

1.   Jungreis, *The Committed Life*.

2.   Ibid., 175.

You have just finished *What Every Woman Wants in a Man* by Diana Hagee. The information you read about marriage was presented from a woman's point of view. The principles the author shared will help you build a loving relationship with your mate.

Now you will want to flip this book over and read *What Every Man Wants in a Woman,* written from a man's point of view by Pastor John Hagee. He will share important principles and stories that, when combined with the information from this book by his wife, Diana Hagee, will help you to build an affair-proof marriage that sizzles with joy and excitement every day of your married life.